SOUL

"Just in time to rescue us from the paralyzing antinomies of essentialism and anti-essentialism, base and superstructure, class and culture, *Soul* arrives to restore Black pleasure to its rightful place in contemporary debates on race, identity, and subjectivity. In a spirit of inclusiveness, this book opens the subject up by providing a rich mix of viewpoints—even those of opposition and contradiction. What comes through above all is the vitality and liveliness of a new generation of scholars and the sense that the heritage of a great civilization is in good hands. And if proof were still needed that we are living in the golden age of African American Studies, *Soul* would be it."

—John F. Szwed, Yale University

SOUL

Black Power,
Politics,
and
Pleasure

Edited by Monique Guillory
and
Richard C. Green

NEW YORK UNIVERSITY PRESS
New York and London

NEW YORK UNIVERSITY PRESS
New York and London

Copyright © 1998
7 by New York University
All rights reserved

Chapter 2, "Afro Images: Politics, Fashion, and Nostalgia" by Angela Y. Davis, published
in *Picturing Us,* ed. Deborah Wills. Copyright © 1995 by Angela Davis. Reprinted by permission of The New Press.
Chapter 18, "Question of a 'Soulful Style': An Interview with Paul Gilroy," copyright ©
Paul Gilroy.

Library of Congress Cataloging-in-Publication Data
Soul : Black power, politics, and pleasure / edited by Monique
Guillory and Richard C. Green.
p.   cm.
Includes bibliographical reference and index.
ISBN 0-8147-3084-1 (clothbound : acid-free paper).—ISBN
0-8147-3085-x (paperback : acid-free paper)
1. Afro-Americans—Race idenity—Congresses.   2. Afro-Americans
in popular culture—Congresses.   3. Afro-American arts—Congresses.
I. Guillory, Monique, 1969-   . II. Green, Richard C., 1967-   .
E185.625.S67   1997
305.896'073—dc21   97-33850
CIP

New York University Press books are printed on acid-free paper,
and their binding materials are chosen for strength and durability.

Manufactured in the United States of America

10 9 8 7 6 5 4 3 2 1

CONTENTS

ACKNOWLEDGMENTS

Much of the material for this book was culled from or inspired by a conference of the same name held at New York University in spring 1995. That event marked the pilot project of the new Black Graduate Studies Association at NYU, which had not been active on campus since the late 1970s. Because the conference lies at the heart of this project, we feel as indebted to those who made the conference possible as we do to those who contributed to the published text. Along with the contributors, we would also like to thank Makungu M. Akinyela, Amiri Baraka, Paul Beatty, Tish Benson, Naadu Blankson, Eloise Jacobs Brunner, Mary Schmidt Campbell, Ephen Glenn Colter, Manthia Diawara, Glenda Doyle, Cornelius Eady, David Ebert, David Ellis, Donette Francis, Alex Garrison, Steven Gregory, dream hampton, Fatima Legrand, Mario Lucineo, Lavern McDonald, William Mills, Sarah Morse, Robin Nagle, Jennifer Joy Radford, Toshi Reagon, Roger Richardson, Andrew Ross, Suzanne Smith, Pam Sneed, Annette Weiner, Jennifer Wicke, and Patricia Williams.

Monique would like to express sincere thanks to St. Jude, her parents and family, and Mel, and a very special hug to Gwen, Natalie, and Tanya, who have been a tireless tag team of love, support, and inspiration.

Richard would like to send special thanks to his family for providing him with a rich soul-filled upbringing, to friends & colleagues such as John M., Anna B., Jeffrey P., Carl R., Tommy D., Andre L., and so many others for their wonderful support and encouragement, and of course to Mark Seamon—for always being there.

BY WAY OF AN INTRODUCTION

MONIQUE GUILLORY AND RICHARD C. GREEN

Who
can be born black
and not
sing
the wonder of it
the joy
the
challenge

Who
can be born
black
and not exult?
—Mari Evans

A magazine reporter once asked Aretha Franklin to define soul.

"Soul is black," Ms. Franklin replied.

And she should know. As the reigning Queen of soul, Aretha Franklin's life attests to that sweet sensuality that lends power to the voice, spirit to the body and depth to understanding. Soul is the stuff of our dreams and marks that magical domain of powerful nothingness where fantasies and ancestors live. Aimé Cesaire recognized the revolutionary potential of such surrealist manifestations; but at the same time, everybody's favorite soul-brother-number-one, James Brown, embodies a gritty, gut-wrenching reality which has transcended national boundaries and crossed generations. Through such timeless, omni-present icons as Franklin and Brown, soul lies embedded in the sacred and the profane, the sublime and the sensational.

But given Soul Queen's very own proclamation, what exactly is black?

Despite the numerous obstacles and trials that have characterized the lives of black people in America (if not elsewhere) we remain unswervingly romantic about the concept of a common black experience. The voices exalting that blackness and the means of celebrating it have shifted with the tides of history. Black Americans no longer sing with one voice or love with one heart, and we have become increasingly doubtful that there ever was a time when we did. We cannot even be certain of who or what is meant by the term "black." Nonetheless, how blacks have come to recognize themselves as a distinct group within the context of America surfaces from an almost ineffable sense of perseverance and vitality in the face of adversity. As Zora Neale Hurston reminds us, "It was an inside thing to live by. It was sure to be heard when and where the work was hardest, and the lot most cruel. It helped the slaves endure. They knew that something better was coming. So they laughed in the face of things and sang, 'I'm so glad! Trouble don't last always.' "[1]

This book seeks to situate the notion of soul within the ongoing discourse over questions of identity and subjectivity. In the sway of cultural studies and other deconstructive winds, many scholars now denounce the reductivist sense inherent in notions of a single black experience, black community, or black history. Such scholars recognize that the experiences, communities, and histories from all corners of the African diaspora may be far too diverse and splintered to lump them into one cohesive group. However, the notion of soul implies a scope of the psyche that exceeds conventional assumptions about those individual motivations which bring folks together. In some ways, the concept of soul may serve us far better than race ever will. While statisticians and clinicians (re: the Census Bureau) discern blackness through a variety of biological and social attributes, soul remains an abstract and evocative site for identity formation. Thus, in critical considerations of black cultural expression, we can appreciate even as we critique Léopold Sedar Senghor's belief that "Africans think with their soul—I would even say: with their heart."[2] We would want to challenge Senghor's linking of African sensibilities with the emotive capacity as opposed to the intellectual, even while we may feel that there is a grain of truth in his observation. As we steadily leave behind the trappings of essentialism, we may more readily recognize soul when we encounter it than we know who, definitively, is black. Certainly, this is not to suggest that the two are in any way unaffiliated. Rather, given the congruence of soul's evolution with the history of blacks in America, one could say that soul is to black what rainbow is to rain.

This is not to suggest that understanding soul is any easier than defining blackness. After reading this collection of essays, short stories, and poems, you may find that you are no closer to defining *soul* than when you started. Although we may not know specifically what soul "is," we still may be able to recognize it. The variety of perspectives mixed (like a good gumbo) in this book demonstrates the extent to which soul speaks to the specifics of personal taste and desire. But is there an essence to soul? Is it linked to a particular social or cultural perspective, or does the presence of soul necessarily attest to some trace of social oppression? Due to the chameleon-like nature of soul, we have intentionally presented the subject from varied and often contradictory vantage points. Therefore, many of the patent considerations of soul fail to encompass the breadth of this study. While we acknowledge "soul" as it is applied to food and music, a particular moment in the history of African America, or a style or aesthetic that is thought to be endemic to black America, at the same time we question the myth of black cultural unity that imbues blacks with a certain quality of being by their race alone. No single understanding of soul is intentionally privileged here; thus, no one figure or moment seems sufficient to serve as a masthead. Rather, we have attempted to grasp soul in some of its many guises and articulations, from James Brown's shuffle to *Schoolhouse Rock,* a children's television show.

Nor have we been particularly fixed on the form or style these explorations of soul should take. Undoubtedly, a book about soul ought to engage the senses and the intellect on every possible level, from photography and visual art to music and contemporary cultural theories (we would like to have included 2 CDs between these covers as well). But even with such vast resources and broad terrain at our command, there remains very little common ground when it comes to individual approaches to soul. Nelson George says soul died with Nixon's reelection in 1972. Others argue that soul never died, it just grew up and got hip with the times. Questions regarding who's got soul and who doesn't, who stole soul and who's faking it, have proven to be legitimate grounds for battle. Soul is a delicate matter, yet it is interesting to note what strange bedfellows surface from beneath its cover. Regardless of one's stance on identity politics, Afrocentricity, or political correctness, commenting on somebody's quotient and quality of soul can be as personal as talkin' 'bout somebody's mama. We have encouraged the contributors here to maintain that personal aspect of soul in their discussions. Soul bears as much relevance to contemporary considerations of identity politics as do race and class, yet it tempers these matters with elements of passion and finesse. As succinctly as Paul Gilroy can rattle off the geopolitical reasons behind divergent means of cultural production in Great Britain and the United States, he can also recall with winsome nostalgia his first encounter with something he recognized as soulful. We have embraced this topic because of its universal appeal. The scholar, the poet, and the person on the street all carry with them a notion of soul, a feel and sense of it as secure and familiar as a mother's touch.

In addition to the broad framework we have laid for the pieces that follow, we have also divided the material into three general categories that are intended to circumscribe various aspects of soul and its historical and social implications. "Black Power" interrogates the revisionist history of the civil rights era and reconsiders its subsequent gains. We also offer here some innovative interpretations of how the notion of "power" might be understood as something other than the Super Soul Brother with fist clenched in the air. "Black Politics" examines the soul-inflected movements of people and commodities in the public sphere. And "Black Pleasure" approaches soul from its most celebrated and often most complicated sources—excessive, demonstrative black bodies gettin' out of hand (and body). We conclude the book with two important possibilities: "Ain't We Still Got Soul?" and "From This Ivory Tower: Race as a Critical Paradigm in the Academy." Given the nature of the following project, these two closing sections could be reformulated as "Ain't We Still Got Soul in This Ivory Tower?" It is, perhaps, our own anxiety and discomfort over this issue that has fueled this conference-turned-book. Familiar questions plague us: what is the black intellectual's debt to the community? How do we not lose touch with the folks we never see in academia's halcyon halls? What happens to soul in degreed and disciplined hands? The following musings mark our humble attempt to grapple with the rich stuff of our souls. Like Rapunzel, confined to her tower, we are letting our locks grow long in the hope that the (Artist formerly known as) Prince will someday save us from ourselves.

NOTES

1. Zora Neale Hurston, "High John de Conquer," in Langston Hughes and Arna Bontemps, eds., *Book of Negro Folklore* (New York: Dodd, Mead, 1958), 93.

2. Léopold Sedar Senghor, *The Foundations of "Africanite,"* trans. Mercer Cook (Paris: Présence Africaine, 1971), 44.

Part One

BLACK POWER

INTRODUCTION: ON BLACK POWER

STEVEN DRUKMAN

For a white middle-class child of the seventies, Black Power ran in color on three major networks. Its "power" was ignited on cathode ray tubes or was motored at 33 1/3 r.p.m. I was aware of Stokely Carmichael's coinage mostly through the sexy-but-safe denizens of *Room 222,* or through downcast, dark-skinned malcontents being preached to by a pious Joe Friday on *Dragnet*. Or, I heard the phrase as anthem-like, its exclamation point coinciding with Sly Stone's at the end of "Stand!" It was later, in high school, when I learned about the Student Nonviolent Coordinating Committee (SNCC) and how white students felt disenfranchised from a movement that didn't seem to want them anymore, no matter how much they liked certain music, or fashion trends, or even exotic recipes (with flavors more enticing than my mother's burnt brisket, for example). Reading Stokely Carmichael and Charles V. Hamilton's book *Black Power* exactly three decades late, I realize that I can't help but be caught in the Jamesonian web of nostalgia, that "Black Power" is always already a pastiche-driven refraction of images, styles, riffs, film dissolves, and so on. The essays in this section all attest to Black Power's postmodern punch—a "Black Puissance," really—while they worry about the consequences of its ongoing transition, from a 1967 "political framework and ideology that represents the last reasonable opportunity for this society to work out its racial problems short of prolonged destructive guerrilla warfare," to—what, exactly? Or, as Anna Scott asks in her conclusion to "It's All in the Timing": "We gotta 'move somethin',' but what will it be: records and tapes or liberated black bodies?"

All the pieces in this section ask that question in one way or another. Angela Y. Davis takes a brave new look at the recontextualization of her hyper-glam "revolutionary" image into fashion fetish. Carl Hancock Rux "cong-cong-congas" all my favorite music (interspersed with recipes, again, cooking up "transition") but remembers Eric Dolphy and Archie Shepp in a very different context from mine—his reminiscence more scary and violent, "taking place in a circle of frenzy." And lest I feel too soulful, Gayle Wald in her essay "Soul's Revival" (in part 2) persuasively reminds me that "narcissism is the only possible outcome of white cultural mimicry" that fails to account for its—er, my—privileged position, granting me permission to cross the line and appropriate some Black Power for my own.

These reminders are important, in our so-called postmodern condition, where the boundaries set up by identity politics yield to a boundless play of surfaces. As Nathan L. Grant points out (in his essay on another of my boyhood heroes, James Baldwin), Black Power decreed that "before a group can enter the open society, it must first close ranks." But the explosive performativity of Black Power has shown that closing ranks is not an option, as the essence of Black Power—the very soul of soul—defies appropriation be reemerging along various axes of definition and employment. Davis is right to feel alarmed about a potential subsuming of the movement's contestatory nature into mere style, but the very concept of Black Power—as it emerges in these pages—has already clearly irradiated beyond its original defining strictures. It will always be a movement in that it is always in movement, so its transition can never properly be called complete. This is Black Power's power, a sort of eternal half-life, an uncontainability. In this respect, all these authors are true to the pages of *Black Power,* wherein Carmichael and Hamilton conclude not only by calling for new forms, but demanding a "bold readiness to be 'out of order.' "

It's All in the Timing

The Latest Moves, James Brown's Grooves, and the Seventies Race-Consciousness Movement in Salvador, Bahia-Brazil

ANNA SCOTT

The "Afro" style of movement and performance began in Brazil in the seventies among radicalized sectors of the Black-mixtured community as a way to recuperate and politicize inherited African cultural practices that had been co-opted by the dictatorship as simply folklore, part of "our Brazilian Heritage." Twenty years later, it appears that this particular style of dance has a fixed set of codes from which the dancer may construct/choreograph meaning into a performance. This position, however, reinstates the paradigm of the "folk" into a dynamic process of identification, communication, and insertion within transnational discourses about the various cultures of people of African descent, a politics of aesthetics. A politics oriented toward and based on a Black aesthetic, however, is a debilitated politics that is restrained by language differences, culturally bounded notions of taste, and external market forces. Black "de/ciphering practices" as an organizing concept potentially moves us beyond those boundaries, allowing the "tenacity of practice," *tenaxis,* rather than cultural products, to become the focal point. In this examination of a fieldwork experience that took place July 13, 1994, in Salvador, Bahia-Brazil, during a two-month visit, I will develop aspects of this process through a performative text, eschewing common tendencies to fixate on the products of this cultural production.

The Space

Having stayed just a little longer than necessary while waiting for a fashionably late moment past 11 P.M., I hurriedly left friends to the vagaries of the new Pelourinho, drinkiñg in front of the cantina Abará Rô, where they were playing salsa on atabaque drums for wealthy, overdressed tourists from São Paulo. As usual, O Cravo Rastafari was jam-packed with black people from the old neighborhood. Across the way, the new Casa de Olodum cranked reggae music from between its bared teeth, through which one could pass only with money or a membership card. The street in between had become the dance floor itself, the Cravo getting the majority of the business. It was almost 1 A.M. Ilê Aiyê had begun its rehearsal sometime after 11 P.M. but, as my roommate's boyfriend had warned as I departed the apartment earlier that evening, hoping to get off cheap by taking an early bus to Pelourinho rather than a taxi, "É melhor de esperar e de ir mas tarde pra o Ilê. Eles só começam a partir das veinte-tres."

Ilê Aiyê was the first *bloco afro* organized in the city of Salvador, yet it was continually having image problems. At the forefront of developing an "Afro" consciousness and culture in Salvador, the organization steadfastly holds to the "black is beautiful" ideology of the black arts movement developed in the United States in the late sixties. Since 1972 Ilê Aiyê has extolled the beauty of black skin by deciding what shade of skin was black enough to represent beauty; this has not garnered them many allies in this land of so-called racial democracy. After a *briga* (battle) for the direction of Ilê in the mid-eighties, some of the leadership jumped ship while others went to work for Olodum. Some directors allegedly felt the politics were too tied to superficialities and wanted to make a broader statement about liberation that would make a space for organizing across color lines.

I decided I needed to end my infatuation with Olodum, one of Ilê's main competitors, the first day I went to its brand-new headquarters in the newly renovated Pelourinho, where Olodum owns five buildings. I witnessed white tourists clamoring for advance tickets, afraid they would miss the great spectacle of Olodum in rehearsal. It wasn't so much the advance ticket sales, which was an improvement over the dangerous money-at-the-door-in-the-alley set-up they used to have; rather, it was that almost every tourist sported some new article of clothing in the combined colors of the Rastafari and United Negro

Improvement Association's liberation flag, purchased at the Boutique de Olodum. In addition to this spectacle of voguing liberation, each ticket purchaser received a copy of a book about Olodum, printed and distributed by Olodum, written by a Brazilian journalist working on his Ph.D. at the Sorbonne. The book, *Olodum: um "holding cultural,"* amounts to an extended fact sheet. I decided that I had better get to know Ilê; maybe then Olodum's "We Are the World" posturing would make sense.

A comparative analysis of the two organizations might rid me of my growing suspicion that in the end there was nothing liberatory at all about dancing and singing about liberation. So I headed out of Pelourinho in the direction of Forte Santo Antonio. Descending the *ladeira* well over the advisable speed for walking down a steep, five-hundred-year-old cobblestone road, I made notes in my head about needing to make a "racial usage" map of the former neighborhood. Onward, downward, upward, past the charming tiled Portuguese façades of crumbling inhabited houses that had not yet been renovated; past sundry stores run out of former living rooms; past peanut vendors who looked as if peanuts were all they had to eat; past lively *cantinas* that had illegally extended their business out to the street; past the point where the cobblestone ended and the twentieth century took over (kind of) I continued up a long, slow incline, the kind that goes on forever but makes you think it's about to end at any moment. Soon I could feel the pulse of the surdo drum section shaking the plaster off the old fort. I crossed the plaza, where the music was already at an enjoyable volume, and entered the fort.

For a brief moment there was silence as I passed through the arched gateway. I emerged from the lime-covered passageway into the midnight-blue sky of the courtyard, greeted by the impact of a single solitary wail from the vocalist atop the concrete stage, leaning just so to the right so he could hear the spirits better. He finished the line, and the *repique* (snare drum) of the band leader started up, giving the phrase that would select which rhythm to play. The band gave a false start; the singer kept on wailing, and the musical director shouted out, "Abre os olhos!" ("Open your eyes!") because the cipher has an aural and *visual* cue to it. The small audience was getting annoyed; they came to see authentic Afro-Bahian culture, and the natives couldn't get their act together. A smallish crowd lingered at the peripheries of the courtyard on all sides, milling about, casually talking among themselves; they had faith. Once

11

more the director played the *repique,* all eyes upon him, ears alert, sticks at the ready. Braa ka bra braakaka, braa ka braakaka bra ka bra ka . . . and the rest of the band jumped on the line. The singer's voice stuttered across the beats, breaking up the big heaviness of the samba reggae swing. I was right on time.

The Place

Built originally as a prison for political insurgents, the Forte is now known as the Nucléo da Cultura Negra. In 1990 it housed four organizations and at least six individual artists and artisans. The offices and ateliers were actually in old cells and cell blocks; the old refectory was converted into a dance studio. There was even a boutique where you could buy the latest in Afro fashion. Ilê, Grupo Capoeria Angola do Pelourinho (GCAP), and one other *capoeira* group currently use the space on a regular basis. The other organizations and groups have left because the reform of the historical district is making its way toward Forte Santo Antonio. The building is slated to become a mall.

GCAP is currently negotiating with the city to get a space in Pelourinho. Although it already runs a boutique in Pelourinho, Ilê Aiyê wants no part of the impending "touristicization" of its organization and music and has decided to relocate rehearsals back in the "ghetto" of Curuzu, a black stronghold of rebellion since the early 1970s and the place where Ilê was born. Curuzu is one of the many neighborhoods that comprise Liberdade, a happening barrio of blackness since the 1950s. While most of Liberdade is in the Ciadade Alta, you must descend a steep hill to get to Curuzu; no buses enter this part of Liberdade.

Spectacle, Spectating

Back in 1990, the last time I was in Salvador conducting research on the dance and culture of *bloco afro* groups, I usually found myself the only or one of few strangers or foreigners at these nighttime rehearsals. It was apparent that many things had changed since my last trip, primary among them the introduction of portable tables and chairs. For the most part, these were occupied by nonparticipant observers—mainly tourists. It is, however, very difficult not to participate, given the force and volume of the music. The audience was situated directly across from the gateway, close to the bar and restaurant. The tables appeared to be placed haphazardly as needed. Older members of Ilê had commandeered some close to a back corner, almost in the shadows, away from the audience. The tables were used to leave large workout bags, purses, jackets (it was winter, after all), and beer under the watchful eyes of resting friends. The participant observers were visibly separated from the nonparticipant observers by a pathway filled with a steady stream of thirsty folks making their way to the bar.

The courtyard was lit with strings of light bulbs; on a clear night such as this, the moon and starry sky illuminated the situation all the more. Hanging out in the peripheries, younger people eyed each other daringly or bopped up and down in their best imitation of B-Boy ennui. The drummers were steadily pumping out the intricacies of samba reggae and the singer was holding "church," switching between Portuguese and Yoruba. The lyrics of samba reggae songs are mainly in what is known in black revolutionary circles as "Pretoguese"—*preto*-, black; -*guese,* from the end of Portuguese—a mixture of African languages and a creolized form of Portuguese that lilts. After introducing a potential song for next year's *carnaval,* the singer launched into an old standard, the crowd having been less than moved. That's when I saw them.

Emerging from the shadows on the GCAP side, a small group of women started to cheer and dance. Gu g'hum dhum dhum ga, ga dhum dhum ga . . . Gu g'hum dhum dhum ga, ga dhum dhum ga. This Suingue Bahiano (Bahian Swing) was doing it for them. At first each was just moving to the music in her own way. After a couple of refrains of the song, one of them emerged as a whimsical stepper, and she soon had the rest following in her funky footsteps. The drumming had switched up just a enough, creating that soulful sway that Ilê is cherished for: "No me pegue no me toque por favor nã me provoque,"and the crowd answered, "eu só quero ver Ilêêê paaassar." Soon, everyone standing was doing something or other, but nothing beat what was happening over in the dark corner where the women were dancing. I realized that I was somewhat lording over a very large empty space near the middle of the courtyard. People were staring, trying to place me: I didn't go sit down immediately, no one came up to meet me, grinning; I had on big, black baggy jeans and a t-shirt, a sure not-from-here look; my hair was "Rasta," but then again, not; I was not white; and I was dancing in the middle of the courtyard with a huge smile on my face.

Thinking to myself, "Now what are they doing?" I began to imitate the line of women, who were cutting up by now, as did the rest of the crowd on that side of the courtyard. The tourist audience realized that the show was behind them and began to slyly rearrange their seats, so they could see both the *bateria* and the dancers. The dangling hundred-watt bulbs made peeping difficult, and the audience had to settle for occasional flashes of teeth and laughter. I couldn't take it any longer. I walked over to the women and got into the new back line that had formed to accommodate those of us eager to learn the latest moves. The songs were continuous now; not even the singer was demarcating the changes—just sheer flow.

Dances

Meanwhile, in the back, we grooved on, hooting and howling for the more intricate steps, intently gathering our stamina and breath during the simple ones, still thinking on the complex ones. Each step was comprised of at least two to six parts, mostly in 4/4 time; this necessitated a good sense of rhythm, since the drumming was in 12/16. A few steps included hops and drop squats, but most were two-step slides, pivot turns, or an "inverted" samba simply known as an injunction— *balança,* "swing it." This dance was a basic step, one that we returned to for rest or to really throw down with the rhythm. Most steps make boxes or lines and emphasize long, articulated arms, like Senegalese dance or reminiscent of Bob Marley's backup singers, the I-Threes. In actuality, the arm uses and positions are from the Candomblé.

Long articulated arms in Candomblé ritual dancing can signify the sky, snakes, ocean waves, rain calling, machete slashes, holding the reigns of a galloping horse, or flashing a saber, staff, or bracelets, to name a few. These movements are "quoted" at will, but are "deployed" when the singer sings the call of a specific *orixá,* Candomblé deity, which happens to be your *ori,* the one that rules your head, that is, your actions, temperament, and destiny. Waves are *Yemanjá,* "motherhood;" Machete slashes are *Ogun,* "iron and war," and so on. The rituals and dances of the Candomblé are the basis of the Afro dance style and arts movement.

The Afro Look

I had forgotten that I was rigged for sound recording and must have slammed the microphone about five times before I realized what it was. In an attempt to conceal the mike from thieving eyes, I had worn my big baggy black jeans. No one else had on baggy jeans. One of the things women who participate with Ilê are known for is their Afro style. "Women-childs" and " 'omans" alike sported African-inspired, loose, batik cotton jumpsuits, with slightly flared pants legs. Others had on *boubas*, West African one-piece gowns, with a slit from shoulder to shoulder instead of a collar and sleeves that hang just above or below the wrists. These *boubas* were the shorter version, worn over a tightly wrapped piece of old *carnaval* fabric, African print, or tie-dyed fabric. Still others worked the standard jeans and t-shirt, both freshly ironed for the evening's events, and neither very tight. Sandals and clogs or very white sneakers seemed to be the foot coverings of choice. As I looked down at my dingy white and black Nikes, I realized how foolish I must have looked; I should have been seated dressed like that—"tourist sensible."

The Dance

People were beginning to comment on that strange black woman who came alone and was picking up the steps rather fast, "mas ela não é nosso." Just then a tall, buxom woman stopped us all by waving her hands and mentioned to her eye. We watched intently as she broke it down: (1) kick to the right with the left foot; (2) step open to the left twice, drag-sliding the right foot along, the first step larger than the second; (3) step open with the right foot, kick left to right with the left foot. Repeat this four to six times if you have no leader; if you have one, she gives the call for the change. Our girl was really messing with us, calling the change on the third or fifth time, making it difficult to get back into the rhythm. The "breakdown" after the call: (1) on the last kick, walk to the left two paces; (2) hop turn, landing on the left foot with the right knee bent up so that the right foot is presented from behind; (3) step out with the right into a lunge; (4) shift the weight back and forth through the hips three times while swinging the arms.

If it sounds very difficult, that's 'cause it is! Intricate rhythm play

15

and weight shifting allows you "stay on beat." The kick is actually on the one, but it doesn't feel that way because it happens at the end of a phrase in the drumming—gu g'hum dhum dhum *ga*. So by the time you get to the breakdown, that kick is still the one, but feels like the "and," making it rather confusing as to how you could possibly "walk it out" for two instead of three steps. The final portion of the breakdown is not set, but meant to mutate each time you do it. As long as you hold for four counts after the lunge (the first step into the lunge is the one), everything should work out fine. Needless to say, we were stumped. Just as we back-liners thought we had it, the leader would switch it up. The most spectacular breakdown she dared us to duplicate was a drop squat that came up in a high kick with the right leg.

Watch Me—Uh, Ah Got It

After almost falling several times on the cobblestone, it hit me *who* this dance was. We were getting on the good foot! James Brown, Godfather of Soul, helped to galvanize the masses and revolutionaries on the dance floor in the 1970s, giving them a new and very black way to "move somethin'." Reclaiming their African heritage from the maws of the folklore factory called the "Department in Defense of Brazilian Culture," these young soul rebels of the seventies sought to differentiate themselves from integrationists and those who believed that Brazil was a racial democracy by developing a black ethos visible through and on the body itself.

During my 1990 visit, I had the good fortune of being introduced to a famous *carnaval* dancer named Negrizú. In the late 1970s and early 1980s he "made" *carnaval* with the popular *afoxé*, Badauê. Badauê was known for its very strong and visible tie to the Candomblé as well as the soul music scene. While chatting with Negrizú, I learned that James Brown's famous open step slide (that one-foot shimmy) was considered an essential Black dance in Salvador in the early seventies. It was called "Blek Sol" (Black Soul). Negrizú rendered an impeccable imitation of the step, explaining the power surge that people experienced when executing it. That James Brown and his music were important icons of the nascent *bloco afro/neo-afoxé* movement was a constant in various circles where other "facts" varied from person to person or even time to time with the same person. But why James?

Paul Gilroy has written, about James Brown's impact on the black British-Caribbean political scene, that the "danceability" of soul music, in particular that of Soul Brother Number One, made it accessible to lower- and working-class blacks, whereas the concomitant jazz revolution did not reach such a wide audience (Gilroy 177). Antonio Risério's *Carnaval Ijexá* has an extremely vivid account of the impact of soul music in the very dwellings built during that era in Liberdade. Apparently, the need to dance à la James required a larger floor space to precisely duplicate that slide, comically described as "agility in the suds", so people constructed their houses with small bedrooms in order to make room for large Blek Sol living rooms (Risério 28). While attending a Congolese dance camp in California in 1989, one of the instructors, who was just learning to speak English, explained to me how important James Brown's music had been to him when he was a youngster. Even though he didn't understand a word of what was said, "it felt important and powerful."

No one was entirely clear as to exactly what James was saying, but everyone knew he was *feelin'* it. A master showman and band leader, James Brown was definitely the "Hardest Workin' Man in Show Business." His economy of lines, his knack for onomatopoetics and double and sometimes even triple entendre—dished out in a driving rhythm that would not be stopped—crystalized many of the political slogans of the time into jewels of sweat on the bodies of thousands of new "Black and Beautiful" people throughout the world. Reflecting on the social unrest and proclamations of self-love of the U.S. black community in the 1950s and 1960s, songs like "The Big Pay-Back," "Sex Machine," "Poppa's Got a Brand-New Bag," "I'm Black and I'm Proud," and "I Got Soul (Superbad)" not only told like it *was,* but like it *should* and was *gonna* be. But the message was beyond the words. Each grunt, repeated syllable, cry, holler, unh, screech, and scream racked his body with a tension that felt like it would be a painful beauty once it got out. And when the voice wasn't enough to make all that sweet and sour soul power known to the world, James Brown got down and delivered the message of Black Power through blurs of body parts.

Whatever he's doing now, Godfather made us all funky. Whether it's pushing a product or providing break beats, the well of James seems to spring eternal. By far one of the most sampled musicians, physically and musically—folks forget that Prince was getting over doing his best "James Brown" with some Little Richard thrown in for good measure before MC Hammer went and put the Godfather hisself in a rap music video (1989)—James Brown continues to be a force in black popular culture youth movements. So much so that in 1994 an African American could go to Salvador, Bahia-Brazil, and relearn his steps in a context so different from the "grits & gravy–candied yams–smothered steak" soul land of his birth that she had to jump back and kiss herself when she finally got the moves.

Gu g'hum dhum dhum ga, ga dhum dhum ga . . . Gu g'ghum dhum dhum ga, ga dhum dhum ga. Still working out the step, I suddenly recognized our teasing leader from a dance class I used to take with Augusto Omolu, director of the dance wing of the *bloco afro* Muzenza and principle dancer with the Ballet Teatro Castro Alves. We talked for a while, shouting over the heavy bass. She introduced me to other people as "uma Americana." Astonished, people seemed to relax after it was explained that I'd been to Bahia before and was studying "Afro" with various dance teachers in the city. "Aie, nega! Isso mesmo!" As with all great dance moves, a few of us suddenly found ourselves floating over the rhythm, nailing each slide, turn and hop, even adding our own end to the breakdown. Too pleased with ourselves, we danced on until the drummers had to break to switch personnel. It had been at least an hour and a half since I'd flipped my sixty-minute tape.

While the next band was setting up, a recording was played to make sure we didn't loose our groove, "Sene sene sene Senega-al." The voice of a woman rang out from the speakers and my newfound group hollered "Queremos-a ao vivo!" ("We want her live"), pointing to one of the women who had earlier corrected us on our use of our arms and hands. As far as I know, Graça is the only female samba reggae singer connected with a *bloco afro*. Several female pop stars sing covers of specific *bloco afro*'s, since it is believed that the music as it is played in the rehearsals is too ugly for mass distribution and consumption. Embarrassed, she half expected the musical director to come get her, but the *bateria* had already dispersed, thwarting our sisterhood desires. It began to rain. Dreadlocked men rushed to cut the juice to the microphones and remove the equipment from the stage. The rest of us took cover in the bar and under the entryway.

In a typical winter Bahian storm, the rain came in a gush and soon settled into a fine mist. Our fearless leader announced to anyone who wanted to hear that she didn't come here this late at night to stand under some stinky old stones; she planned to get hers and she wasn't satisfied just yet. She marched us back to our spot, demanding that the band get their behinds back on the stage. And they did.

It was now about 2:30 A.M. The last of the tourist audience had left about half an hour ago, while the ranks of the crowd continued to swell. The new band was outfitted with congas and *atabaques* (a cousin of the conga but taller and slenderer, often played with a stick). They looked as if they were going to serve up some *pagôde,* a new-old samba from Rio that was taking the country by storm again, but they started in aiming to finish what the *bateria* had begun: *suingue.* "For por a causa do Ilê, menina / For por a causa do Ilê / For por a causa do Ilê, menina / que me faz esquecer de você." People lost their minds, myself included.

We were working on a frontal version of the James Brown thing when one of the leader-ladies said, "Bote um." "O que?" I asked, uncertain what she wanted me to put and where. "Bote um de seus passos." One of my steps? You mean they've been making this stuff up as they went along? Taken aback, I gave it a go, showing a Senegalese dance called *lamba,* since it emphasizes long articulated arms similar to their own dance idiom. We did the basic walk: to the right three steps, arms swinging in alternation; skip switch foot with arms extended up and back; walk to the left, same thing. Then I showed the variation on that step. The woman who'd asked me to show a move asked in her curt way, "Quantos vezes?" "I don't know, how ever many you want." She was exasperated now. I was not understanding the process. I had not given the parameters of the steps I'd shown. No counts, no transition step between the two, just some movements.

Trying to redeem myself, I gave a torso-popping move that was a variation on one of their shoulder-popping ones. This time I included counts, a couple of transitions and variations. They could not figure it out, however, even though the feet never moved. The torso isolation was tripping them up. Most Afro dance does not make use of torso isolations, and those that do use it as a very small constant pulse around which the arms and feet move in counter and half tempo. Even though she couldn't make it work, my girl in the jumper enjoyed the movement nonetheless because of its difficulty. She now had an idea for a move that she could work out at home, then come back and make everybody admire her skills. We split a beer while the band took a break. I looked at my watch and decided I needed to leave. It was 3:30 A.M.

What You Gon' Do Now? An Open Ending

An explicit analysis of this Ilê Aiyê rehearsal would probably miss the point. Nonetheless, I do have several questions about liberation and ass-shaking. If the James Brown period of the worldwide Black Power Movement is any indication, then there is in fact some deciphering of code that happens between various points of the black Atlantic and is translated through the body itself. What those codes are is determined by the decipherer herself and the community of "de/cipherers" to which she belongs. These are not "blood memories" or "retentions," as they are sometimes defined in certain scholarly circles.

Retention theory obscures the tenacity of cultural practitioners who pass on their knowledge in a systematic, continuous way by displacing that tenacity onto the object, making the object and its reproduction by future generations symptomatic of breaks or lacks in cultural awareness. What is missed by being transfixed by the object's appearance and disappearance is the continuous use of a culture-specific process that adapts or encompasses different material production as the material reality of the practitioner changes. This is known as "makin' do." There is no accidental memory; recollection is purposeful and productive. Unfortunately, it is precisely this aspect of Afro-Bahian culture (and arguably black world culture) that has been frozen by police, anthropologists, ethnomusicologists, folklorists, and those more influential practitioners connected, usually economically, to the power structure that these various "collectors" represent. A more recent addition to that list is the tour guide.

Within a rententionist paradigm, it is incomprehensible that dance moves from James Brown's repertoire were actively sought out, added and interrogated on the dance floor, and thus continuously modified. But I want to problematize "ciphering" itself, especially in the instance of His Funkiness, by posing the question of gender to the cipherer James Brown, the cipher "James Brown," and the "movements" that inspired many of his songs. Given the sexual politics of the black arts and Black Power movements in the United States, what does it mean for the women at Ilê Aiyê to be dancing in the shadows? How has the phallocentricity of Black Nationalism embedded in James's body and lyrics been de/ciphered or reproduced in Salvador?

Various radical academics are working toward a paradigm for "reading" these and other codes, understanding them as "texts" with specific contexts. Sylvia Wynter has pointed out that reading a code does not destabilize Western European hegemony, but reinstates it in the very act of confronting it. I have taken the position of black arts makers, most of whom have chosen to identify the process at work rather than solidify the codes into a fixed "read," thereby destroying their potential to traverse time, space, language, and national boundaries. In his article "Notes on an African Diaspora Symbolic Language," Philip Mallory Jones, a mysteriously uncelebrated but well-funded avant-garde Pan-Africanist video artist, has listed elements that for him constitute an "African Diaspora aesthetic" (what I am calling a de/ciphering practice), including symbolism, metaphor, music, performance, drawing on collective memory and lore, appropriation, signs and ritual gesture, story/telling/witnessing, fragmentation, interruption, polyrhythms, incorporation of text, density, and interval.

If I were to become transfixed by the various movements I witnessed that night at Forte Santo Antonio, I could quite easily state that the dancers were misusing sacred dances in a profane place. And it is perhaps in that moment of mono-processing that Afro-consciousness expresses its political intentions. There are no binary constructions with which to contend. The sacred can be placed in the service of social commentary just as easily as a funk rhythm. The new dance move is, in fact, the old as well as the not-yet-new. The development of the Afro-consciousness is traceable through bodies in motion: from soul singers like James Brown and reggae superstars like Bob Marley and his I-Threes to the Black Power movement in the United States. However, it is also connected by language and history to bodies in struggle in Mozambique, Guinea Bissau, and Angola. Aside from a refrain in a *carnaval* song, are these connections/codes evident and critical in the lives of the "crowd"?

Given that the aim of *bloco afro* performance is to change consciousness and then to mobilize, the vitality of the movement can be measured on a personal level through anecdotes. For example, on my way to another Ilê Aiyê rehearsal, the cab driver told me that he always makes *carnaval* with Ilê because they are "more" as he rubbed his dark brown arm. He said that he was moved to tears by Ilê *carnaval* theme this year, "Black America, the African Dream," a tribute to past civil rights leaders in the United States. A sidewalk painter who used to be a drummer with the Community Dance Workshop run by Olodum, when I asked him why he was selling *faux naif* art instead of playing, said,

"They didn't want to pay anybody over there. They ain't nothing but the Mafia, using people's talents to make money for themselves!"

Confounding black aesthetic products with its production, Olodum is successfully shutting out the competition as it enters the capitalist market. Ilê Aiyê is making an attempt to continue creating a space for the "crowd" to work the process free of the restraints of the product, yet the organization struggles for money. Invariably, Afro culture and consciousness are at a critical juncture. Yes, we gotta "move somethin'," but what will it be: records and tapes or liberated black bodies?

REFERENCES

Gilroy, Paul. *"There Ain't No Black in the Union Jack": The Cultural Politics of Race and Nation.* 1987. Chicago: University of Chicago Press, 1991.

Jones, Philip Mallory. "Notes on an African Diaspora Symbolic Language." *Felix* (spring 1992): 38.

Risério, Antonio. *Carnaval Ijexá: notas sobre afoxés e blocos do novo carnaval afrobaiano.* Salvador, Brazil: Corrupio, 1981.

Afro Images

Politics, Fashion, and Nostalgia

ANGELA Y. DAVIS

Not long ago, I attended a performance in San Francisco by women presently or formerly incarcerated in the County Jail, in collaboration with Bay Area women performance artists. After the show, I went backstage to the "green room," where the women inmates, guarded by deputy sheriffs stationed outside the door, were celebrating with their families and friends. Having worked with some of the women at the jail, I wanted to congratulate them on the show. One woman introduced me to her brother, who at first responded to my name with a blank stare. The woman admonished him: "You don't know who Angela Davis is? You should be ashamed." Suddenly a flicker of recognition flashed across his face. "Oh," he said, "Angela Davis—the Afro."

Such responses, I find, are hardly exceptional, and it is both humiliating and humbling to discover that a single generation after the events that constructed me as a public personality, I am remembered as a hairdo. It is humiliating because it reduces a politics of liberation to a politics of fashion; it is humbling because such encounters with the younger generation demonstrate the fragility and mutability of historical images, particularly those associated with African American history. This encounter with the young man who identified me as "the Afro" reminded me of a recent article in the *New York Times Magazine* that listed me as one of the fifty most influential fashion (read: hairstyle) trendsetters over the last century.[1] I continue to find it ironic that the popularity of the "Afro" is attributed to me, when, in actuality, I was emulating a whole host of women—both public figures and women I encountered in my daily life—when I began to wear my hair natural in the late sixties.

But it is not merely the reduction of historical politics to contemporary fashion that infuriates me. Especially disconcerting is the fact that the distinction of being known as "the Afro" is largely a result of a particular economy of journalistic images in which mine is one of the relatively few that has survived the last two decades. Or perhaps the very segregation of those photographic images caused mine to enter into the then dominant journalistic culture precisely by virtue of my presumed "criminality." In any case, it has survived, disconnected from the historical context in which it arose, as fashion. Most young African Americans who are familiar with my name and twenty-five-year-old image have encountered photographs and film/video clips largely in music videos, and in black history montages in popular books and magazines. Within the interpretive context in which they learn to situate these photographs, the most salient element of the image is the hairstyle, understood less as a political statement than as fashion.

The unprecedented contemporary circulation of photographic and filmic images of African Americans has multiple and contradictory implications. On the one hand, it holds the promise of visual memory of older and departed generations, of both well-known figures and people who may not have achieved public prominence. However, there is also the danger that this historical memory may become ahistorical and apolitical. "Photographs are relics of the past," John Berger has written. They are "traces of what has happened. If the living take that past upon themselves, if the past becomes an integral part of the process of people making their own history, then all photographs would acquire a living context, they would continue to exist in time, instead of being arrested moments." [2]

In the past, I have been rather reluctant to reflect in more than a casual way on the power of the visual images by which I was represented during the period of my trial. Perhaps this is due to my unwillingness to confront those images as having to some extent structured my experiences during that era. The recent recycling of some of these images in contexts that privilege the "Afro" as fashion—revolutionary glamour—has led me to reconsider them both in the historical context in which they were first produced (and in which I first experienced them) and

2.1. FBI Wanted Poster

within the "historical" context in which they often are presented today as "arrested moments."

■ ■ ■

In September 1969, the University of California Regents fired me from my post in the philosophy department at UCLA because of my membership in the Communist Party. The following summer, charges of murder, kidnapping, and conspiracy were brought against me in connection with my activities on behalf of George Jackson and the Soledad Brothers. The circulation of various photographic images of me—taken by journalists, undercover policemen, and movement activists—played a major role in both the mobilization of public opinion against me *and* the development of the campaign that was ultimately responsible for my acquittal.

Twenty-five years later, many of these photographs are being recycled and recontextualized in ways that are at once exciting and disturbing. With the first public circulation of my photographs, I was intensely aware of the invasive and transformative power of the camera and of the ideological contextualization of my images, which left me with little or no agency. On the one hand I was portrayed as a conspiratorial and monstrous Communist (i.e., anti-American) whose unruly natural hairdo symbolized black militancy (i.e., anti-whiteness) Some of the first hate mail I received tended to collapse "Russia" and "Africa." I was told to "go back to Russia" and often in the same sentence (in connection with a reference to my hair) to "go back to Africa." On the other hand, sympathetic portrayals tended to interpret the image—almost inevitably one with my mouth wide open—as that of a charismatic and raucous revolutionary ready to lead the masses into battle. Since I considered myself neither monstrous nor charismatic, I felt fundamentally betrayed on both accounts: violated on the first account, and deficient on the second.

When I was fired by the UC Regents in 1969, an assortment of photographs appeared throughout that year in various newspapers and magazines and on television. However, it was not until felony charges were brought against me in connection with the Marin County shootout that the photographs became what Susan Sontag has called a part of "the general furniture of the environment." [3] As such, they truly began to frighten me. A cycle of terror was initiated by the decision of the FBI to declare me one of the country's ten most-wanted criminals. Although I had been underground for over a month before I actually saw the photographs the FBI had decided to use on the poster, I had to picture how they might portray me as I attempted to create for myself an appearance that would be markedly different from the one defined as armed and dangerous. The props I used consisted of a wig with straight black hair, long false lashes, and more eyeshadow, liner, and blush than I had ever before imagined wearing in public. Never having seriously attempted to present myself as glamorous, it seemed to me that glamour was the only look that might annul the likelihood of being perceived as a revolutionary. It never could have occurred to me that the same "revolutionary" image I then sought to camouflage with glamour would be turned, a generation later, into glamour and nostalgia.

After the FBI poster was put on display in post offices, other government buildings, and on the television program, *The FBI, Life* magazine came out with a provocative issue featuring a cover story on me. Illustrated by photographs from my childhood years through the UCLA firing, the article probed the reasons for my supposedly abandoning a sure trajectory toward fulfillment of the middle-class American dream in order to lead the unpredictable life of a "black revolutionary." Considering the vast circulation of this pictorial magazine,[4] I experienced something akin to what Barthes was referring to when he wrote, "I feel that the Photograph creates my body or mortifies it, according to its caprice (apology of this mortiferous power: certain Communards paid with their lives for their willingness or even their eagerness to pose on the barricades: defeated, they were recognized by Thiers's police and shot, almost every one)."[5] The life-size headshot on the cover of the magazine would be seen by as many people, if not more, than the much smaller portraits on the FBI poster. Having confronted my own image in the store where I purchased the magazine, I was convinced that FBI chief J. Edgar Hoover had conspired in the appearance of that cover story. More than anything else, it seemed to me to be a magnification and elaboration of the WANTED poster. Moreover, the text of the story gave a rather convincing explanation as to why the pictures should be associated with arms and danger.

The photograph on the cover of my autobiography,[6] published in 1974, was taken by the renowned photographer Phillipe Halsman. When I entered his studio with Toni Morrison, who was my editor, the first question he asked us was whether we had brought the black leather jacket. He assumed, it turned out, that he was to recreate with his camera a symbolic visual representation of black militancy: leather jacket (uniform of the Black Panther Party), Afro hairdo, and raised fist. We had to persuade him to photograph me in a less predictable posture. As recently as 1993, the persisting persuasiveness of these visual stereotypes was made clear to me when I had to insist that Anna Deavere Smith rethink her representation of me in her theater piece *Fires in the Mirror,* which initially relied upon a black leather jacket as her main prop.

So far, I have concentrated primarily on my own responses to those photographic images, which may not be the most interesting or productive way to approach them. While the most obvious evidence of their power was the part they played in structuring people's opinions about me as a "fugitive" and a political prisoner, their broader and more subtle effect was the way they served as generic images of black women who wore their hair "natural." From the constant stream of stories I have heard over the last twenty-four years (and continue to hear), I infer that hundreds, perhaps even thousands, of Afro-wearing black women were accosted, harassed, and arrested by police, FBI and immigration agents during the two months spent underground. One woman who told me that she hoped she could serve as a "decoy" because of her light skin and big natural, was obviously conscious of the way the photographs— circulating within a highly charged racialized context—constructed generic representations of young black women. Consequently, the photographs identified vast numbers of my black female contemporaries who wore naturals (whether light- or dark-skinned) as targets of repression. This is the hidden historical content that lurks behind the continued association of my name with the Afro.

A young woman who is a former student of mine has been wearing an Afro during the last few months. Rarely a day passes, she has told me, when she is not greeted with cries of "Angela Davis" from total strangers. Moreover, during the months preceding the writing of this article. I have received an astounding number of requests for interviews from journalists doing stories on "the resurgence of the Afro." A number of the most recent requests were occasioned by a layout in the fashion section of the March 1994 issue of *Vibe* magazine entitled "Free Angela: Actress Cynda Williams as Angela Davis, a Fashion Revolutionary." The spread consists of eight full-page photos of Cynda Williams (known for her role as the singer in Spike Lee's *Mo' Better Blues*) in poses that parody photographs taken of me during the early 1970s. The work of stylist Patty Wilson, the layout is described as " 'docufashion' because it uses modern clothing to mimic Angela Davis's look from the '70s."[7]

Some of the pictures are rather straightforward attempts to recreate press photos taken at my arrest, during the trial, and after my release. Others can be characterized as pastiche,[8] drawing elements, like leather-jacketed black men, from contemporary stereotypes of the sixties-seventies era of black militancy. They include an arrest scene, with the model situated between two uniformed policemen and wearing an advertised black satin blouse (reminiscent of the top I was wearing on the date of my arrest). As with her hair, the advertised eyewear are amazingly similar to the glasses I wore. There are two courtroom scenes in which Williams wears an enormous Afro wig and advertised see-through mini-dresses and, in one of them, handcuffs. Yet another revolves around a cigar-smoking, bearded man dressed in fatigues with a gun holster around his waist, obviously meant to evoke Che Guevara. (Even the fatigues can be purchased—from Cheap Jack's!) There is no such thing as subtlety in these photos. Because the point of this fashion spread is to represent the clothing associated with revolutionary movements of the early seventies as revolutionary fashion in the nineties, the sixtieth-anniversary logo of the Communist Party has been altered in one of the photos to read "1919–1971" (instead of 1979). And the advertised dress in the photo for which this logo is a backdrop is adorned with pin-on buttons reading "Free All Political Prisoners."

The photographs I find most unsettling, however, are the two small headshots of Williams wearing a huge Afro wig on a reproduction of the FBI wanted poster that is otherwise unaltered except for the words "FREE ANGELA" in bold red print across the bottom of the document. Despite the fact that the inordinately small photos do not really permit much of a view of the clothing Williams wears, the tops and glasses (again quite similar to the ones I wore in the two imitated photographs) are listed as purchasable items. This is the most blatant example of the way the particular history of my legal case is emptied of all content so that it can serve as a commodified backdrop for advertising. The way in which this document provided a historical pretext for something akin to a reign of terror for countless young black women is effectively erased by its use as a prop for selling clothes and promoting a seventies fashion nostalgia. What is also lost in this nostalgic surrogate for historical memory—in these "arrested moments," to use John Berger's word—is the activist involvement of vast numbers of black women in movements that are now represented with even greater masculinist contours than they actually exhibited at the time.

Without engaging the numerous debates occasioned by Fredric Jameson's paper "Postmodernism and Consumer Society,"[9] I would like to suggest that his analysis of "nostalgia films" and their literary counterparts, which are "historical novels in appearance only," might provide a useful point of departure for an interpretation of this advertising genre called "docufashion" as "[W]e seem condemned to seek the historical past," Jameson writes, "through our own pop images and stereotypes about that past, which itself remains forever out of reach."[10] Perhaps by also taking up John Berger's call for an "alternative photography" we might develop strategies for engaging photographic images like the ones I have evoked, by actively seeking to transform their interpretive contexts in education, popular culture, the media, community organizing, and so on. Particularly in relation to African American historical images, we need to find ways of incorporating them into "social and political memory, instead of using [them] as a substitute which encourages the atrophy of such memory."[11]

NOTES

1. *New York Times Magazine,* date unknown.

2. John Berger, *About Looking* (New York: Pantheon Books, 1980), p. 57.

3. Susan Sontag, *On Photography* (New York: Farrar, Straus and Giroux, 1978), p. 27.

4. During the 1960s *Life* magazine had a circulation of approximately forty million people. (Gisele Freund, *Photography and Society* [Boston: David R. Godine, 1980], p. 143.)

5. Roland Barthes, *Camera Lucida* (New York: Hill and Wang, 1981), p. 11.

6. *Angela Y. Davis: An Autobiography* (New York: Random House, 1974).

7. *Vibe* 2, no. 2 (March 1994), p. 16.

8. I use the term *pastiche* both in the usual sense of a potpourri of disparate ingredients and in the sense in which Fredric Jameson uses it. "Pastiche is, like parody, the imitation of a peculiar or unique style, the wearing of a stylistic mask, speech in a dead language; but it is a neutral practice of such mimicry, without parody's ulterior motive, without the satirical impulse, without laughter. . . . Pastiche is black parody, parody that has lost its sense of humor." (Fredric

Jameson, "Postmodernism and Consumer Society" in Hall Foster, ed., *The Anti-Aesthetic: Essays on Postmodern Culture* [Port Townsend, Wash.: Bay Press, 1983], p. 114.)

9. Jameson's essay has appeared in several versions. The one I have consulted is referenced in note 8. I thank Victoria Smith for suggesting that I reread this essay in connection with the *Vibe* story.

10. Jameson, p. 118.

11. Berger, p. 58.

3

Notes of a Prodigal Son

James Baldwin and the Apostasy of Soul

NATHAN L. GRANT

We have only begun to hear of Martin Luther King, Jr. Malcolm X has yet to be taken seriously. No one, except their parents, has ever heard of Huey Newton or Bobby Seale or Angela Davis. Emmett Till has been dead two years. Bobby Hutton and Jonathan Jackson have just mastered their first words, and, with someone holding them by the hand, are discovering how much fun it is to climb up and down the stairs. Oh, pioneers!

—James Baldwin, *No Name in the Street*

James Baldwin, as a developing essayist and thinker, sought to fashion the Black reaction to anti-Black racism by iterating and reiterating the risk of genuine freedom for whites who refused to relinquish their hatred. Baldwin desired to dissolve the horror of American racism in the crucible of love, and thus pass to his brothers and sisters the cup of understanding. This idea was at the heart of his first collection of essays, *Notes of a Native Son* (1955), which was hailed by many as an enduring view on the Black condition in America. But perhaps the severest criticism was that its examination of the African American condition was too narrowly fashioned by its Euro-American perspective.

Less than a decade later Baldwin's formula for racial harmony would wear even thinner to the proponents of Black Consciousness, who externalized their anger and defiance in ways that were considered dangerous at the time that Baldwin began to write. Their ethos of soul, which was in part the ultimate projection of Black anger, would no longer allow what appeared to be the softer criticisms of American life. Soul, as a concept, would seek the hard edge of critique and shape as targets every manifestation of the American capitalist impulse, looking to smash these in an effort toward Black revolution. As a behavior, forged by Black men and women in Harlem or Watts or Chicago's South Side, soul was boldness with a Black veneer; it was the urban Black mind projected in ways that had not been seen before. Soul was more than anti-establishment; it was Black badness, new, tough, and aggressive. Its long list of heroes, including Huey Newton, Eldridge Cleaver, Bobby Seale, and Rap Brown, reflected the attitudes of urban Blacks. Soul tested the horizon of the cultural frontier defined for Blacks by white America.

Though soul perhaps was not a realizable phenomenon until the mid-sixties, its most enduring literary prototype was Bigger Thomas, the tortured Black youth of Richard Wright's *Native Son* (1940). Bigger's fear and hatred of the white world that hemmed him in would rise to the fore in the sixties and seventies and would be largely manifest in the behavior of disenfranchised urban Blacks. Baldwin's first two essays in *Notes of a Native Son*, "Everybody's Protest Novel" and "Many Thousands Gone," written in 1949 and 1951, respectively, decry the validity of Bigger Thomas's experience, asserting that the only value of the protest novel is in separating us from our shared heritage of liberty. For Baldwin, the protest novel is "a mirror of our confusion, dishonesty, panic, trapped and immobilized in the prison of the American dream." [1]

The young Baldwin felt that he had much to learn from the older Wright, and he appeared to come to terms with this tutelage in his sequel to *Notes, Nobody Knows My Name* (1962). Baldwin's coming of age here included the visitations of Wright's terrible sensibilities upon the younger man's intellect, and Baldwin's recognition of himself in Wright's work would apparently serve to make and remake his vision:

We were linked together, really, because both of us were black. I had made my pilgrimage to meet him because he was the greatest black writer in the world for me. In *Uncle Tom's Children*, in *Native Son*, and above all, in *Black Boy*, I found expressed, for the first time in my life, the sorrow, the rage, and the murderous bitterness which was eating up my life and the lives of those around me. His work was an immense liberation and revelation for me. He became my ally and my witness, and alas! my father. [2]

Father terrorizes child in this instance, however, for Wright in *Native Son* (and similarly, in the autobiographical *Black Boy*) presents to Baldwin the unmasked face of Black rage, the gnawing, absolute, and unendurable hunger that ensues with the denial of every support of citizenship. Baldwin's response is to seek the citizen in both the Black and the white; the discovery of the citizen in each is itself the promise of America. But this is a conflicted response, for the abyss is already known to Baldwin, already in him: If the novel of protest is to him "trapped and immobilized in the sunlit prison of the American dream," then he is certainly aware of the terror of which Wright speaks and is, however reluctantly, prophesying the era of soul.

Along with a new political sensibility, debates about Black identity, and a sense of creativity blended with nationalistic sentiment that often mirrors that of the Harlem Renaissance, the era of soul rendered an attitude of expression that previously had been hidden from the eyes of not only white America but Black America as well. This attitude—this soulful "badness"—was itself a rejection of everything about America to which Baldwin determined all Americans had a claim. Bennett Berger's commentary on soul defines it as an ideology of African American lower-class culture, which sees itself as the ultimate rejection of middle-class American culture. So defined, *soul* is "an attempt to strike at the heart of the ethic of success and mobility, which is as close as this country comes to having any really sacred values."[3] Soul repudiates capitalism in all of its representations; it denies the very system that historically has demanded the disenfranchisement of nonwhite peoples and continues to maintain itself as the system to which nonwhites are not admitted. But soul seeks to go a step beyond: Relying on its distinction from capitalism for its self-definition, soul imposes itself finally as capitalism's fullest antithesis.

The inevitable consequence of such movement is a stasis beyond simple nonparticipation. Capitalism has rhythms that are unique to it, but it is insufficient to say that these rhythms are our rhythms; as a tenet of Marxism, capitalism is time itself.[4] That capitalism actually does thematize life means that its rhythms—of commerce, influence, politics, and power—are the rhythms to which we move, even breathe. This idea inheres in Stokely Carmichael and Charles Hamilton's dictum that "before a group can enter the open society, it must first close ranks."[5] But the closing of ranks may mean that many on the inside are trapped by the new order. The suddenness and force with which soul wrenches itself from the capitalist ethos means that it develops no rhythms of its own. The legions of the soulful are forced to live outside the structures and systems of the modern world, and as was the case with Bigger Thomas, the consequences for urban Black men and women are severe indeed.

Baldwin, of course, is fearful of such consequences and had expressed that fear by the early fifties. If Bigger Thomas is a precursor of the soulful Black man because he is hurled tempestuously beyond American society through its fears, then the flaw in Bigger is also irreducibly society's flaw:

We do not know what to do with him in life; if he breaks our sociological and sentimental image of him we are panic-stricken and we feel ourselves betrayed. When he violates this image, therefore, he stands in the greatest danger (sensing which, we uneasily suspect that he is very often playing a part for our benefit); and, what is not always so apparent but is equally true, we are then in some danger ourselves—hence our retreat or our blind and immediate retaliation. (*Notes*, 19)

But Baldwin was slightly outpaced by the sixties, that decade of unrest, of assassination, of one damned thing after another, which also saw the very different perspective Blacks in the United States were taking toward their condition. Though soul was born of the political and social upheaval of the sixties, its literary and aesthetic manifestations would play a significant role in its definition. Amiri Baraka (LeRoi Jones), one of the principal figures of the Black Theater Movement, notes in his famous *Blues People* that soul, whose essence can also be linked to Black music, represented a shift from Black cultural and political values that prevailed during the forties and fifties. Soul marked "a form of social aggression," he writes. "It is an attempt to place upon a 'meaningless' social order, an order which would give value to terms of existence that were once considered not only valueless but shameful. . . . Soul means a new establishment." [6] Genevieve Fabre finds that the very militancy of soul mobilizes people; it "creates a climate of confidence and fellowship and recognizes a control over destiny." [7] But while soul can have these creative and generative attributes—while it can foster and maintain cohesion and an in-group relatedness that has aspects of healing that Blacks cannot hope to find in the larger society—it also has its nightmarish quality, which itself is paradoxically the result of its irreducible separation from the values of the larger society. What replaces soul is the internecine quality of life in the Black community—the community's newly found ability to feed upon itself. This new society has new prey: women, the emotionally weak, and middle-class Blacks all become the usual fare for a new generation of Bigger Thomases.

Many writers of the sixties and seventies thus both enjoined and embellished Wright's representation. In Iceberg Slim's autobiography *Pimp: The Story of My Life*, it may easily be said that no one in this milieu has successfully escaped the core value of capitalism, its ethic of acquisition; in fact, capitalism's most dastardly mask is baldly in evidence here. But what is at immediate issue is the sense that any form of separateness from Euro-America and its structures is far preferable to life lived by white men's rules. Here, Slim compares his life as a pimp who is presently trying to build his stable to what that life would be had he not chosen crime. Clearly, he likes his chances:

I went down to the street. I got into my Ford. It roared to life. . . . felt good. I wasn't doing bad for a black boy just out of the joint. I shuddered when I thought, what if I hadn't kept my ears flapping back there in the joint? I would be a boot black or porter for the rest of my life in the high walled white world. My black whore was a cinch to get piles of white scratch from that forbidden white world.[8]

Later, Slim witnesses from another pimp some of the ordinary control of women without which the pimp cannot claim his "badness":

The crowd stood tittering and excited like a Salem mob watching the execution of a witch. . . . Again and again he slammed his size-thirteen shoe down on the witch's belly and chest. She was out cold. Her jaw hinge was awry and red frothy bubbles bunched at the corners of her crooked mouth. At last he scooped her up from the pavement. She looked like an infant in his arms. He looked into her unconscious face. He muttered, "Baby, why, why, do you make me do you like this? Why don't you hump and stop lushing and bullshitting with the tricks?" (*Pimp*, 96)

The subjugation of women is as totalizing as slavery itself and even depends upon a doubly ahistorical removal from the twin senses of capitalism and whiteness:

I got to find out the secrets of pimping. I don't want to be a half-ass gigolo lover like the white pimps. I really want to control the whole whore. I want to be the boss of her life, even her thoughts. I got to con them that Lincoln never freed the slaves. (*Pimp*, 104)

The drama of playwright Ed Bullins dominated off-Broadway for more than a decade with expressions that readily bespoke the need for a Black separateness whose inexorable result was alienation and stasis. In his famous play *The Duplex,* the passion of Steve Benson's dilemma rests in his wanting to escape with and provide for his landlady Velma, who lives with her abusive husband in the same building. Steve aspires to the middle-class life because education, health care, and a decent income are desirable things, but a stultifying sense of absurdity closes in when he begins to see a compromised Black self:

[No one will know] that she'll never really know me . . . this black man . . . with this mind . . . they'll never understand the thoughts that flash through my head and scorch the back of my eyes . . . these eyes that see her being beaten and raped, these eyes that see the flames of the hell that we all live in . . . in our cool dark little lives . . . getting ready to become something we ain't now or will never be . . . really. Some names like what? Colored insurance man, postal clerk, negro journalist, teacher, lawyer, afro-american dentist, actor, horn blower, whiskey pourer . . . clown? [9]

These scenes displaying the anguish of an entire race were largely suppressed during the pre–Civil Rights years, but to the extent they were considered at all, Baldwin was the period's most eloquent spokesperson:

Negroes live violent lives, unavoidably; a Negro press without violence is therefore not possible; and, further, in every act violence, particularly violence against white men, Negroes feel a certain thrill of identification, a wish to have done it themselves, a feeling that old scores are being settled at last. It is no accident that Joe Louis is the most idolized man in Harlem. He has succeeded on a level that white America indicates is the only level for which it has any respect. We (Americans in general, that is) like to point to Negroes and to most of their activities with a kind of tolerant scorn; but it is ourselves we are watching, ourselves we are damning, or—condescendingly—bending to save (*Notes,* 53)

Of course, he begins this statement with the caveat that the negro press is, in form and purpose, merely an outgrowth of the white press, and thus struggles interminably for recognition in white America; this is part of the rhetoric Baldwin used to define the cultural space that Blacks had bestowed upon them by whites. The other aspect of Baldwin's strategy, however—the ploy for which he is best known—adopts the perspective of the thinking white American, thus seducing that reader into thinking about the condition of Black Americans. If his readers had never before considered the Black condition, then Baldwin, as his biographer David Leeming suggests, is more than prepared to inveigle then to do so. But Baldwin's strategy has become famous for its inherent flaw: the fact that it is finally too comforting to many whites. Rather than provoke thoughtful debate, it too readily polishes the shield of denial. Even though white Americans (and many middle-class Black Americans) can here be persuaded to be reflective, perhaps the supreme challenge is in the pausing to bend to save a Bigger Thomas, a Steve Benson, or an Iceberg Slim. In this connection the young social critic seems to have allowed himself sufficient room for the dissatisfaction with white America that was probably already creeping up within him. What must it have meant to adopt this persona time after time on behalf of a majority who, for all its well-intentioned spirit, refused even to see the problems? The evolution of James Baldwin becomes slightly more apparent in the group of essays *Notes, Nobody Knows My Name*. Here the author begins to describe the phenomenon of cultural space—when Black life exists on the margins through white demand. In "Fifth Avenue, Uptown," Baldwin describes for a white intellectual the conditions in both the Southern town and the Northern ghetto:

My recital disturbed him and made him indignant; and he asked me in perfect innocence, "Why don't all the Negroes in the South move North?" I tried to explain what has happened, unfailingly, whenever a significant body of Negroes move North. They do not escape Jim Crow: they merely encounter another, not-less-deadly variety. They do not move to Chicago, they move to the South Side; they do not move to New York, they move to Harlem. The pressure within the ghetto causes the ghetto walls to expand, and this expansion is always violent. . . . [I]nevitably the border which has divided the ghetto from the rest of the world falls into the hands of the ghetto. The white people fall back bitterly before the black horde; the landlords make a tidy profit by raising the rent, chopping up the rooms, and all but dispensing with the upkeep; and what has once been a neighborhood turns into a "turf." (*NKMN*, 68)

A sometime exile in Europe, Baldwin was able to see most clearly into the cauldron of soul when he was farthest away from it. Even though the essay "The Black Boy Looks at the White Boy," a treatise on Norman Mailer, appears directly after the confessed filial connection to Richard Wright, Baldwin attacks both Mailer and his adoption in "The White Negro" of the soulful Black man as the ego ideal of the "hipster," the white male whose disaffection with the hypocrisy of American society seeks an existential release:

He could have pulled rank on me because he was more famous and had more money and also because he was white; but I could have pulled rank on him precisely because I was black and know more about that periphery he so helplessly maligns in The White Negro than he could ever hope to know. Already, you see, we were trapped in our roles and our attitudes: the toughest kid on the block was meeting the toughest kid on the block.... At the same time, my temperament and my experience in this country had led me to expect very little from most American whites, especially, horribly enough, my friends: so it did not seem worthwhile to challenge, in any real way, Norman's views of life on the periphery, or to put him down for them. I was weary, to tell the truth. I had tried, in the States, to convey something of what it felt like to be a Negro and no one had been able to listen: they wanted their romance. And, anyway, the really ghastly thing about trying to convey to a white man the reality of the Negro experience has nothing whatever to do with the fact of color, but has to do with this man's relationship to his own life. He will face in your life only what he is willing to face in his. (*NKMN*, 219, 221)

Indeed, in the second half of *Nobody Knows,* beginning with "Notes for a Hypothetical Novel," Baldwin drops the strategy of employing the white mask. His narrative preference is now for the first person, perhaps in broader recognition of the sorrow, rage, and bitterness that Wright had bequeathed to his consciousness so long before.

Baldwin's most powerful statements on the condition of soul are to be found in *The Fire Next Time* (1962) and *No Name in the Street* (1972), especially the latter. Well before the appearance of *No Name,* the worst aspects of the American condition had been exacerbated to define the nihilism that became soul. In the years between the publication of *Fire* and *No Name,* Medgar Evers had been brutally slain; so had John and Robert Kennedy, to whom the cup of understanding had been passed; and Malcolm X and Martin Luther King Jr. had also died for the noble but elusive—and for this, seemingly indefinable—cause. These events would change Baldwin forever in the sense that they forced the dreaded realization of the denied citizen that had been planted by Richard Wright so many years before, as Baldwin himself described in *Notes*. The crucial, interior, yet vaguely articulated duality that overtook him after having read Wright now metamorphosed into an externalized meditation, perhaps a platform from which to act. Gone is the studious third-person usage that in previous writings had blended the thinking of whites and Blacks:

Incontestably, alas, most people are not, in action, worth very much; and yet, every human being is an uncontested miracle. One tries to treat them as the miracles they are, while trying to protect oneself from the disasters they've become. . . . One could scarcely be deluded by Americans anymore, one scarcely dared expect anything from the great, vast blank generality; and yet one was compelled to demand of Americans—and for their sakes, after all—a generosity, a clarity, and a nobility which they did not dream of demanding of themselves. . . . Perhaps, however, the moral of the story (and the hope of the world) lies in what one demands, not of others, but of oneself.[10]

For what revolutionists would call his sins, Baldwin would have to endure their execrations. Perhaps the most famous, as well as the most devastating, attack came from Eldridge Cleaver, who in *Soul on Ice* sees Baldwin's homosexuality as a threat to Black creativity:

The case of James Baldwin aside for a moment, it seems that many Negro homosexuals, acquiescing in [a] racial death-wish, are outraged and frustrated because in their sickness they are unable to have a baby by a white man. The cross they have to bear is that, already bending over and touching their toes for the white man, the fruit of their miscegenation is not the little half-white off-spring of their dreams but an increase in the unwinding of their nerves—though they redouble their efforts and intake of the white man's sperm.[11]

But Baldwin was nevertheless bound to the movement he had once indirectly scorned, and had only come late to a reading of *Soul in Ice*—ironically, while working for the release of the incarcerated Huey Newton and Bobby Seale.[12] Baldwin, now feeling himself to be at a different stage in the campaign for justice, had not abandoned intellectual fidelity while supporting the spirit of revolution. Rather than succumb to the glorification of the antirhythm of soul, he sought to give it dimension by interrogating the abuses of power. His anger and frustration with the ordinary and flagrant abuse of police power comprise the rhetorical engine behind *No Name,* and after several sojourns to Europe he has acquired a finer understanding not only of Americans but of American power, as he sees the injustice of the West manifested daily in the nonwhite world.

For a very long time . . . America prospered—or seemed to prosper: this prosperity cost millions of people their lives. Now, not even the people who are the most spectacular recipients of the benefits of this prosperity are able to endure these benefits: they can neither understand them nor do without them, nor can they go beyond them. Above all, they cannot, or dare not, assess or imagine the price paid by their victims, or subjects for this way of life, and so they cannot afford to know why the victims are revolting. They are forced, then, to the conclusion that the victims—the barbarians—are revolting against all established civilized values—which is both true and not true—and, in order to preserve these values, however stifling and joyless these values have caused their lives to be, the bulk of the people desperately seek out representatives who are prepared to make up in cruelty what both they and the people lack in conviction. (*No Name,* 88)

Another, bitterer cup of understanding had been passed to him: He had begun not only to comprehend the ethos of soul, but also to see its antirhythm in a double sense as a consequence of the abuses of power. He understands the case of a Bigger Thomas, who is swept along by a series of events he rarely fully understands; and in the present, he sees the intellectual response, the conscious obedience to the impulse to tear away from American middle-class institutions and mores. He is also finally fully conscious that Bigger has been steadily growing up, nourished on the finest grade of American hatred: "It is true that even those who taught at Columbia [University] never saw Harlem, but, on the other hand, everything that New York has become, in 1971, was visibly and swiftly beginning to happen in 1952: one had only to take a bus from the top of the city and ride through it to see how it was darkening and deteriorating, how human contact was endangered and dying" (*No Name,* 34).

As if borrowing from the literary purveyors of the wish-fulfillment heroes of the era of soul, Baldwin experiences a real-life excursion through badness in the person of Tony Maynard, who, before enduring a trumped-up charge for the murder of an American serviceman in New York, had been Baldwin's chauffeur and bodyguard. Tony's innocence seems compromised by his bearing. Seeming to have stepped from the pages of an early seventies' Black novel, Tony is a big man and can be very loud, is far from discreet, and has done his share of street fighting . . . "he has, in fact, a kind of pantherlike, street-boy elegance—he walks something like a cat—and a tricky, touchy, dangerous pride, which, in the years we worked together, kept him in all kinds of fruitless trouble; and he had a taste for white women (who had a taste for him) which made him, especially given his aggressively virile good looks, particularly unattractive for the NYPD" (*No Name*, 100).

Maynard often disagreed philosophically with Baldwin's stance on nonviolence and through his anger had at times placed Baldwin in embarrassing social situations. But Baldwin understood the passions that drove his friend.[13] They were simply organic responses to a hostile world. In the ordeal of Tony Maynard, a more personal anger and frustration envelops Baldwin as he struggles with the meaning of this tempestuous period. The story of Baldwin's fight against Tony's extradition (he was charged in Hamburg, West Germany), his imprisonment, and his subsequent brutal beating at the hands of the police are told in the effort to explain one man's initiation to the horrors of the absence of citizenship, the worldwide reach of those horrors, and the millions of Tony Maynards who daily endure this treatment and, for enduring it, become all the more determined to exist beyond the bonds of capitalist time. From the new perspective of the revolutionary, Baldwin sees the juridical aspect of the "sunlit prison of the American dream":

I agree with the Black Panther position concerning black prisoners: not one of them has ever had a fair trial, for not one of them has ever been tried by a jury of his peers. White middle-class America is always the jury, and they know absolutely nothing about the lives of the people on whom they sit in judgment: and this fact is not altered, on the contrary it is rendered more implacable by the presence of one or two black faces in the jury box. (*No Name*, 113)

Understanding the myriad frustrations that drive the ethos of soul to its instantiation, however, is not to condone the strong self-destructive influence that flourishes in the Black community. Something cries out to be said about "the closing of ranks" when Black anger becomes self-hatred and self-destruction. Baldwin is not silent on this issue, and somehow, despite his efforts in another direction, never had been. If we read him carefully, we first understand the affinity he felt to Bigger Thomas after having read *Native Son*. No understanding of Bigger's self-destructive confusion is possible without understanding his deepest wish to end it, a wish that is at war with the impulse toward self-annihilation. Wright tells us that Bigger "knew that the moment he allowed what his life meant to enter fully into his consciousness, he would either kill himself or someone else. So he denied himself and acted tough."[14]

Beneath this act is Bigger's inexorable desire to change his situation, and given the resistant nature of his oppression, that change would be cataclysmic. Baldwin's intellectual bearing has made him what he always said he wished to be—a witness. But as the hope for unity appears lost—indeed, thrown away—he, like the apostle Paul, looks through a glass darkly, intimating to us the conflagration to come: "A historical wheel had come full circle. The descendants of the cowboys, who had slaughtered the Indians, the issue of those adventurers who had enslaved the blacks, wished to lay down their swords and shields. But these could be laid down only at the Sambo's feet, and this was why they could not be together: I felt like a lip-reader watching the communication of despair" (*No Name,* 185).

NOTES

1. James Baldwin, *Notes of a Native Son* (Boston: Beacon Press, 1955), 14. Hereafter cited in the text as *Notes.*

2. James Baldwin, *Nobody Knows My Name* (New York: Dell, 1962), 191. Hereafter cited in the text as *NKMN.*

3. Bennet Berger, "Black Culture: Lower Class Result or Ethnic Creation?" *Soul.* ed. Lee Rainwater (Chicago: Aldine, 1970).

4. "The time of economic production is a specific time (differing according to the mode of production), but also that, as a specific time, it is a complex and nonlinear time—a time of times, a complex time that cannot be read in the continuity of the time of life or clocks, but has to be constructed out of the peculiar structures of production. . . . It is an invisible time, essentially illegible, as invisible and as opaque as the reality of the total capitalist production process itself. This time as a complex 'intersection' of the different times, rhythms, turnovers, etc. . . ., is only accessible in its concept, which, like every concept is never immediately 'given,' never legible in visible reality: like every concept this concept is produced, constructed" (Louis Althusser and Etienne Balibar, *Reading Capital* [London: Verso, 1979], 101).

5. Stokely Carmichael and Charles V. Hamilton, *Black Power* (New York: Vintage, 1967), quoted in Norman Harris, *Connecting Times: The Sixties in Afro-American Fiction* (Jackson: University Press of Mississippi, 1988), 91.

6. LeRoi Jones (Amiri Baraka), *Blues People* (New York: Morrow, 1963), 218.

7. Genevieve Fabre, *Drumbeats, Masks, and Metaphor* (Cambridge: Harvard University Press, 1983), 150.

8. Iceberg Slim, *Pimp: The Story of My Life* (Los Angeles: Holloway House, 1969), 86. Hereafter cited in the text as *Pimp*.

9. Ed Bullins, *The Duplex* (New York: Morrow, 1971), 121.

10. James Baldwin, *No Name in the Street* (New York: Dial Press, 1972), 9, 10. Hereafter cited in the text as *No Name*.

11. Eldridge Cleaver, *Soul on Ice* (New York: Dell, 1968), 100.

12. David Leeming, *James Baldwin: A Biography* (New York: Alfred A. Knopf, 1994), 304.

13. Ibid., 290.

14. Richard Wright, *Native Son* (New York: Harper and Brothers, 1940), 9.

4

Fragmented Souls

Call and Response with Renée Cox

ARTRESS BETHANY WHITE

The electric narrative structure of this interview reflects a desire to communicate the ways in which history constantly informs and is reinformed by contemporary life and art. When I first encountered the work of Renée Cox I found myself standing in front of a seven-foot framed photograph of a naked black woman in pumps holding a baby titled Yo Mama. *Here stood a woman daring the viewer to make her someone's mammy, bed warmer, or doormat. Cox challenges viewers to leave historical stereotypes about black female sexuality by the wayside and to engage in the act of reinventing the black female body. She is not alone in this endeavor.*

In my exploration of black sexuality I wanted to take a cross-genre look at visual and literary images from slavery to the blues divas of the 1920s and 1930s to the Black Power Movement. Rather than doing an exhaustive survey, I picked moments at random to exemplify the character of some popular culture dialogues. I want to thank Renée because our conversation was an invaluable catalyst to this mission, and because the three sections of this chapter are titled after two of her more provocative pieces and a work-in-progress, which serve as a means of establishing thematic structure.

■ ■ ■

Renée Cox is a thirty-seven-year-old visual artist and entrenched resident of the SoHo arts community. Her photography has been exhibited at such coveted spaces as the Whitney Museum and the Jack Tilton Gallery, as well as galleries in Denmark. In the summer of 1995 she stepped away from the gallery scene briefly to engage in guerrilla street art tactics by initiating the Poster Project under the auspices of the Negro Art Collective, which she co-founded with video artist Tony Cokes.

■   ■   ■

WHITE: Do you feel like you carry on a meaningful dialogue with other artist through your work?

COX: Oh yeah, I think so. It basically stems from what I respect in the work of other artists that echoes what I strive to realize in my own work. Like directness. With Adrian Piper I really like the in-your-faceness she achieves. With Carrie Mae Weems, it's the way she integrates text to illuminate certain discourses. Lorna Simpson . . . well I wouldn't say it's so much directness, it's the way she uses photography in a different way, like the photography isn't more important than the text. When I look at someone like Kara Walker, well the first time I saw her work I said to myself, "Oh damn, this is hot!" I guess what interests me is those twists. My whole sensibility with my work is about sticking in and turning the knife a little bit and keeping it in people's faces. Not letting them get away with a whole lot. I think one of the things that's important about my work is that it's direct but it's also multilayered. It's not a one-liner. That's where I think the whole idea of dialogue comes in.

It Shall Be Named

When I am thirteen I will be punished for disassembling every doll I own and reassembling them so that black dolls have white arms, white dolls have black legs and none of them have clothes or hair.
—Jacqueline Woodson, *Autobiography of a Family Photo*

I distinctly remember the chill that went through my body as I read Gayl Jones's novel *Corregidora*[1] for the first time. I was shocked by the notion of two generations of women fathered by the same man, though forced miscegenation during slavery had certainly been added to my store of historical facts by this time. I realized that what made the fictional depiction resonate more than references to the same act in slave narra-

4.1. "It Shall Be Named," by Renée Cox

tives was the fact that Jones made the reader privy to, and held captive by, the chilling psychological effect of the dual crimes of miscegenation and incest on this family of black women. She gave them voices. And certainly I felt a sense of satisfaction when the great-grandmother finally escaped because she had done the "unthinkable" to the Portuguese slaveholder Corregidora. The "naming" of the unthinkable doesn't occur until the last page of the novel; my imagination, however, would not accept any punishment less than the great-grandmother castrating him. Jones makes it clear that there is a demon in this story; but it was also clear to me how much displaced demonization of black men had led them to a fate similar to that of the slave owner. In effect, I was reveling in the joyful satisfaction of a reverse lynching.

The sexualization, or perhaps more accurately the fetishization, of black bodies in American culture has been an ongoing obsession for white America. As a result, African Americans have found themselves revisiting sites of sexual trauma, such as those manifested by slavery, as a road to healing from or desensitizing themselves against the power of dysfunctional memories.

The directors of two recent films, *Pulp Fiction* and *Sankofa,* have also chosen to revisit some of these sites of sexual trauma. Unlike Cox, however, they ultimately end up voyeuristically capitalizing on these legacies of violent physical encounters between blacks and whites. In *Pulp Fiction,*[2] white director Quentin Tarantino exposes and exploits white phallic anxiety by depicting the rape of a black man (who is bound and gagged) by a white security guard. In *Sankofa,*[3] African filmmaker Haile Gerima enacts his story of sexualized violence primarily on the bodies of black women. His depictions of an extended rape scene of a black female slave and the brutal whipping of another black pregnant slave serve less to heal than to incite and excite audience members. Unlike Tarantiño, who continues to problematically link black emasculation to white male empowerment, Gerima attempts to use sexualized violence to reevaluate psychic dissonance for African Americans.

■ ■ ■

WHITE: Can you talk a little bit about the way you deal with historicity in your work?

COX: Take the cross piece *"It Shall Be Named"* [which appeared in the Whitney's Black Male show]. The cross piece for me was very academic, intellectual . . . me going to the Schomburg [Center for Research in Black Culture] and spending a lot of time there just going through things randomly. They had piles of scrap books with the actual newspaper clippings from all these lynchings down South. That left an indelible mark on me. It's like you learn it at school but you don't really learn it at school. Nobody really dwells on it, so until you go through this stuff and you finally see how many people actually died. . . . The state that did it the most: Florida. The day that they usually did it on: Sunday. It was a picnic. You know, you see the little white girls, six- and seven-year-olds dressed in their Sunday best with a big smile, and you have the black guy hanging down from the tree with his neck cocked to the side. Then you read further and you find out that what they would do was cut off the penis, sell it as a souvenir. Cut of the toes and the fingers— all sold as souvenirs. I'm like "Where are all these dead black penises?" That was one of the reasons why my [black male] figure [*It Shall Be Named*] has no genitalia.

48

■ ■ ■

Where Cox's image explores what was extracted from blacks physically, the work of artist Kara Walker explores what was extracted psychically. At a recent gallery show at the Wooster Gardens, her almost life-sized figures were cut out of black paper and pasted on the white walls of two interconnecting rooms. What was most striking about Walker's exhibit, entitled "From the Bowels to the Bosom," was its resistance to providing the viewer with an easy historical read. For example, a silhouette image of a trio of bare-breasted black women and a black child suckling each other could connote sisterhood as easily as a shared history of psychic aberration around the role of perpetual wet nurse. In another silhouette, a young black boy blindfolds a white boy who has his hands bound behind his back. Though fully clothed, the white boys buttocks are thrust out as if awaiting a spanking. Is the white boy a symbol of the penitent white master who desires to be cleansed of his role in slavery, or is this a role reversal symbolizing black revenge or retribution? Walker continues this tactic of manipulating historical content and context not only for the subjects of her pieces but also for herself as an artist. Using language similar to that of nineteenth-century slave narratives, she refers to her herself as "a Free Negress of Noteworthy Talent" in publicity material for the show. These various images—filmic, photographic, and artistic—point to reckoning with a history and bodies riddled with not only maternal, but sadomasochistic tendencies.

Yo Mama

my work
attempts to ferret out
what i know & touch
in a woman's body . . .
> **—Ntozake Shange, introduction to *For Colored Girls Who Have Considered Suicide when the Rainbow Is Enuf***

It is easy to assemble myriad examples of the two roles that black women have been able to occupy in Western culture: desexualized mammy or ravenous seductress. The late sixties and early seventies saw the emergence of television dramas featuring black women. Diahann

4.2. "Yo Mama," by Renée Cox

Carroll assumed the role of professional single mother in *Julia* while Teresa Graves became the sexy, butt-kicking detective in *Get Christy Love*. There was perhaps some promise here, but a plot that would have made greater strides toward black female empowerment would have been the integration of these roles into one badass taking-care-of-business woman and her equally badass taking-care-of-business male partner—something akin to Shaft meets Christy Love and at the end of the day they go home to the kids and . . .

Perhaps the most provocative example of self-defined black women are the blues divas of the 1920s and 1930s. In *Black Pearls: Blues Queens of the 1920s,* Daphne Duval Harrison summarizes why these blues queens were so influential: "I view the blues as the driving force with which the women could act on personal and artistic agendas simultaneously. In short, the blues is life which is art."[4] The blues lyrics composed by women such as Sippi Wallace and Bessie Smith spoke of a sexual autonomy and self-realization that resisted traditional values and social mores:

I come to you, sweet man, falling on my knees,
I come to you sweet, pretty papa, falling on my knees,
I ask, if you ain't got nobody, kind daddy, take me please.[5]

You can send me up the river or send me to that mean ole jail,
You can send me up the river or send me to that mean ole jail,
I killed my man and I don't need no bail.[6]

Though both women here explore intimate relationships between women and men, there exists a duality that addresses the complexity of desire: the woman who sublimates herself and the woman who chooses to rid herself with no remorse of a man gone bad. This oscillating reality led to the perception of blues women as empowered women. As Duval Harrison asserts, "Through the blues, these women became the principal spokespersons for black women in the North and South."[7] In effect, blues queens served as early models for a black feminist expression that incorporates the good, the bad, and the ugly. This was a proto-feminist expression that demonstrated the power of choice, a dynamic that first necessitates confronting stereotypes of black womanhood.

■ ■ ■

WHITE: Can you comment on how, say, *Yo Mama* and *Yo Mama at Home* explore notions of black women and art?

COX: *Yo Mama at Home* is a reactionary piece. I did it when I was in the Whitney Program and seven months pregnant. I was the first woman in twenty-five years to be visibly pregnant in the program. When I told people they looked at me like I was crazy, as if to say, "Well, why are you doing this?" I came out of the fashion industry. In the fashion industry people don't care. "Great, you're having a baby. Can you work next week?" I felt scared for myself. I had made this major career change and educational commitment to fine art only to find out that I could possibly be rejected because I'm married and have children. So once I figured that out, I realized I'd have to do whatever I had to do, which meant I have to be in your face and be as clear as possible. Direct. Hence we have *Yo Mama at Home* with me sitting there very pregnant, legs partly spread, head wrapped, and giving you "I own the place honey and I'm still having my baby." And the attitude for *Yo Mama* [a head-on shot of a nude Cox holding her year-old son and wearing black pumps] is "Come on girl, put your pumps on, look cute, pick up your child and keep on pressing."

■ ■ ■

Tony Morrison gives a deftly rendered tale of politically motivated infanticide in her novel *Beloved*.[8] Rather than face the threat of being returned to slavery, the protagonist Sethe attempts to kill all of her children; but she succeeds only in killing the baby Beloved. Although infanticide is generally considered a criminal act, during slavery it was also an act of resistance.

Julie Dash's film *Daughters of the Dust*[9] provides another unique narrative thread around black female choice. When Yellow Mary returns to the island on which she was born, the young girls there are in awe of her. When one character asks. "What kinda woman Yellow Mary?" another responds, "She a new kinda woman." As Yellow Mary tells her story, the viewer begins to get a clearer sense of what "new" means. Yellow Mary had left her native island to seek her fortune in the real world. She ended up becoming a wet nurse to a wealthy family in Cuba, after supposedly losing her own child. After taking her leave, the viewer is left to assume she either became a prostitute to support herself or in some way became a kept woman, corroborated through her fancy dress. The idea of the new woman becomes in reality the economically independent woman, the woman freed from all binds of domesticity and child rearing. However, the "new" woman is still trapped because her explorations are limited to what are deemed socially as selfish pursuits, which can rarely accommodate motherhood. Dash complicates Yellow Mary's "independence" by having her return to stay on the island (the motherland) to nurture herself. This, too, can be viewed as an independent woman simultaneously engaged in maternal empowerment in order to heal herself.

Rage (a Work in Progress)

**This one is about dignity, they all
are. Hattie was an awful big
maid. Her cannon shape was appropriate
for what came out of her. She
gave context to Gone with the Wind.**
—Thylias Moss, "Hattie and the Power of Biscuits"

In terms of the search for black selfhood, the Black Panthers and proponents of the Black Power Movement make an interesting case study. First there was the attire: basic black leather and shades, often accompanied by weapons. The physical intimidation factor alone led to outrageous Hooveresque estimates as to the number of Panthers inhabiting the nation. Second, here was a group of men and women who stood unified behind a race-based fight for equality. Third, this mission dedicated them to changing the world.

In her controversial book *A Taste of Power*, Elaine Brown documents her initial involvement with the Black Panthers and her eventual rise to the role of "chairman." Many female participants in the movement have noted the lack of attention paid to women's issues in the interest of maintaining a façade of racial unity. Brown describes what she feared as she attempted to save the Black Panther Party at the behest of Huey Newton:

A woman in the Black Power movement was considered, at best, irrelevant. A woman asserting herself was a pariah. A woman attempting the role of leader-

53

ship was, to my proud black Brothers, making an alliance with the "counter-revolutionary, man-hating, lesbian, feminist white bitches." It was a violation of some Black Power principle that was left undefined. If a black woman assumed a role of leadership, she was said to be eroding black manhood, to be hindering the progress of the black race.[10]

■   ■   ■

WHITE: What boundaries do you push in your work?

COX: Again, I'll go back to The Poster Project. It was inspired by my son, whose question to me actually became the title of the project: "Mama, I thought only black people were bad." I felt it necessary to put a message out there to counter that. The text for the other poster referenced Charles Murray, *The Bell Curve*,[11] stating, "Surprise, sur-prise, in raw numbers European American whites are the ethnic group with the most illegitimate children, the most people on welfare, the most unemployed men and the most arrests for serious crime." The text was supplemented with photos of Ivan Boesky and Charles Manson. At the bottom of each poster was the tag "This message is brought to you by The Negro Art Collective, fighting cultural misinformation about Afri-can Americans."
Before my number was made unlisted, I received phone calls from Caucasian folks saying, "You must be an angry nigger," and "Don't you niggers realize you've lost? You all need to just shut up." There were two articles written about the project, one in the *Daily News* the other in *New York Newsday,* and I know that at least one of the writers received death threat letters. So, in a way I guess I was successful because I wanted to provoke people. I wanted to initiate another kind of dialogue.

WHITE: Did you see yourself as a revolutionary in that sixties kind of way?

COX: Well I didn't go out and get an Angela Davis patch. I mean the revolution has to be approached differently these days. But I think the media is a powerful tool to that end.

WHITE: What projects do you have coming up?

COX: The next project I have coming up is going to be called *Rage*. Rage is an African American superhero who goes back into history and changes things around. For example, maybe she will save Jean-Michel Basquiat from his drug overdose. She's going to definitely take Picasso to task and throw him down on the continent of Africa so he'll learn how to credit his sources. She's going to be involved in the liberation of Aunt Jemima and Uncle Ben from their boxes. I attribute this idea to Bettye Saar, who did a piece called *The Liberation of Aunt Jemima* back in the sixties. When I first saw her piece I thought it was brilliant. I thought to myself, That's the kind of work I want to do. Sort of take all these historical wrongs and turn them into rights.

NOTES

1. Gayl Jones, *Corregidora* (Boston: Beacon, 1975).
2. *Pulp Fiction.* Dir. Quentin Tarantino. Miramax, 1994.
3. *Sankofa.* Dir. Haile Gerima. Mypheduh Films, Inc., 1993.
4. Daphne Duval Harrison, *Black Pearls: Blues Queens of the 1920's* (New Brunswick, N.J.: Rutgers University Press, 1988), 8.
5. Sippi Wallace, quoted in ibid., 132.
6. Bessie Smith, quoted in ibid., 53.
7. Ibid., 9.
8. Toni Morrison, *Beloved* (New York: Penguin, 1987).
9. *Daughters of the Dust.* Dir. Julie Dash. Kino, 1990.
10. Elaine Brown, *A Taste of Power* (New York: Random House, 1992), 358.
11. Charles Murray and Richard Herrnstein, *The Bell Curve* (New York: Simon and Schuster, 1994).

5

Wailin' Soul

Reggae's Debt to Black American Music

GRANT FARED

Reggae is Jamaican soul music, a sort of tropic rock 'n' roll.
—Stephen Davis, *Reggae Bloodlines*

Imported African-American music informed the evolution of Jamaican popular music just as exported DJ-ing allowed recombinant possibilities.
—Carolyn Cooper, *Noises in the Blood*

At the height of his experiment in democratic socialism in the 1970s, Prime Minister Michael Manley coined a stinging retort to those Jamaicans opposed to his government's restructuring of this Caribbean island's economy. "We have five flights to Miami every day," he tartly reminded these disgruntled Jamaicans, the majority of whom were white and Creole. The prime minister's information about the frequency of flights to Miami was, of course, redundant, since these disaffected citizens were infinitely more familiar than Manley with the plane schedules. However, the Jamaican leader's contempt for both these malcontents and the U.S. city for which they were bound is easily understandable. By virtue of geography, Miami forms the sharp end of the long shadow of Yankee imperialism—a foreboding cloud that blankets the entire Caribbean. The closest port of entry for Jamaicans en route to North America, Miami epitomizes U.S. economic, ideological, and cultural interventions in the Caribbean. In the 1970s Jamaica and its neighbor, socialist Cuba, bore the brunt of these Yankee incursions. Manley and Fidel Castro were keen supporters of each other, a bond frowned upon by the anti–communist United States.

But Miami's location served to naturalize its status as the center of exchange between Manley's country and the American mainland. It is in this southeastern U.S. city that business deals affecting the Jamaican economy are transacted, West Indian family ties are renewed, and U.S. dollars are acquired. Miami has become a bustling international hub where, among other Latin and Caribbean folk, Jamaicans of all racial groups, cultural orientations, and generations stock up on the latest U.S. cultural accessories. On their way to Kingston and Montego Bay, Jamaicans shop for these commodities—everything from oversize Fila T-shirts to slim Gucci handbags, from Karl Kani's hip-hop jeans to tailored Chanel suits.

However, had Manley reflected more carefully for a moment, he might have spared the south Florida metropolis in his jibe. Jamaica, and Manley's People's National Party (PNP) government in particular, owe the American cities of Miami and New Orleans a considerable historical debt. Inadvertently, these two cities were responsible for the development of Jamaica's most powerful and dynamic form of black self-expression: reggae music. One of reggae's core antecedents, black American soul music, can be directly traced to the radio stations of Miami and New Orleans. Dick Hebdige maps this cultural link succinctly in *Cut 'N' Mix:* "Throughout the 1950s the interest in black American music was fuelled by American radio—particularly in the small r&b stations situated in and around Miami. . . . And in West Kingston, the r&b produced in New Orleans in the southern part the US became something of a craze amongst those rich enough or lucky enough to have access to a radio." [1]

Reggae emerged from the experiences of west Kingston, a collection of impoverished ghettoes that included the now famous Trench Town, as well as the lesser-known communities of the Dungle and Back O' Wall. West Kingston is home to the poorest black Jamaicans, that constituency most responsible for the election of Michael's Manley's PNP government. In 1972, Manley's party wrested power from the Jamaican Labour Party (JLP) primarily because of the votes of Trench Townians and the endorsement of the island's premier reggae stars—Dennis Brown and the Wailers, particularly the group's lead singer, Bob Marley. The PNP's subsequent electoral triumph in 1976 owed a great deal to Bob Marley's performance at the "Smile Jamaica" concert. This supposedly nonpartisan event was represented as an effort on the part of the entire ruling elite—both the incumbent PNP and the opposition JLP—to re-store a measure of peace to west Kingston life, which had been disrupted by factional political violence. Manley, however, hijacked the "Smile Jamaica" event of December 5, 1976, for his own party by calling for a general election just days after the Kingston concert. Because of the dramatic events preceding Marley's participation in the songfest at the National Stadium, his performance registered as an emphatic stamp of approval of the PNP. Two days before the concert there was an assassi-nation attempt against the reggae star, some of his band members, and his manager at his Kingston home. Popular rumor had it that JLP gunmen were responsible for the attack; to date no one has been arrested for the crime.

This "music of the ghetto," as Bob Marley defines reggae, marks the clear and unprecedented public enunciation of Jamaica's African roots. Reggae transformed the black working (and unemployed) poor's cultural practices—their patois, their form of personal address, their religion, their dress codes, their various accoutrements—into national (and inter-national) Jamaican symbols. While reggae has dramatically remade the island's cultural persona, it continues the struggle to substantively change the liminal status of the black majority in the state's political apparatus. Jamaica is still a black majority nation ruled by the Creole elites of the PNP and the JLP. Nevertheless, the music has consistently functioned as a space where several intense ideological contestations about Jamaican society have been conducted. Crucial issues such as national identity, Jamaica's racial hierarchy, political philosophy, eco-nomic inequities, postcolonialism, and religious beliefs, to name but a few, have been engaged in the lyrics of reggae songs.

However, as the trajectory outlined in *Cut 'N' Mix* indicates, any examination of reggae would be incomplete without an account of black American soul. This essay maps the routes Hebdige delineated through an exploration of the relationship between these two black musical forms in the work of Robert Nesta Marley. In no reggae artist are the strains of soul—a subtle, critical, and evocative musical discourse about the black experience—more resounding than in the work of Trench Town's most famous son. The myriad ways in which the Marley *ouevre* signals the dependence upon, fusion of, and divergences between these two forms enables us to examine fully the complex relation of soul to reggae. What musical techniques do soul and reggae have in common? What is the political significance of those similarities? At which cultural point does reggae deviate from soul? Why do these divergences occur? Which elements of soul are most important to Bob Marley? How does Marley incorporate and transform soul in his music? These are some of the core issues this chapter will engage. This project, however, relies on a fuller representation of reggae's history. As entangled and complicated as the soul-reggae intersection is, it is itself preceded and succeeded by the formation of other Caribbean musical genres. Reggae emerges as the hybrid end-product of these cultural exchanges. The development of these other musical forms—mento, ska, and rocksteady—will be surveyed and their contribution to the shape and content of reggae evaluated.

The umbilical bond between reggae music and the Rastafarian faith is largely presupposed. One is presumed to be metonymic of the other. The ways in which Rastafarianism provides the moral, cultural, religious, and racial foundation for reggae is taken for granted; so is the way in which both were both integral to Marley's political identity. In truth, he rendered the two indistinguishable. The message was not only in his reggae music, but could also be read off his personal appearance and identified in his personal habits—the dreadlocks and the Rasta colors he wore and the ganja he smoked so publicly all reinforced how intertwined reggae and Rastafarianism was in Marley's universe. However, a question that derives from the reggae-Rasta conjuncture, and one that will be raised only tangentially here, is the position of women in this nexus. The problem of gender, a shorthand for misogyny in this instance, is of course not a condition unique to reggae or Rastafarianism—it is as disturbing feature a of soul (and the soulful 1960s) as it is of contemporary hip-hop and dancehall. However, the religious and metaphorical deployment of misogyny in reggae lyrics lends it a critical pertinence.

Soul, the dominant black American musical genre from the late 1950s through the mid-1970s, can be understood as a highly stylized vocalizing of black experience in this period. Buried not far beneath the surface of rich melodies and the smooth, dance-inducing rhythms of soul is the articulation of the black community's struggle against economic, political, cultural, and gender disenfranchisements in white America. Encapsulating both the high moralism of the Civil Rights era and the militance of the Black Power Movement, soul envelops these contestations in smoky vocals and silky harmonies. However, the slick musical arrangements disguise but never undermine the various politics of opposition encoded within soul. Two of the finest recordings of black America's battle in the 1960s are Nina Simone's haunting "Mississippi Goddamn" and Marvin Gaye's lush "What's Goin' On?" Simone's song is an angry protest against the burning of a black church in Birmingham, Alabama, in 1963. Gaye's is an epic cry against injustice—"Don't punish me with brutality," he implores American society in the most luxurious of voices. But no other track captures the spirit of soulful resistance with quite the seductive brilliance that Aretha Franklin does in her rendition of "Respect." In her version of this Otis Redding number, the soul diva literally spells out the struggles black Americans were waging: "R-E-S-P-E-C-T / Find out what it means to me," she challenges her audience. In the 1960s, however, white America was surely intended to hear in those lines more than a sexy spelling lesson. Franklin's song was an indictment of the appalling conditions prevailing in black communities all over the nation; the strength of her voice was a barometer of black anger. In addition to all this, of course, Franklin inserted into "Respect" a feminist critique absent from Redding's rendition.

Although Bob Marley's immersion in soul music is well chronicled, his appreciation for Aretha Franklin has never been fully understood. This oversight is understandable, particularly since it has only recently come to light that the prince of reggae recorded an (as yet unreleased) album of soul tracks with Franklin's band in the mid-1970s.[2] The regard that Marley, one of the founders of reggae and indisputably its most renowned and revered exponent, had for Franklin reveals the extent to which his career indelibly bore the stamp of black America's rhythms. More than that, through Marley the ideological and musical convergences between soul and reggae, especially the latter's borrowing and reinscription of the former's characteristics, are made manifest. The political overlaps are abundantly evident. The reggae ethics Marley so inimitably crafted subscribe fully to the politics of black resistance at the core of what Cynthia Young calls "soul culture."[3] Young describes the soul era as the funk-infused recording of the black community's struggle, through music and other cultural practices of the 1960s (plays, poetry, grassroots community organizing, and so on), against the institutional racism, economic disenfranchisement, and political marginalization of American society. Soul culture documents the black campaign to radicalize its constituency's political approach, to rethink its political location, to challenge its public representation, and to reconstruct its political self-image—all in the face of white American hegemony.

This struggle for "respect," which is dynamically gendered by Aretha Franklin, is insistently raced by the Jamaican reggae community. The attainment of black dignity and pride is at the very core of reggae. Peter Tosh's ringing proclamation, "Equal Rights, Justice," is a theme reflected upon, developed, and nuanced in countless Wailers tracks, most prominent among them, arguably, "Exodus," "Redemption Song," "Africa Unite," and "Zimbabwe." The struggles of black peoples in Jamaica, in the postcolonial metropolises of Europe and America, and in the anticolonial campaign in Africa are some the key issues that shaped, reconceptualized, and sustained reggae. Reggae is rooted in the tradition of Rastafarian protest against Jamaican society's rigid caste system, which privileges Creoles (or "browns," as they are colloquially known) over the black majority; it is also, of course, a protest against anti-Rastafarian prejudice. As reggae developed and gained increasing recognition in the 1970s, it started to include and address Caribbean communities in metropoles such as London and New York. Among reggae artists, Marley was particularly committed to conditions of struggle in Africa. He turned his attention to the continent with marked frequency after his 1976 exile from Jamaica, and the three trips he made—to Ethiopia, Gabon, and Zimbabwe—between 1978 and 1980. Marley attacked the racism of Ian Smith's white minority government in Rhodesia and the apartheid regime in South Africa. He was also publicly supportive of, respectively, Frelimo and the Popular Movement for the Liberation of Angola's battles against Portuguese imperialism in Mozambique and Angola.

It is clear from Marley's move toward a postcolonial Pan-Africanism that for all the crucial similarities between soul and reggae, there is a pivotal distinction. Reggae not only absorbed the politics of soul, it exceeded them. Although it occasionally borrows the muted political reverberations of soul, especially in its love songs, reggae is marked more by direct confrontation and protest. Trench Town's music is a series of direct challenges. This difference does not undermine the links that bind blacks in the diaspora in the Americas, but it does enable us to understand how a phenomenon such as the growth of black cultural expression in the Caribbean engenders more militant forms of opposition. Much of this can be explained, of course, by contextual specificities, such as the numerical majority black Jamaicans enjoy as opposed to the minority status of African Americans. The subtlety of soul's resistance, however, is never abandoned by reggae. It simply becomes a single arrow in a multi-stringed musical bow, rather than the dominant form of cultural engagement. Reggae's Jamaican resources were such that subtlety could be employed selectively interspersed among the more prevalent trenchant protest songs, insurrectionary anthems, and gospel tunes. Soul was not without its incendiary moments. Stevie Wonder and Marvin Gaye, among others, contributed their share of such tracks, but these were the exceptions, not the rule. Marley, that most linguistically agile of Rasta poets, used subtlety frequently but for a different effect. It lends lyrical sophistication and ideological reinforcement to his protest; it does not constitute his challenge. Reggae issues a dual lyrical threat, through affronting as well as through insinuation and nuance. The most striking instance of this lyrical strategy can be found in "Zimbabwe," a song that could be read as Marley's clarion call for postcolonial Africa. Embedded in this track, which celebrates international black unity and the southern African revolution. ("I-n-I will liberate Zimbabwe") is inscribed a dire warning about postcolonial elites. "Zimbabwe" contains a telling but nonetheless surprising political cynicism, a distrust that seems anachronistic within the upbeat lyrical and ideological confines of Zimbabwean freedom:

**No more internal power struggle
We come together to overcome
The little trouble
Soon we'll find out who is
The real revolutionaries
Cause I don't want my people to be
Tricked by mercenaries**[4]

Much of Marley's well-disguised skepticism was, in all likelihood, informed by the experience of his native Caribbean. It is, nevertheless, still a moment of remarkably subtle and powerful critique in the Marley musical canon. Postcolonial leaders not only have their revolutionary credentials called into question—are they "real" or not?—but also find themselves implicitly depicted as "mercenaries." "Zimbabwe" is as much emblematic of Marley's postindependence optimism as it is a statement about the gravity of his reservations.

While soul's politics echoes in and is extended by reggae, the black American art form is no less influential artistically. Musically, the original Wailers—Marley, Peter Tosh, and Bunny Wailer—started out in the west Kingston yard of singing coach Joe Higgs trying to emulate Brook Benton, the Drifters, and the Impressions. Amid the wailing of the Trench Town poor, among which they numbered, these Rastafarians-in-waiting diligently practiced their harmonies. In those formative Wailer years, this Trench Town group performed at local venues in their tight-fitting black suits, trying for all the world to make like the Impressions' Jerry Butler and Curtis Mayfield. In an early Wailers track, "Guava Jelly," we see how Marley's songwriting is thematically saturated by the sensuality of soul. Although "Guava Jelly" is more rocksteady than reggae (in the Marley songbook it is euphemistically described as "moderate reggae"), it reveals the ways Marley adapts the concerns of soul to a Jamaican variation of this music.

You said you love me.
I said I love you.
Why don't you stop your crying?
Dry your weeping eyes.
You know that I love,
I love, I love, I love you so, Damsel.
Here I am.
Me said, "Come rub it 'pon me belly
With you guava jelly, Damsel." [5]

Love, relationships, emotional pain—the standard tropes of most popular music and soul in particular—are all on display here. But Marley's sex jam (no Anglophone pun intended) is spared from inanity by the unusual combination of the linguistic anachronism of addressing the woman as "damsel" (a term which qualifies as an Anglo relic even in a colonized society) and Jamaican idiosyncrasy—where else would a citrus fruit be employed as a sexual lubricant? Played against the backdrop of a unique beat, inflected by the ethos of black American music, Marley transforms his early sounds into a "tropic soul" that is positively saccharine.

In exploring the depth of the relationship between black U.S. soul and the reggae of Bob Marley, however, we have to listen beyond the unmistakable soul traits of the young Wailer(s). In the post–Bunny Wailer and Peter Tosh era, when Marley was officially installed as *the*

Wailer, harmonizing became even more crucial to the group's reggae format. Remarkable as Bob's voice was, he had benefited from soul-like harmonies in which he, Peter, and Bunny had engaged. From 1975, Bob's lead was underscored and softened by that of the I-Threes, the Wailers' trio of backing vocalists. The all-female group was composed of Bob's wife, Rita Marley, Judy Mowatt, and Marcia Griffith, three of Jamaica's top female vocalists. The earlier harmonizing among Bob and the other two Wailers was now replaced by a pattern of call-and-response between the lead singer and the I-Threes. The singularity of Marley's tenor was enhanced, and thrown into relief, by the higher reaches of the women's voices.

Some of Marley's most powerful and resonant songs were produced within this musical format, one amply indebted to soul. Outstanding among the tracks released in this period, the poetically and ideologically mature Marley era, are his soul-based, gospel-like anthems "Africa Unite," "Natural Mystic," and, of course, the immensely moving "Redemption Song." The first of these songs, "Africa Unite," owes much to the Mosaic tenor of the Old Testament that is so characteristic of the Rastafarian faith:

Africa unite,
'Cause we're moving right out of Babylon,
And we're going to our Father's land.[6]

Nowhere, however, is Marley's immersion in the culture of soul music so pronounced as in his mellow love songs. The Rastafarian dedication "One Love" and "No Woman, No Cry," his lament for the most enduring love of his life, Trench Town, stand as poetic declarations of emotional and psychic commitment. "No Woman, No Cry" is a Trench Town Rasta's contemplations on the joys and costs of living in the ghetto:

'Cause I remember when we used to sit
In a government yard in Trenchtown.
Oba-Observing the hypocrites
As they would mingle with the good
People we would meet;
Good friends we have had, Oh good
Friends we've lost along the way.[7]

"Waiting in Vain," however, demonstrates the considerable range of Marley's love ballads. The song is Marley's reflection on the disintegration of his relationship with Cindy Breakespeare, the Jamaican beauty queen who won the 1975 Miss World title. It is a somber creation, a tribute to Breakespeare that is filled with pain—and one without self-reflexivity about the reggae star's infidelity, since he had been married to Rita for almost a decade at the time of his relationship with Miss World. In this song, Marley can contain neither his impatience nor his bitterness at his itinerant lover:

But I know now that I'm way down on your line,
But the waiting feel is fine.
So don't treat me like puppet on a string,
'Cause I know how to do my thing.
Don't talk to me as if you think I'm dumb
I wanna know when you gonna come.[8]

Throughout his adulthood, Marley's treatment of women was highly problematic, mirroring much of the misogyny of Rastafarianism (and Jamaican society).[9] In his fifteen-year marriage to Rita (they were married in 1966 and remained so until his death in 1981), Marley claimed as his sexual prerogative the right to have very public relationships with other women. This aspect of his life is acknowledged but largely unremarked upon by Marley's biographers and cultural commentators alike. The absence of a gender critique cannot be explained away by Jamaican or Rastafarian misogyny. It is an ideological lack that has to be redressed, especially in view of the reggae star's iconic status in contemporary music and popular cultural circles the world over. To not engage this issue is tantamount to endorsing this misogynistic behavior. Ironically, it is precisely Marley's appetite for sexual licence that lends "Waiting in Vain" such rare sting as poetic rebuke. Bob Marley, father of some ten children (only four with Rita) and the ultimate "Mr. Rasta-Loverman" (as Shabba might have it), has been defeated in the game of passion and infelicity. He is certainly not "dumb," but he has become a mere "puppet" on Breakespeare's cruel "string."

A great deal of Marley's mature work was produced while he was in exile from Jamaica, a deracination that culminated with his death in Miami in 1981. This compels us to turn our glance momentarily northward again, to look anew at that tropical 1950s conjuncture: the Kingston–Miami/New Orleans axis. At this terminus of incipient U.S. neo-imperialism (Jamaica was at this point still a British colony), black American music intersected with, was appropriated by, and gave previously unimagined new form to working-class black Jamaican cultural traditions. Not unlike hip-hop and dancehall, reggae is the product of the intersection of technology and oppression: a musical form that develops from an encounter between the airwaves and conditions of on-the-ground impoverishment. From the AM radio stations in the American port cities of Miami and New Orleans, rhythm and blues mutated into soul and then wended its way through ska and rocksteady into reggae.

Like most cultural practices, reggae is hybrid in its form and variegated in its roots. The different sources of reggae are indigenized African religious rituals (such as Kumina), mento (the Jamaican version of Trinidadian calypso), and soul. Reggae's development is the narrative of cultural exchange (often on unequal terms), internal migration, and insistent transformation. Prior to the sound invasion from Miami and New Orleans, Jamaican popular musical consciousness was dominated by mento—in itself an interesting and a telling story. Mento was a politically anemic cultural practice. Adopting the bounce and beat of calypso, mento was the deliberate evacuation of the Trinidadian tradition of stinging social criticism. Despite its grievous lack of political content, mento marks the first reluctant and tentative steps toward the Caribbeanization of Jamaican radio. Jamaican calypso signals the slow process of substitution of black West Indian music, however sanitized, for white British tunes. This politically diluted, though occasionally bowdlerized, calypso reflects the ideological uncertainties of a pre-urbanized (though just barely so), late-colonial Jamaican society. Mento reflects a Caribbean society in the throes of transition; as Antonio Gramsci might have put it, this was a society suspended awkwardly in the interregnum. Jamaica was located in that interstitial moment between the end of colonialism and the achievement of national independence. The mass migration of rural blacks was clearly about to begin, though it was as yet not underway.

Jamaican calypso's domination of the nation's state-controlled airwaves in no way, however, undermined the alternative musical traditions of the ghetto. All the while, the cultural inheritance of West African slaves—the drumming and percussive rituals of Kumina and *nyabinghi* (played at Rastafarian gatherings)—thrived in the ghetto, available neither on vinyl nor on any Jamaican radio frequencies. Both these musical practices, as well as the political constituencies they represented, were crucial to the rhythm upon which reggae would be built. But it would take more than the demise of mento to allow for the incorporation of these traditions into a national Jamaican popular music. The eclipse of mento in the early 1950s heralded the introduction, via the sound system and the radio, of black American music. The outmoding of Jamaica's emaciated calypso coincided with increased migration to the cities and the rise of the famous Kingston sound systems. Sir Coxsone Dodd, Duke Reid, and Prince Buster's outfits started to rule the musical roost in the ghettoes and beyond. Fiercely competitive, and not without an attendant violence as Dodd and Reid vied for paying customers, the sound systems mixed the latest black American singles from Miami, New Orleans, and New York—always, of course, trying to keep one hot record release ahead of one another.

While the sound systems kept Jamaicans dancing on the weekends, the disc jockeys in the Crescent City and Miami were busy all week long. Stephen Davis, reggae historian and biographer of Bob Marley, provides a decidedly neocolonial reading of this relentless musical invasion. "American rhythm and blues," Davis writes, "was pumped without mercy into the culturally vulnerable Caribbean islands nightly by fifty-thousand-watt clear-channels in New Orleans and Miami."[10] Jamaica in the 1950s was technologically and culturally vulnerable, in no way able to repel this massive attack on the tiny nation's airwaves. The island lacked the electronic resources to rebuff the nightly incursion of black American artists who jammed the local stations. With the influx of transistor radios, Sam Cooke, Fats Domino, Amos Milburn, Louis Jordan, Alvin Robinson, and Huey "Piano" Smith quickly became household names. Toward the end of the 1950s, as R&B was transformed into soul, these artists gave way to a whole new set of American artists, and solo performers such as Otis Redding, James Brown, and Aretha Franklin and groups such as the Drifters and the Impressions quickly took their compatriots' place at the top of the Jamaican charts.

However, at the turn of the decade the flow of soul tracks suddenly dried up. It is difficult, as the region's foremost cultural historians have discovered,[11] to account precisely for why black American music suddenly became unavailable in Jamaica in 1960. The reasons could not have been economic, because Jamaica remained a lucrative market. The soul artists were as popular as their R&B predecessors and there was every indication that their records would sell well. While Jamaican independence was only two years off in 1960, there was no nationalist impulse closing the door on imported culture from either the U.S. mainland or the European colonial center. The unexpected drought of American music, however, had pivotal spinoffs for local Jamaican music. Thwarted by the lack of American records, the sound system men were compelled to turn to the resident musicians and to pay closer attention to the trends emerging from inner-city Kingston and Montego Bay— trends that clearly evinced the effects of black American music. Derived from the soul sounds that had been dominating the airwaves, ska was well placed to fill the vacuum left by the Impressions and the Drifters. Musically eclectic and technologically innovative, ska mimicked the optimism and uncertainties of the nation's anticipated independence. Borrowing from the music the sound systems had previously played, ska was a bouncier and more unpredictable version of black American soul. Ska was "cheerful, riddled with funky brass sections, disorganized, almost random. Ska was mento, Stateside R&B, and Jamaicans coming to terms with electric guitars and amplification." [12] In 1964 ska made a stunning international debut with Millie Small's "My Boy Lollipop." Produced by Anglo-Jamaican Chris Blackwell (who would later work with Marley), Small's ska tune hit number one on the British charts, the first Caribbean song to achieve that distinction.

Locally, the Skatalites, Justine Hines and the Dominoes, and the Vikings put out ska tracks. The newly constituted Wailin' Wailers also cut several ska singles, most notably "Judge Not," "Terror," and "One Cup of Coffee." This last song was similar to, but not exactly of a cover of, R&B star Brook Benton's "Another Cup of Coffee"—showing clear evidence of Bob Marley's admiration for Benton, the Jamaican's favorite R&B/soul artist. Some of the most innovative ska was recorded by a teenage Jimmy Cliff. He was fourteen when he made his debut with "Daisy Got Me Crazy," which he followed up a couple of years later with the hit "Dearest Beverley." In the summer of 1966, however, Jamaican political life became more fractious and violent. In Trench Town the rude boys, small-time gangsters packing German ratchet knives and no modest amount of *joi de vivre,* became a major feature of ghetto life for the first time. Jamaican music recorded the change in sociopolitical climate in its tempo. Ska was quickly phased out and replaced by " 'stickier,' more sinister rhythm. A completely new dance style emerged. Gone were the fast, jerky movements of ska. Instead, a slinkier, cooler dance called the *rocksteady* became popular."[13] Rocksteady, the handmaiden of reggae, was born.

Because of the contradictions inherent to cultural and economic imperialism, reggae's relationship to American soul riddled with ambivalences. This uniquely Jamaican musical form is in considerable measure the product of a historical paradox. (Reggae emerged from a cultural process that could reductively be construed as a historical contingency—it is the result of sound system necessity.) Reggae is at once dependent upon the importation of R&B and soul for its form—and to a lesser extent for its content—and inconceivable without the inexplicable suspension of American exportation. On the one hand, if American cultural hegemony had continued unabated and the sound systems had predominated, reggae may very well have been stillborn. On the other hand, without the influx of those soul sounds from the colossus to the north, reggae may not have emerged—or, it may have emerged in a very different and possibly even less efficacious form. Without soul, the Rastafarian practice of nyabinghi drumming and percussion, so fundamental to the rhythm of reggae, would have continued to be an integral part of life in the poorer haunts of west Kingston. These are powerful rhythms that echo ominously, and sometimes eruditely, the disenfranchisements of the ghetto *sufferahs*.

Although soul did not produce reggae, it did provide the musical conditions crucial for the overlay of intricate vocal harmony onto a 2/4 Jamaican beat. The 2/4 beat is not an exceptional musical form, but reggae's accents on the second and the fourth beats are complicated—some would say distorted—by the intricate percussive pattern in which it is played. Reggae's 2/4 is part of "a metric system so flamboyant and unique that only seasoned Jamaican drummers can keep it together and flowing."[14] However, as part of soul's political similitude to reggae, the black American music's most significant contribution to its Jamaican cousin may be its capacity to serve as a template for the verbalization—or vocalization, if you will—of the Rastafarian beats that resonated through Trench Town. The harmonizing of the Drifters, the Stylistics, and the Impressions provided the musical model for the Wailers, where Marley sang lead with Bunny Wailer as "high harmony" and Peter Tosh as "low harmony."[15] This musical format became the basis for the young Trench Town Rastamen, as Joe Higgs taught them to use harmony to play off each other. (In the 1950s Higgs had been an R&B artist, forming one half of a fairly successful duo called Higgs and Wilson.)

Marley's lead tenor, distinctive in its versatility and range, was picked up and clarified by the unaffected spirituality of Bunny's soprano and occasionally overridden or amplified by the moral resonance of Tosh's bass. (In a Wailers group where Bob and Peter were occasionally at loggerheads, especially toward the end, Bunny's voice held the tenor and the bass together in more ways than one.)

The lyrical vocabulary of reggae was pure black west Kingston patois, or "Trench Town rock," as Marley hailed it. Reggae did not so much craft an indigenous musical vocabulary as it rendered poetic the anger of the ghetto. This music empowered the black Jamaican masses by lyricizing their everyday language, transforming patois into sonorous song. Reggae validated not only the language, but the very experience and the history of the ghetto people. In the process, reggae enabled the uniquely black Rastafarian linguistic patterns to be set to music. Terms such as "Jah" (the black deity whom Rastas believed to be the Ethiopian emperor Haile Selassie) and "I-n-I" (the Rasta plural for "we") were more than new verbal formulations that became an integral part of this lyrical vocabulary—they transformed the way people in the Carribean, European metropolises, the United States, and Africa conceptualized black history, religion, culture, and self-representation. Old Testament biblical terms such as "Babylon" and "Zion," for centuries the preserve of white Christianity, were ideologically reinscribed. These words have become loaded cultural markers, terms now inseparable from their reggae/Rasta usage.

"Babylon," a recurring trope in reggae music, points to a multifaceted, biblically gendered, oppositional politics. It is an expansive term, including colonialism, neo-imperialism, and the entire apparatus of Western government. Marley's critique of this sociopolitical construction is stark and unrelenting in the aptly titled "Babylon System," a track from the 1979 album *Survival:*

Babylon system is the vampire
Sucking the children day by day.
Babylon system is the vampire
Sucking the blood of the sufferers.
Building church and university
Deceiving the people continually.
Me say them graduating thieves and murderers,
Look out now[16]

In this song "Babylon" is transfigured from the whore of Saint John's Revelation into a symbol of the Western nation-state. Through careful application and dissemination in circles outside the religion, "Babylon" is rendered an ambivalent term: it signifies both reggae's misogynistic representations of women and the remaking of the term into a tool for anticapitalist critique. (Within Rastafarianism, "Babylon" retains only its New Testament meaning.) However, we keep the term's antagonism to women in focus only in so far as we remember its biblical roots.

In the struggle against colonial powers, the postcolonial state has long been feminized—the "Mother of the Nation" is a powerful rallying cry. One of the dubious achievements of reggae is that it has so effectively disguised Babylon's feminine identity, not through deception but through selective presentation and decontextualization. Reggae has subjected "Babylon" to particularistic evacuation—the term's biblical genesis and its negative depiction of women are not explained to reggae's non-Rastafarian audiences. Since many audience members do not know who "Babylon" was, she can function as if she has always been the State. It is precisely through obfuscation and the overuse of Marx at the expense of Jah, if you will, that we move surreptitiously from the Revelation to reggae's anti-capitalism. Because reggae has identified "Babylon" so closely with the oppressive state, the metaphor has assumed a neo-Marxist persona. Outside of Rasta enclaves, "Babylon" is not a "whore" as much as she is representative of capitalism's war on the disenfranchised, especially black people. This is the meaning that "Babylon System" invokes, indicating how reggae ideology was transformed through its exportation from the periphery to the metropolis and the postcolonial motherland. The impoverished "sufferers" are exploited to inhumane extremes, bled dry by a "vampire" capitalism that spares neither adults nor their offspring. The education system and religious institutions are equally culpable, represented by Marley as post-Althusserian ISAs, state apparatuses that specialize in the arts of deception, theft, and murder. "Babylon" is truly a vampire, a soul-less and genderless, but not an un-raced, miscreant. "Babylon" is always implicitly white, or a shade thereof, as in the Jamaican Creoles.

Much like soul, reggae's critique of white injustice, incarceration, violence, and oppression is never more resonant or rhetorically efficacious than when it is delivered as a gospel song. Marley's work includes several outstanding gospel tracks. None, however, achieve the anthemic heights, the moral fortitude, and the resilience of spirit of "Redemption

Song." It is a soaring tune and, perhaps appropriately, the reggae star's final cut on his final album, *Uprising*. (All the subsequent Marley LPs were released posthumously.) "Redemption Song" is a commentary on the brutalities of slavery, a protest against a pain that is four centuries old:

Old pirates, yes, they rob I.
Sold I to the merchant ships
Minutes after they took I from the bottomless pit.
But my hand was made strong
By the hand of the Almighty.
We forward in this generation triumphantly. [17]

The images of suffering are vivid, with the "bottomless pit" as the central metaphor for the cruelty of slavery. However, remarkable about this song are the ways in which the legacy of pain is offset by faith, a belief system that sometimes doubles as an optimism borne out of a sense of inevitable historical justice. In its gospel tracks, reggae not only incorporates the struggle its adherents are waging, but also offers a prescription for overcoming these battles. In the reggae universe, redemption is eminently achievable in the here and now:

Emancipate yourselves from mental slavery.
None but ourselves can free our minds.
Have no fear for atomic energy,
'Cause none of them can stop the time.
How long shall they kill our prophets
While we stand aside and look?
Yes, some say its just a part of it.
We've got to fulfill the book. [18]

"Redemption Song" negotiates that uneasy philosophical relationship between faith and individual accountability. We move easily between individual action and an omniscient spiritual authority. While personal accountability is paramount ("None but ourselves can free our minds"), we are guaranteed protection from nuclear disaster ("Have no fear for atomic energy"). In this Christian Rastafarian universe, the latter is apparently dependent upon the former. God helps those who help themselves. Historical inevitability is at once a sacred promise ("none of them can stop the time") and contingent upon human intervention ("We've got to fulfill the book"). "Redemption Song" is a typical tract of religious faith, underpinned by the belief that morality will prevail.

"Redemption Song" is Marley's imagining of a just environment. But it is a conception that can only be attained through communal effort. "Won't you help to sing these songs of freedom?" he invites all of us. Marley needs all the help he, like any radical cultural activist, can get. Even in its most spiritual mode, Marley's struggle is still a materially deprived and embattled one. His faith is useful, making him as unafraid of "atomic energy" as only a true believer can be, but he nonetheless finds himself in possession of only two resources: the community he constructs (and reconstructs) and the music that helps that social edifice.

In historical, ideological and geographical scope, Bob Marley surpasses Aretha Franklin's call for respect. Marley's was a unique and expansive view of the world, spanning the Caribbean diaspora, the postcolonial metropolis, and independent Africa. He attacked Trench Town poverty unrelentingly; he unsettled the elites of independent Africa. His vision was informed by a flexible Rastafarian faith, one that was made to accommodate neo-Marxism and a critique of postcolonial rulers. Bob Marley's reggae was, by turns, trenchant, mellow, and up-tempo. But it remained remarkably free of the compromises of commercialism and the sensual civility of black American soul. His own particular Trench Town rock resisted the gloss of Motown. It is in that spirit of political commitment that Marley sang one type of song more than any other: those songs of freedom so deeply rooted within reggae's very soul.

NOTES

1. Dick Hebdige, *Cut 'N' Mix: Culture, Identity and Caribbean Music* (New York: Routledge, 1987), 62.

2. Roger Steffens, a Marley historian, revealed this information at the February 1996 induction of the reggae artist into the Rock n' Roll Museum and Hall of Fame in Cleveland.

3. Cynthia Young is currently engaged in a project that attempts to explain the connections—as well as the differences—among the various cultural practices that predominated in the black community in the 1960s. I am grateful to her for her definition and for her permission to use it in this essay.

4. Lyrics transcribed by the author.

5. Bob Marley, *Songs of Freedom* (Milwaukee: Hal Leonard Publishing Corp. 1992), 60.

6. Ibid., 10.

7. Ibid., 131.

8. Ibid., 196.

9. The debate about misogyny in Rastafarianism and Jamaican society as a whole is one of some standing. It has, however, taken on particular importance in Carolyn Cooper's engagement with the related issue of homophobia—another problematic aspect of reggae—in dancehall culture. See Carolyn Cooper, Noises in the Blood (Durham, N.C.: Duke, 1995.

10. Stephen Davis, *Bob Marley* (Rochester, V.: Schenckman Books, 1990), 29.

11. See, for example, Stephen Davis and Peter Simon, *Reggae Bloodlines: In Search of the Music and Culture of Jamaica* (New York: DuCapo, 1992); Davis, *Bob Marley;* Hebdige, *Cut 'N' Mix;* and Timothy White, *Catch a Fire: The Life of Bob Marley* (New York: Holt Rhinery Winston, 1983). In all these accounts of reggae's transformation, the authors declare themselves unable to explain the 1960 dearth of black American music in Jamaica.

12. Davis and Simon, *Reggae Bloodlines,* 14.

13. Hebdige, *Cut 'N' Mix,* 71.

14. Davis and Simon, *Reggae Bloodlines,* 12.

15. Ibid., 32.

16. Lyrics quoted from Carolyn Cooper, *Noises in the Blood: Orality, Gender, and the "Vulgar" Body of Jamaican Popular Culture* (Durham, N.C.: Duke University Press, 1995), 123.

17. Marley, *Songs of Freedom,* 156.

18. Ibid.

6

Aunt Emma's Zuni Recipe for Soul Transition

CARL HANCOCK RUX

I. The Holy Ghost & Son House Blues

- August, Sunday, 9 A.M.

Celery (seven sticks)
Garlic (seven cloves—save some for altar space)
Pork Sausage (made immediately after the death of the beast)
Cayenne Pepper (seven dashes)
Bell Pepper (from someone else's garden)
Fresh Tomatoes (from your own garden—crushed to the consistency
    of blood and pulp)
Fresh Chicken Livers (store the body of the bird for later consump-
    tion)
Onions (sliced in seven rings, then chopped)
All-Purpose Flour (three tablespoons)
Bay Leaf (save some for altar space)
Salt from your tears
Season with the blood of your last flow
Sweat (seven dashes) from the last breast to give last offspring suck

*Gather ingredients into the tips of your fingers on the day of the death
of your first son. Store in a cool place. On the morning of interment, in
the presence of your son who still breathes, combine ingredients in one-
gallon cast iron pot. Simmer. Pour into an unwashed bowl last used for
the last meal served before the day of death. Wait. Return to cast iron
pot. Stew.*

. . .

Brother lay dead in a box. We sit living in a box. Inherited house. Zuni, Virginia. A southern box, facing northern light, with one window. One soulless chair. A bed for quaking. A stove. No music. Bland food. Ghosts give recipes for soul. I be nothing, unrecognizable child; watching television. Waiting for the hour when Father and Mother take my hand to kiss the cold face of Brother. I be without my self today. Brother, he be fixed, hushed. Waiting for the hour when the spirit divorces itself from the flesh. Hebetudinous young man in slumber. Hands crossed, palms face down. White suit. Flower. Quiet. Asleep in Apostolic Holiness . . . across the ditch . . . just outside the window. Waiting for roar of tears and thunder of clap and stomp and "Save me, Lawd! Hep me Jeezus!" Father be drinking Wild Turkey too early this morning, staring out of window—impatient with Mother's disjointed scurry. He be drinking Johnnie Walker Black when Wild Turkey finished, and cursing her nonsense to himself, and cursing her cooking. Father likes to believe he can control his emotions. "This is the northern way," he has informed us all. He and me, we wear identical suits and shoes, and parted hair. We wait, like the apostles on the Mount of Olive. Mother, she be skittish, jumpy, tremulous woman in fear. Mother be dressed early this morning:

Hair controlled and arrested in pins and net, perfectly pressed black suit trying not to fall from thinning frame. Legs want to move. Want to shout. Throw themselves up and out again, like they did in the days of birth pains. Stockings say *no*. Say *quiet*. Say *still*. No soul. Don't lose it. Feet try to move, try to pound heel into wood floor, try to grieve like other women. Women who can't care about how their panties show when they fall over pews and drape themselves over caskets. Patent leather pumps rationally ask *why?* Request sensible steps. Careful walk. From here to there. No throwing our of voice or flinging up of hands. No Holy Ghosts. Ignore the quake and quiver and tremble of hand. Mother likes to believe she can control her emotions. "This is the better way," she says to Father in agreement.

"Wife," Father asks in perfect pitch through drunken slur, "Are you doing all right?"

"Yes," Mother replies in normal octave. "Yes, I am. Thank you."

"Have you finished?" Father asks, poised and sure with unsteady stance, "Have you finished pr-preparing?"

"Not yet," Mother replies in soft tone and broken heart. "Not yet." Mary outlived Jesus. Sometimes mothers outlive their sons. Yes. Sometimes mothers do. Aunt Emma outlived four. Lost one to fever. One to a woman's tumultuous husband. One to homemade whiskey. One to an angry union of men. Aunt Emma outlived four and called on Jesus till she heard from Mary. Mother says Aunt Emma closed her eyes one morning and died. In this house. In the chair where Father sits. On the day of the interment of the final son. Father says the dead are dead for good. Mother says Emma's six-foot frame rushed out into the fields of Zuni, Virginia—barefoot with her machete in her fists—and slaughtered hogs and picked her vegetables from around the yard, and massaged the necks of sleeping chickens so she could slit their throats. Aunt Emma prepared a stew for revival. And changed her garments. Let God change her name. Aunt Emma's been dead now some twenty-five years. She left this house in Mother's name. Father calls it his. Father, Mother, and Brother migrated South, bringing with them boxes of northern ways. I was not yet. That was before now. I have met Aunt Emma before. Years after her death. She is here today. Even now. Ignorant and uneducated sister of Mother's grandmother, born to former slaves and Sha'lako Shamans. Aunt Emma stands in doorways and looks at Mother from mirrors. Looks over her shoulder as Mother prepares the stew.

"Dis' whut be yo' transition now. Ah pray tuh Jesus, hear from Mary. Make da stew. Dip yo fanger in da pot—you be speakin' in tongues aftah while. Tarry some, you be speakin' in tongues aftah while. Ah outlive fo'—you got one in da basket—but ya still got one waitin' tuh be a man. No soul wiffout dis' kine sacrifice, dis' kine rituah."

Aunt Emma, in bloody linen and sweat-soaked head rag, six-foot frame, with the hands of a man, looks at Mother and listens to her careful speech, and northern ways.

"Heh . . . ya need tuh dance tuh da coon shouters! Delta Blues . . . Niggah Blues . . . Leroy Lasses White can hep ya—call on 'em! Call on 'em! Albert King, Mamie Smith, Charlie Patton, Son House—CALL ON 'EM! Did ya add da innards o' da hog to da stew? Ya 'member to stir whif ya las' flow? Transitional. Change ya gawments, girl. Dat'll be all right. Yep . . . Dat'll be all right . . . change y' gawments. Transitional . . . yep."

Mother hums a gospel song for the first time in years, listening to

Ghosts for instructions, stirring all the while. Father drinks gin and tonics now and stares out of one window. Brother lay silent. Still. Brother left this house some four years ago. I was eight. Mother says he could not contain himself here. His spirit restricted by bloodstained walls and shattered glass spittle spewed from fraternal throat. Danced out the door and up the hill, with busted eye and broken hip. He died somewhere in the hills . . . free. He died for our sins. We all smell of chicken livers and tears and garlic and blood. Father curses Mother's foolishness through tight lips, and Mother sings spirituals louder from tight lips, and Brother sleeps quietly, face drawn back with tight lips, and I say nothing of the smell in this house. I say nothing. Aunt Emma finds the records, piled away some many years. She spins 78's and guides Mother's hands as she stirs the stew. Mother laughs to herself a little. Makes the stew for the day of interment. Hopes for transition. Resists lack of control. About these things Mother knows nothing. The music plays.

Emma says, "Big Bill Broonzy curse Ray Charles for gospel voice and blues rhythm. Heh . . . I say combine de two!"

Mother serves the stew. Aunt Emma blesses the table from behind Mother's eyes. She hovers over us like some great warrior bird from the southern mesas flying at dusk, singing tribal chants and summoning Ma Rainey to bless us all. We eat in silence, except for Emma's blues wail. It is small and private. The stew is thick and smells. We eat in mourning, except for Mother's laughter. When the cedar bowls are empty, with no trace of flesh or soup or spit, the table is cleared and the cloth is cleaned with water and bile. Retiring to the chair facing the window that looks out over the hill, Father drinks and grumbles and curses. He walks toward the kitchen as Mother places the clean white sheet carefully over the dining-room table. Mother is naked—has discarded the suit and shoes. She rends the tablecloth in two. Emma lays out the pattern for new garments. Instructs her hands to cut and rip. To sew and fold. Garments of white, ragged and free. Flowing cottons and head rags. Long skirts and ruffled blouse. Mother drapes herself in grandiloquent silence. Emma's hands pick through Mother's hair. Hair unbound. Hair singing and stomping in percussive wails. Chorus of braid and bush. Clapping.

Father wants to get to the church where Brother sleeps. To say things to the corpse he never said to living flesh. To grieve and hurt and break and bend, without a flinch or blinking eye. To dance and scream and blame himself without a sound or stir or failing gate. But his wife takes her time and wastes the hours. Changes her garments and laughs too much on the day of their first son's interment. His wife has not asked him about his grief. About his apathy toward this thing called life and death. She has not asked why he could not touch or look upon the anomaly that was once his son. The boy integral and elegant in all his manner. She has never inquired why he must sometimes break his holy vow. The loss of control, the beating away of beauty when it is present all around him. She does not care about him, the living. She spends these hours with no concern for the economics of time. Stands in silly attire—and now the waiting and too much drink will surely challenge the steady calm he has worked so hard to maintain today.

Father says, "What the FUCK you wearin'? You done lost yo' MIND?"

Mother says nothing. Hair singing and stomping. His tone familiar. Her feet, still and quiet.

Father says, "People comin' from outta town, you gon' shame me? You gone EMBARRASS ME by wearin' rags?"

Mother says nothing from tight lips. Does not make a sound—only percussive wails come from scalp and root. Nigger blues. Leroy Lasses White. Coon Shouters singing from her tangled bush.

Father says, "Get holdta yourself! COMB your hair! Turn OFF dis music, early in da morning! You tryin' to make me act a fool! I know what you up to! You gonna TELL people it's MY fault the boy left—huh? MY fault he died young—huh? MY FAULT!"

Mother says nothing. Tight lips loosen. Mother sings. Just sings and moves. Mother's hair is dancing. Her feet are bare. Ingredients for the post-funeral coalation meal are placed on the table.

Father curses and yells, "MY fault I lost my job! MY fault we had to move back down here, in YOUR aunt's house! My fault the boy never listened to me! Can only be ONE man in a house."

I say nothing. I see nothing. Aunt Emma's palms veiling my mouth and eyes. Aunt Emma folds me into an unmade bed. My head resides on the pillowcase and I am fully dressed in black suit and black shoes and tie. On my back. Like Brother. Asleep. Aware. Deaf ears to slaps and crashing glass. Brother dances for me from the dark of Aunt Emma's palm. Integral, in all his elegance and fragile ways.

II. *Clifford Jordan & Eric Dolphy: First Mourners to Arrive*

▪ August, Sunday, 3 P.M.

For sores inflicted by someone who wants to take your power:

Lard of Male Hogs (1 pound)
Spignut (½ pound)
Extract of Dandelion (1 ounce)
Seed of Lobelia (1 ounce)
Turpentine (1 ounce)
Beeswax (2 ounces)

Make into a salve and apply until the pain subsides.

▪ ▪ ▪

I think Archie Shepp played *ham bone ham bone where you been?* in our living room, the night faces & fists melded mellifluous melancholy madness into red river carpeting—spurt, splash! Torrent falls, gushing reds, primeval screams crashing through vodka spittle. Sharp tenor sax and subjective alto, trumpet, trombone, hambone bass and Roger Blank . . . drums . . . Blank . . . drums . . . blank . . . Shepp's lyricism lurking behind ficus and forlorn fruit and rhythm patterns lined in gold fringe, clutched in our living room—in, *where you been?* arrangements scattered from kidney-shaped cherry wood coffee table. Camels sleep in red river woven carpeting. Caravans of Camels and Kools and vodka and blood and Shepp and rhythm . . .

▪ ▪ ▪

For bleeding at the nose:

Take birthroot, and cranesbill—pulverize and snuff into nostrils.

▪ ▪ ▪

I think *Garvey's Ghost* came to play with me between Charlie Brown sheets to the percussion of belt-buckle slaps and cracked wall mirrors and ripped Chinese watercolors (or was it *Mendacity?*). Either way, the party was in my pillow, where cut-outs held court with *Right On!* magazine centerfolds. Conversation was had, freely, and maybe Junior Walker interrupted for a moment, or it might have been . . . I think, it was . . . no . . . yes, it was *Mendacity.* It was Abby Lincoln who sent herself into my restlessness and jazz frenzy and comic book high, and quivering and quake. Not sure now what the silences mean after Johnnie Walker Black came crashing down to the harmonic freedom and improvisation of Roach and Mingus and Hawkins and Dizzy . . . Dizzy . . . dizziness . . .

■ ■ ■

For hysterics:

> *Take a portion of mountain tea, white root, and unkum root, pound them, and make into pills with Canada balsam and yellow poplar. Take two with water.*

■ ■ ■

I know Jimmy Garrison summoned a nature boy to come my way. We entertained battering and long fingernails broke against leather strap, against cheek and ass and eye. I played to Jimmy Garrison's plucking, sucking my thumb in corner circle rhythm patterns. Brilliant corners. Creative post bop, Monk's *Brilliant Corners* a hiding place, while ass whoopin's are taking place—like what twelve-year-olds like me supposed to get for stealing or lying, or the kind (maybe) you hear women get. Women who can sing "I Fall in Love Too Easily," Women who can hang tough with "Willow Weep for Me" and take a swing and a hard-hitting fast blow down. Crashing fruit and floral patterns and primeval screams through vodka spittle.

■ ■ ■

For spitting blood:

> *Two spoonfuls of nettles.*

■ ■ ■

The kind of ass whoopin' maybe women (who sing) supposed to get after they done tried to do "Afro Blue"—but you don't hear about broken nails and Jimmy Garrison and split lip and Eric Dolphy and swollen cheeks against red river roads where Camels and Kools caravan away from cherry wooded areas. Spilling themselves away, like the long and vibrant notes of *Yardbird Suite,* with the sweet repose of Holiday on "There Is No Greater Love". . . in our living room. They didn't tell us about this in record jackets; what to expect when Booker Little sings on that trumpet, when Carlos Valdez gets to *cong, cong, conga, cong, cong, congaing* to the beating taking place in the circle of frenzy in our living room.

■ ■ ■

For dizziness:

Peal garlic, dip it in honey, and put into ear with a little black wool.

■ ■ ■

There are no sequins for this diva. No boa. No rhinestone tiara. No pencil black eyebrows arched in pride across her forehead, or gentle shadows softly sleeping above the lid of her falling eye in sweet repose. No straightened hair illuminating lights and gels and go-boes. Not in our living room. Just Charles Tolliver's "Plight" to her modern dance ballet; ronde de jambe of the knee, to the fall, to the fist, straight back, and lip split, side turn, ever so gracefully, ever so soft, and hard, and SWING! and BOP! and BAM! and POW! and Dizzy . . . dizziness . . .

Swelling cheeks. Weak alto sax. Strong bass. I think it was Etta James screaming *James . . . James . . . JAMES . . . JAMES JAMES JAMES*, or maybe not. Maybe it was just the rustling of the knees and elbows, and the matchstick struck across the board. And embers. And smoke rising. And flames, lifting broken body beaten. Beaten the way twelve-year-olds like me are supposed to be beat (or maybe if you Abby Lincoln and sing that good. Maybe if you can do primeval screams to Max's drums).

And then there was nothing there . . . and then nothing . . . no voice . . . somebody hollered one last time and I can't recall if it was Grachan Moncur with Sonny Rollins, and Joe Henderson, but I think maybe it was the silences . . . Moncur's "Intellect" came up next . . . in our living room, with nothing there . . . no voice . . . I think it was the silences . . . a finger turning rotary dial . . . door shut . . . locked . . . running water . . . or it was? . . . no, I'm sure it was Moncur . . . who played with me . . . unveiled trombone taking me up in gentle long notes and tickling vibes. Texture and shape, and safe brilliant corners to suck my thumb in . . . I think it was the silences . . .

■ ■ ■

For the trembling of hands:

Mugwort soaked in water. Wash hands while singing to Morgana King.

III. Eulogy: Libretto for the Living

- August, Sunday, 5:38 P.M.

1 corpse
1 red velvet room
1 lithograph of Jesus and sheep
7 mourners wailing
1 ancient woman on the organ
1,000 songs

Mix and stir, and shake hands and heads. View the body, speak well of the soul.

■ ■ ■

White night. Milky glare. To my left, women in straw and plastic fruit holding pocketbooks and clean white handkerchiefs. This brownstone has been abandoned by the spirit of rhythm. Brick and damp wood exposed. Walls strong and flat, brass candleholders and red velvet draped over platforms and stands. To my right, Mother is blackened and bruised and smiling. Father does not share the front row. He waits in the back, by the door—just in case the walls cave in. Men in shiny polyester shake strong hands and speak in loud whispers while the organ plays a dirge. Brother is the fairest of them all. Reminding me of a pigeon, dead just outside the door—where the hard white pavement meets the foundation of gray mortar. A gravesite for broken neck, and severed wing. Still, beautiful gray and beautiful white feathers are guided by evening gale forces, moving even though the twisted body is still. There is movement in stillness. Movement, still. Brother looks like that to me. All words come from folded hands across the chest. All holy songs come from his painted lips. Can anyone else see the body moving? The dance he did to 45's? The mane of black and twisting walk . . . fashioned smile like young girls on the avenue. There. Liquid and lithe. Mother sees it. I know she does. Father avoids my eyes. I mutter psalms nobody taught me the meanings of.

The man in polyester suit takes the stand to speak, and Emma's hands hush the room. There are no more vain commandments. No disconsolate supplication for the reprobate. Maneuvers are to be graceful. Aunt Emma leans into me.

"You speak. Gon' on."

I have nothing.

"Gon' on. Make it right. Reach. Resurrect. Sow up the pieces. Make it right. Cup the fragments. Make 'em one thing. Whole."

Brother's face sings, *Canaan, I'm on way, and I am well able to posses the land!*

"Gon' on!"

Today is the yesterday we'll glorify tomorrow. Death has escaped me, thus far. Today is the future we stayed up all last night celebrating. Aunt Emma places her palm over my mouth until I speak. Not sure what they mean, but the words, they come. They echo the things I hear. And when I no longer hear the sounds of blues whispers, jazz prayers, and gospel cries, the words leave me. It is finished. The word made flesh. The eulogy was performed by me, from my seat. Brownstone walls echo a jazz fusion. Classical violins are played by spirits like fiddles. Feet pounding into hardwood floor. Ghosts march up and down the aisle chewing tobacco and dancing with their thighs and stomachs. The room is fragrant with cayenne and pork, and Mother's hands throw themselves up and out again, like they did in the days of birth pains. Legs move up and down. Shout precious memories into the carpet. She drapes herself over pew and casket while women in fruit and flower lay white sheets across her legs and fan her face. Quake and quiver and tremble of hand.

The lid of the casket is closed. Father stands in the back, by the door, calling out.

"Wife! Wife! You doing all right? Wife? . . . You . . . doing . . . all . . . ?"

Quake and quiver and tremble of hand.

IV. Final Recipe for Transition

- August, Sunday, 7 P.M.

Mackerel Fish (cut open and cleaned)
1 tablespoon of Olive Oil (save for anointing every member of household)

Medium Leeks (seven)
Spit (three times)

Let cool, then serve. Be cool, then serve. Warm hands in the steam. Rub together until you feel the friction. Until you feel the spirit. Until you feel the soul return to your body. Serve yourself first. Let the guests serve themselves.

■ ■ ■

I be waiting for people to come to the house after they leave the burial ground. Father removes his coat and sits quietly, his foot tapping to rhythm. Brother sleeps in a box underground. This house changes. Aunt Emma dances in blood-soaked smock. Mother holds her hands up in the air, feet stomping into hardwood floors, lips loose and rolling words—unintelligible. Intellectual language between her and the ghosts. The fish is waiting for invited mourners. She speaks in tongues. Father waits for the walls to cave in around us. Brother's body ascends. Carried off in the arms of Eddie Kendricks. Garments, new and flowing—garlic and olive oil and cayenne on our faces. We sit, living in a box, with one window—walls turning. Changed. There will always be music, and seasonings, and free-flowing garments. No shoes. From now on. Mother's steady rhythm and rapid dance dent parquet floors. The walls cave *out*. Open air. We sit, living in open air. Changed. Aunt Emma gathers up the scraps of our prior selves and fashions a doll for me to have.

The head from a piece of chipped brick
The spine, fish bone, reinforced with twine
The heart, a pig's heart, wrapped and frozen
The lungs, pieces of cigarette lumped in two
The skin, pigskin soaked in perfume from broken bottles
The hands, chicken feet
The hair, Brother's mixed with Mother's, combined with Father's, and mine
The mouth, cinnamon bark sweetened with red wine

Father drinks and smokes with trembling eyes to Ottis Redding and waits for redemption. Mother holds onto a doorknob to sustain herself, and dances. Bopping head tilted toward rapid feet. There will always be music and free-flowing garments in this house. Open air. Aunt Emma bustles up a path toward Zuni dirt roads. A bird's secret dance through ancient mesa-top ruins, amid song and prayer and sacred recipe. Ending this offering. Native Negro woman with man's hands, bestowing blessings on us all, moving . . . up the hill . . . bloody linen skirts traversing to a six/eight pulse.

Part Two

BLACK POLITICS

INTRODUCTION: AFROFEM AESTHETIC MANIFESTED

TRACIE MORRIS

I'm flowing with reflections of poetic sisterhood politics and its meaning to this book's theme. Playing with my dense rhyme scheme a tagteam partner in an attempt to marry analysis, opinion, and art. Intense word play is the way we poet types try to understand how we feel. For this artisan, soul is the reflection of culturalists looking for the most alternatives and bearing the most diverse array of accouterments. From my vantage point I see nuanced implications for political direction in Afrofem's literally abstract articulation. The crystallization of hip black culture in general and its connections to the nation's women can be refracted in the prism of the paradigmatic. As constant innovators it's crucial that we don't take our past and present creations for granted. Like the sixties lingua of bedecked heads, soul is natural and, like other U.S. cash crops, specifically black. It is a signifier of shifts in marketing, fashion, and communication with the yin-yang of cynicism and hopes for liberation. Backward and forward searches of soul make it a substantial anthropological marker. Why is this relevant today?

The application of soul, like a cotton pickin' minute, can be looked at as an alternative to Republican flag-waving. Soul serves as more than mere celebration. The inception of bold colors and sounds after the understated reactions to quintidecadence was deliberately sonic and visually shocking. This breakout became multiplicitous framework for affirmations that's pan(d)oramically open and free. Current handling of retro soul iconography speaks more to its former context as revolutionary media than to a desire to go back to good oldies. Its contemporary allure may well be a response to the revisionary, hot-headed conservative tendencies these days. Damn, according to Manning Marable's essay we only had four years off before folks thought we was too loose and plotted to give us Dick in the next election. White backlash assumes that the first whipping really stopped. (For the record, going to fetch the cat-o'-nine-tails is not a respite for the one tied up.) Later for the unhep boys who hem and haw about whether they'll be leftist like Ted Koppel or open to discussion like Rush Limbaugh. We stretch our brown bodies over caverns created by the maw. (Or was that a disinterested yawn?)

For me, Afrofem art determined the debate.

Brother Kazaam notwithstanding, I'm a believer in magical melanin gyns—mainly for nonsupremacy political reasons (and to get even), but also because our unconditional love has historically shored up cultural moorings. When trips back across the Atlantic seem de rigueur if not boring, the aesthete sensibility of temporal diasporic divas demands the antithesis of ignoring. From Queen Hatshepsut's dynastic character, to Harriet Tubman's hardcore emancipation exercises under threat of rearrest, to stunning gun-blazing sexual mackstresses, to down low eighties wannabe corporate sisters who wore braids as Afrocentric anti–Bo Derek cultural front statements, victory depends on style. Winning on any field depends on how, not just what, is done. The di-unital feeling and spiritual adherence to the muse may come off as confusing as we refuse to make either/or political choices about what gives us pain and pleasure. None of this contrived stiffness of the thick upper lipid masking personal anguish like some sixties and seventies women were prone to. Giving what up? To whom?

Girls prefer strong blackbone exorcism of painful macrocosmic and interrelational power. We sayin' commitment's got to be thorough. Curtis Mayfield, ever the articulate helmsman, once said, "If there's a hell below and we're all gonna go," we may as well be rooted in the fruit of knowledge. Afrofem artists seriously cut down on attacks of the coronary by melding solo and group issues, disintegrating contradictions with the light of day. Love in struggle is no digression. It is an investigation of all aspects of true liberation and the problematic nature of whatever gets in the way. Nobody loves deeper than we do. For all the talk-show-complaining, headrolling urban girlfriends (who won't ever get any of their issues dealt with unless they're highlighted in the extreme), who's been hanging tough through the centuries? Some of us may be like Sapphires, but can you blame us for being a bit jaded? No excuse for community recluses who use isolation not to deal with longstanding sexism, to aid and abet the racism confronted by the group. That lowest common demeanor played itself like Dino. Something about bright futures in the wake of rape, lynchings, and castrations links up the nice but rough in us, as it did in Tina. As life-givers who too often take it, we have an innate understanding of the disastrous implications of inaction.

All the while we continued to make contributions, including howto's on remaining stylistically gracious. (You are everything, and everything is you.) Can I get a witness? Jeez, we be nurturing the troops from the side of Sunday greens to loaves of blue fish to feed a million marchers. Talk about nourishment and propagation. Wading through the misty to the clear truth ain't easy, especially as you see gradual yet consistent forays in to the mainstream. What I mean? It's inevitable that poetry, like every other sentiment, will be out the box and be marketed like the cash crop prize for new jack crackers. Standard-bearing agitpropists, serving as reference for the real, will probably be distanced in exchange for the nonthreatening familiar (the kind that sits on the desk pretty and you can pet on the head).

If there's a conspiracy to be had, it's the threat of a plethora of poetry records that can raze a seller's system without so much as reference to pocketed entertainment industrial complex protectors. This is because the poetic constructions, whether two-dimensional or oracular, are more established and much older. So poetry's explosion has been reduced to a leak through the ceiling (some lead traces). The mainline three or four record companies aren't going for a variation of the "nation of millions" attack arrogance. The constraint probably won't be that blatant. Drama is a high commodity. Buoying up an industry (or philosophy) under the premise of aesthetic edginess underscores the malleable political applications of soul to regulate the inter- or intrarelations of agitation among African-identified natives (as May Joseph explains). Even if a few do "tear the roof off," it'd behoove them to check their charms. The rabbit whose foot was rubbed didn't feel lucky. While this age's spoken word tries to negotiates its place on the sociocultural landscape, it is related, beholden to, and confused by the rough ride of its contextualizer, the unpredictable resistance trends inextricably tied to hip hop's zig-zag development (for the antimisogynists: I acknowledge that movement doesn't exclude the possibility of going backwards). The wordspoke in the wheel of fortune may turn out the ever verboten conservative. Industrial largess may tend toward either the vaguely well-put descriptive or the patently (and predictably) offensive political variety. (I want to be optimistic. Maybe if Savion clicks his heels it'll be better.)

Poetry's potential to resonate serious issues and offer legitimate analysis of the mainstream is heavy. Combine it with performance art's ability to compellingly convey sentiments by using a good beat and you have something which makes the genre particularly unique. Some Sepias in the disciplines seek to fit the format; other pan-Afro penners attempt to wreck shit. Sisters saying like it is could be a bitch even if the operandi is sweet. Some honey in your coffee? A Tracy Chapman type in poetry would be hype, but reality bites this delicate umbilical thread to the information web. Rhetorical devices ain't part of it so far. With government funding of the arts cut out, the power of all work will be in the hands of the same companies that own everything else you may want to write on. Do we generate more tension for uncolored men when we push their luck or let go? Depends and don't matter. Our very standing is intimidating. Any aspect of the dogged masses still alive and creating under the pressure cooker of circumscribed stances is daunting. I got a glance of this fact while I was being saved by the vibes of George Clinton's horns and Tribe Called Quest in Lollapalooza tour of 1994. Folks was floored by the intractable bottom dancing to "in joke" sophisticated laid-back snapping. All praises. (While being daily resurrected, I was also hoping for a surprise guesting by, say, rocker Nona Hendrix.) Stop beggin'. I mistook tokenism for representin'. This was not the love train. More like a chain of foolishness. Sometimes, between Lazarus episodes, I foundered. Blackchicks like Cheryl Boyce Taylor, two Boom Poets, and me bucking on the vaudevillian white boy fantasy rock tour ride was so disorienting for this East New Yorker, I started running with the resident drag queen. (We'd bonded via a mutual respect for rum-raisin lipstick—he, for the Cindy Crawford vamp; me, giving it dap for matching my peeps in phenotype and nomenclature.) *C'est la vie.* Whether white Americans are introduced to us through commodification or by presumptive knowledge based on exclusion, permeates and permeates the environment in interesting ways. Interior decorating of the womb. Who's germinating whom? David Serlin's essay seems to be investigating this peregrination. Tactility cannot be equated with grabbing the reigns of terra firma, however. Formerly suckled southerners made this point abundantly clear. Choose your weapons. Rather, don't choose. The developmental alternative of Orwellian commercial craft for pressing parlance is not just in the safety of the Net but the resurgence of more tangible multimedia. In this section, visual applications are clarified by examples from Marilyn Nance. As my personal muse informed me, multifaceted approach is the way and is lately what I've been called to add to the stew. Flygirls are more than just kinte window dressing where the boys are. Wasn't your mom's job more than dilating and contractions?

Surely sisters contribute with sex-specific making and nurturing.

Not that pushing doesn't have its advantages when guided, as Salt-n-Pepa made clear years ago. One of the longest standing rappers of any hormonal balance, they did a lot to embrace proud female sexuality in hip hop. Yeah, they could literally throw down. When their sound came out, it was earth-shaking. Along with then guru Herbie Azor, they made distinctions between overt sexuality and demeaning depiction of the hoe/skeezer and hottie. Even among those of similarly situated backgrounds, they demonstrate the ability to be physically strong and pleased. They follow the tradition of blues women who generated a new state of being. This is part of the catechism that breaks the questionable links of woman-hating by associating various aspects of a powerful Venus. This trinity is just one part of the consortium of hierophants at the temple of tough love, the gatekeeper being the gangsta bitch who finds justification to temporarily sublimate sexuality: to get the job done. Mack wants to be hard and step to the plate? "Hell hath no fury . . ." Ya damn straight.

Ah, the myriad methods of a girl. Me'Shell's ambiguities revel and rebel in combined methods of sex, pointed comments, and music. Speaking became one of the ways she got open and expressed complexity while maintaining the direct rootedness of seventies music through bass playing. Because everyone's talking there's a freedom to not be as heavily invested in what the mainstream thinks. Jessica Care Moore, the multiple Apollo Amateur winner, got in kids faces with her desire and rage as explicit as Chuck D's. She got the freelove. Can't underestimate the people. The management eventually had to move her away from the stage, claiming it was breaking the rules of monopoly. Black fem poetry has woven into the recorded mainstream in a seamless yet underpaid way. Some more sonic sirens like Lauryn Hill reinforce Afrofem power with drama in the eardrum—mnemonic, pounding and resounding musically. In my role as double band leader I also see sister musicians as an intrinsic part of the artistic atmosphere. Like MC's, they have to wax prolific with proficiency.

In every intersecting circle I've been in there's been an overflow of melanin XX combinations. So much for naysayers proclaiming their discriminating missives that there ain't no "good womyn" available. (You want a list? It's too long, so ask me.) Those that don't fall into convenient creative formats should also be added to the mix. They underscore and create environments for the aesthetically dispossessed. Complected maidens roam the full range of art administration, visual commentators, fiction dictators, patrons (and regular, poorer supporters), dancehall queens, fly poetic stylists, open-minded alternative lifestyle strivers, hip hop heads, and intellectual, well-read Dark Room types. (Many are inbetween these nonexclusive categories). African-based women's art (and for my part, performance poetry) has a multifocused approach, and when honestly addressed it's like a good enema. It'll remove the bullshit, cultivate the flora, and take some weight off. I'm not saying it's easy, but hopefully it's one of a myriad of ways in which the entire African community is being forced to release baggage and get closer to home, to our truer selves. Afrofem art manifested invokes remembrances of captured Lucumi, who stored apatakis to concretize abstract ideologies into a workable foundation for complete freedom.

7

From Freedom to Equality

The Politics of Race and Class

MANNING MARABLE

It has been more than a generation since Fannie Lou Hamer's eloquent and moving plea for freedom and civil rights before the 1964 Democratic National Convention in Atlantic City. More than thirty years have elapsed since Dr. Martin Luther King Jr. led thousands of nonviolent protestors across the Edmund Pettus Bridge in Selma, Alabama, to confront the racist phalanx of state police troopers defending segregation. The politics of resistance at that turbulent moment in our history gave new meaning to our sense of identity. The politics of soul in the 1960s was the personal and collective decision to fight for freedom.

Since the 1960s we have witnessed a series of racial and political reactions designed to undermine and erode the reforms achieved during the Civil Rights Movement. The 1994 congressional campaign victories of the Republicans only represented the culmination of a historical process that began more than a generation ago. After the political reforms of 1964 and the defeat of Jim Crow segregation, racial politics and a white backlash helped elect Richard Nixon in 1968. He subsequently pursued a "southern strategy" of appealing to the supporters of segregationist George Wallace and opposed school desegregation. Through his policies of "benign neglect," Nixon tried to slam the door on the movement for racial equality; but the Watergate scandal undermined his conservative strategy. In 1980, racial politics crystallized behind white ethnic voters and the middle class, which overwhelmingly endorsed the conservative candidacy of Ronald Reagan. This was the second phase of race/class reaction. As president, Reagan aggressively tried to roll back affirmative action, equal opportunity legislation, women's rights, and the rights of labor—remember the administration's repression of the air traffic controllers strike in 1981. However, the Iran-Contra scandal shattered the conservative offensive momentarily. By the 1990s, with the Republicans controlling the national legislature and the federal courts, yet another wave of reaction has transpired. Affirmative action, minority economic set-asides, minority scholarships at colleges and universities, and minority-controlled legislative districts are now all on the endangered species list.

To understand what is behind the most recent racial backlash, however, we must examine the contemporary structure of America's economic system. The polarization of wealth and poverty, the decline in wages, and the growth of unemployment and a sense of crisis are now defining the economic foundations of reaction. In the 1980s, millions of new jobs were created in the U.S. economy, but relatively few were at wage levels that could support families. Eighty-five percent of all new jobs created during the decade were in low pay or part-time service work. Nearly 20 percent of all workers had no health insurance, and two out of five had no pension coverage. In 1979, the average wage of a U.S. production worker was $12.06 per hour, in inflation-adjusted dollars. By 1989, that average had dropped to $11.26 per hour; in 1993, it was $10.83 per hour. According to Children's Defense Fund research, the greatest losses of real income have occurred among families with children under the age of eighteen where the household head was under the age of thirty. White households in this category fell 22 percent in inflation-adjusted income between 1973 and 1990. For young Latino families with children, the decline during these years was 27.9 percent. For young black families, the drop has been a devastating 48.3 percent.

During the Reagan administration, the United States witnessed a massive upward redistribution of wealth unequaled in our history. In 1989, the top 1 percent of all U.S. households received 48.1 percent of the total financial wealth of the country. In other words, the top 1 percent controlled a significantly greater amount of wealth than the bottom 95 percent of all U.S. households (27.7 percent). These trends produced a degree of economic uncertainty and fear unparalleled since the Great Depression for millions of U.S. households. White working-class families found themselves working harder, yet falling further behind. In this uncertain political environment, "race" easily became a vehicle for orienting politics toward the right. If a white worker cannot afford the modest home in the suburbs that his or her parents could have purchased thirty years ago, the fault is attributed not to falling wages but to affirmative action. If the cost of public education spirals skyward, white teenagers and their parents often conclude that the fault is not due to budget cuts, but because "undeserving" blacks and Hispanics have taken the places of "qualified" white students.

There is another racial dimension to this class struggle. Unprecedented numbers of white people are confronting what many African-Americans and Latinos have known for years, namely, unemployment, poverty, and hunger. About half of Americans living in poverty, nearly eighteen million people, are white. More than one in three white female–headed households is poor. Between 1979 and 1991, the poverty rate nearly doubled for white families headed by twenty-five to thirty-four years olds. Whites comprise nearly half of those receiving Aid to Families with Dependent Children and food stamps. In 1991, 12.6 million whites received Medicaid.

For millions of white middle-class Americans, "whiteness" used to mean a relatively privileged lifestyle, a standard of living superior to that of most racial minorities. As these Americans lose ground, they are desperately trying to understand why their "whiteness" no longer protects them. In this uncertain economic environment, Patrick Buchanan appeals to alienated, angry white workers for whom the "American Dream" has become a nightmare.

The primary response by the U.S. government, elected officials, and the corporate elite to the growing crisis of inequality has been the massive expansion of public and private security forces and the incarceration of millions of black, Hispanic, and poor people. Between 1980 and 1990, the number of police in the United States doubled. As of 1995, state and local police forces employed 554,000 officers. An additional 1.5 million private security officers are currently employed to guard office buildings, stores, affluent neighborhoods, and corporate headquarters all over the country. Private patrol cars now cruise entire communities of upper- and middle-class Americans whose streets are closed off to outside traffic. Much of the new suburban housing being built today in "planned communities" is surrounded by walls and gates, wired for electronic surveillance, and guarded twenty-four hours a day by private security personnel.

It was in this context that Congress passed President Clinton's $30 billion Omnibus Crime Bill in 1994. The Crime Bill's draconian provisions included $10.8 billion in federal matching funds to local governments to hire one hundred thousand new police officers over the next five years; $10 billion for the construction of new federal prisons; an expansion of the number of federal capital crimes from two to fifty-eight (the bill also eliminated an existing statute prohibiting the execution of mentally incapacitated defendants); a so-called "three strikes" proposal that mandates life sentences for anyone convicted of three "violent" felonies; a section that allows children as young as thirteen to be tried as adults; and the creation of special courts able to deport noncitizens alleged to be "engaged in terrorist activity" on the basis of secret evidence.

Even more striking has been the recent massive expansion of the U.S. prison system. From 1980 to 1995, the prison population tripled from 500,000 to 1,500,000. In the state of California alone, between 1977 and 1992, the prison population soared from less than 20,000 to over 110,000.

The racial oppression that defines U.S. society as a whole is most dramatically apparent within the criminal justice system and the prisons. Today, about half of all inmates (more than 750,000) are African Americans. Of black men thirty to thirty-four, 6,299 are imprisoned for every 100,000; for black men aged twenty-four to twenty-nine, the number of prisoners is 7,210 for every 100,000. About 30 percent of all African-American males in their twenties are either in prison or jail, on probation, on parole, or awaiting trial. What does this mean in the daily experience of an average black male in the United States regarding the criminal justice system?

On any given day in Washington, D.C. in 1991, 15 percent of all black men between the ages of eighteen and thirty-four were in prison, 21 percent were on probation or parole, and 6 percent were being sought by the police or were on bond awaiting trial. Thus, the total involved with the criminal justice system was 42 percent. One study estimates that 70 percent of black men in the District of Columbia will be arrested before the age of thirty-five, and that 85 percent will be arrested at some point in their lives. Washington racist pattern of arrest is not unusual: in nearby Baltimore on any given day in 1991, 56 percent of the city's African-American males were in jail or prison, on probation or parole, awaiting trial or sentencing, or had warrants issued for their arrest.

These statistical profiles of racial oppression should not obscure the class dimensions of who is arrested and imprisoned in the United States. In 1989, more than 14 million Americans were arrested. About 2 percent of the total male population in the United States today is in prison. According to a 1991 survey by the U.S. Department of Justice, about one-third of all prisoners were unemployed at the time of their arrests. Only 55 percent held full-time jobs. About two-thirds of all prisoners have less than a high-school-level education, and therefore few skills with which to compete in the labor market. The study, which surveyed 14,000 inmates in 277 state prisons throughout the Unites States, found that "70 percent of all prisoners legally earned less than $15,000 in the year before their arrest, with 32 percent earning less than $5,000." U.S. prisons are vast warehouses for the poor and unemployed, for low-wage workers and the poorly educated, and especially for Latino and African-American males. White-collar criminals who embezzle hundreds of millions of dollars are rarely given prison sentences. The wealthy and powerful almost never go to prison for the crimes they commit. But for the most oppressed, prison is often an improvement in one's life circumstances: free health care, three meals a day, shelter, and some modest training programs. Today, hundreds of thousands more black men are in prison or within the criminal justice system than are enrolled in colleges or universities. Statistically, a young black man is more likely to be jailed or arrested than to obtain a job that adequately supports himself, his partner, or his family.

The prison industry has become one of America's biggest and most profitable businesses. Between 1979 and 1990, prison construction nationwide increased 612 percent and annual expenditures for corrections soared by $14 billion. Today, more full-time American employees work for the prison industry than any Fortune 500 corporation except General Motors.

According to the research of the Office of Urban Initiatives, based in Buffalo, New York, prisons are now the site for tens of thousand of new jobs. In California, the use of prison labor generates $1.3 million in profits per year. Most prisoners are hired at subminimum wages, usually $2.00 or less per hour. In Oregon, inmates are marketed through state-sponsored tours of prisons. Ten percent of Arizona's prison inmates work for private companies at subminimum wages. In New York State, Governor George Pataki is demanding three new maximum security prisons by the year 2000 at a cost of nearly $500 million.

Another crisis compounding the difficult situation of people of color is the state of public education in this country. In many states, the dropout rate for nonwhite high school students exceeds 50 percent. Across the United States, more than 1,500 teenagers of color drop out of school each day. Many of those who stay in school do not receive the training to prepare them for a computer-driven, technologically advanced labor market. In short, thousands of people applying for jobs as cashiers and bank tellers cannot do simple arithmetic. Thousands of high school students are unable to read the simplest instructions. Meanwhile, the new jobs generated by high technology increasingly demand the ability to operate computers and analyze complex data. The gap is steadily growing between the technical qualifications and academic background necessary for such jobs and the actual level of ability of millions in the educational underclass.

A new form of "segregation" will soon surface threatening the prospects of millions of black youth. Rather than the Jim Crow signs of "white" and "colored," the segregation of the twenty-first century will be the division between the educated "haves" and the uneducated "have nots." Those who lack scientific, mathematical, and computer skills are already disproportionately nonwhite.

The present social and economic crisis is having a devastating impact on our young people. Growing up black in white America has always been a challenge, but never more so than today. To be young and black in the 1990s means that the basic context for human development—education, health care, personal safety, the environment, employment, and shelter—is increasingly problematic. To be young and black today means fighting for survival in a harsh and frequently unforgiving urban environment.

The frightening prospects for African-American children and youth have been identified by Marian Wright Edelman and the Children's Defense Fund. Today, compared to white children, black children are one and one-half times more likely to grow up in families whose household head did not graduate from high school. They are twice as likely to be arrested for property crimes, to be unemployed as teenagers and later as adults, and to become teenage mothers. African-American infants are two and one-half times as likely to die in the first year of life and to be born at low birth weights. They are three times more likely than white young people to live in single-parent homes, to live in group quarters, to be suspended from school, and to endure corporal punishment. African-

American young people are four times more likely to be born of mothers who have had no prenatal care, mothers who died during childbirth, or mothers dying from HIV infection. They are five times more likely to be arrested by the police for violent crimes and nine times more likely to become victims of homicide.

The Institute for Research in African-American Studies at Columbia University, which I direct and from which my data are gathered, is only six blocks away from the heart of Harlem, 125th Street. Every day, in our immediate neighborhood, I can see the destruction of an entire generation of our young people. In New York City, 45 percent of all African-American youth dwell in poverty. In Central Harlem, one out of eight households has no plumbing or toilet facilities; 87 percent of all households lack any form of air conditioning; more than half live in buildings with more than four floors that lack elevators; and one-third have no telephones. Every day in New York, an average of 70,000 children, mostly Latino and black, use illegal drugs. Black and Hispanic youth unemployment exceeds 40 percent. The spectre of violence pervades everything. In Central Harlem, the mortality rate for children from birth through age four is almost triple the national average.

Black America stands at a challenging moment in its history: a time of massive social disruption, class stratification, political uncertainty, and cultural ambiguity. The objectives for black politics in the age of Jim Crow segregation were relatively simple: full equality, voting rights, and the removal of "white" and "colored" signs from the doors of hotels and schools.

Today's problems are fundamentally different in scope, character, and intensity: the flight of capital investment from our central cities, with thousands of lost jobs; the deterioration of the urban tax base, with the decline of city services; black-on-black violence, homicide, and crime; the proliferation of single-parent households; and the declining quality of our public schools. To this familiar litany of problems, I would add one more: the crisis of the spirit. A growing pessimism within our ranks asserts that there are no solutions to our overwhelming social problems, that government cannot help us, that voting and participation within the political process are irrelevant, and that no allies exist outside the African-American community who will help us. And the greatest doubt of all is the question of leadership—whether we have the capacity or the will to generate women and men who will rise to our contemporary challenges.

The place to begin reconstructing contemporary black politics is the terrain of memory. The collective histories of African-American people reveal a consciousness of survival and resistance. In the 1960s the militant awareness of identity and collective energy was captured by the term *soul*. Engaging in the struggle to redefine the world and one's community meant that each person had an obligation to history and memory. We were part of a larger process, challenging structures of inequality and power. Spiritually and esthetically, the meaning of soul pushed us toward new definitions of self and new possibilities for our politics. We need to recapture that degree of commitment and struggle in the reconstruction of new progressive political identities for black people as we enter the twenty-first century.

We must build a new black leadership to tackle today's problems, one with original analysis and a new level of programmatic and policy sophistication. First, this new black leadership must develop policy initiatives in concert with the best scholars and researchers, to construct alternatives in health care, education, housing, and the environment. At the new Institute for Research in African-American Studies at Columbia University, we are developing a center to promote constructive interaction between black elected officials and their staff members, research scholars, political analysts, and representatives from the unions, churches, public schools, civic associations, and other institutions. Sound public policies that address the black community's problems must come from a collaborative process of recognizing and critiquing the weaknesses of previous policies while identifying those that have worked.

Leadership in a multicultural environment means having the courage to make connections, bringing together people of radically diverse class backgrounds, ethnic groups, languages, and cultural and social traditions. Those who think that U.S. politics will always be decided by white conservative males ignore the multicultural reality of contemporary American society. In the past ten years, there has been a 40 percent increase in the number of Americans who speak a language other than English in their homes. In New York City, more than 40 percent of all residents consider English a second language. It is estimated that by the year 2000, one-third of all Americans will be people of color: Latinos, Asian Americans, Pacific Island Americans, American Indians, and African Americans. The Asian-American population is projected to grow from 7.2 million in 1990 to over 20 million by the year 2020. Latinos will outnumber African Americans by the year 2010. By the year 2050, the majority of Americans will be people of color; white Americans will simply become America's largest "minority group."

As we have seen, the contradictions within American capitalism are more profound than ever before. What, then, should be the basis for constructing a new radical democratic politics, a politics of social transformation? A politics of liberation should ground itself in the actual conditions and perspectives of those who suffer most from the disempowerment created by globalized capitalism. The common points of experience and struggle, resistance and suffering, and hope and human emancipation among those classes and communities defined by racial and gender domination, political oppression, and social control, create the context for a unified social force. They may speak different languages and have different cultural and ethnic traditions, but they still must come together to fight the power.

I recently spoke with Ossie Davis about the challenges and problems confronting the African-American community as we enter the twenty-first century. "Every generation needs a moral assignment," Davis insisted. "We have yet to define that moral assignment for ourselves and in our time."

African-American people were challenged 150 years ago by the harsh realities of slavery. The great moral and political question of that era was the abolition of human bondage. Black abolitionists such as Frederick Douglas and Martin Delany pursued a vision of freedom that mobilized the energies of the black community, north and south. Nearly a century later, the great moral challenge confronting black people was the oppressive reality of Jim Crow segregation. African Americans were denied access to schools, hospitals, hotels, and many other public establishments. The Fifteenth Amendment was a dead letter for several generations. Martin Luther King Jr. and the Civil Rights Movement represented the courageous struggles of a people who yearned to be free. This struggle for freedom was like crossing a turbulent river. In the religious imagination of black folk, the river was frequently identified as the River Jordan. Like the ancient Hebrews who escaped Egyptian bondage, black Americans courageously crossed their own River Jordan to seek and claim the promised land of freedom.

Now we are in an uncertain time, filled with dangerous and destructive social forces: violence, drugs, unemployment, poverty, social alienation, and fear. Our leaders seem unsure of how to articulate a new agenda for progressive change. Many voices within our community call on us to turn inward, away from potential allies with whom we can work to achieve positive change. What is required is the definition of a new moral assignment, a new vision of human emancipation.

Davis said, "We must cross a second river, the river of equality. We must insist that the Constitution create the conditions for genuine equality. But equality is an economic function, first and foremost." It is important to distinguish between the goal of freedom and the goal of equality. Freedom is about "rights"; equality is about social justice and the material realities of human fairness—universal health care, quality education, housing, and jobs—as human rights. Equality is the power to restrict the prerogatives of the corporations, the shutting down of factories, the economic destruction of urban communities. Equality is about having a living wage for all people. Equality ultimately means power to the people.

Our movement must cross that second river of equality. In doing so, we must wage the same principled struggles that were fought during the desegregation campaigns King led throughout the South. The same willingness to sacrifice, the same tears, the same determination to challenge unjust laws, and the same impatience with oppression must propel us toward a new politics. The meaning of soul in contemporary terms must translate into solidarity and a renewed commitment to the fight for social justice. To end the oppression of the criminal justice system, to abolish unemployment and homelessness, to uproot discrimination and social alienation, we must move beyond civil rights to the realization of human equality.

8

From *Sesame Street* to *Schoolhouse Rock*

Urban Pedagogy and Soul Iconography in the 1970s

DAVID SERLIN

One of the most memorable moments in Spike Lee's quasi-autobiograph-ical and highly underrated film *Crooklyn* (1994) occurs just as the Lee children are watching an episode of *The Partridge Family.*[1] Crowded around the television set, secretly, in an upstairs bedroom of their Bed-ford-Stuyvesant rowhouse, the Lee children are mesmerized by the image of David Cassidy and company pounding through the harpsichord-driven white psychedelia of "I Woke Up in Love This Morning." Like the faded, earthy 1970s colors chosen for *Crooklyn* by cinematographer Arthur Jafa—brick reds, denim blues, canary yellows, and greens and oranges that look as if they were left too long in the sun—the television scene mixes memory and desire, nostalgia and embarrassment, into one arresting visual aesthetic.

Watching this rag-tag group of kids watch TV, I thought that I was witnessing a kind of genealogy of personal consciousness: a subtle unraveling of an individual's history by way of his or her earliest televi-sion experiences, the results of which pay tribute to the power of popular culture on prepubescent subjectivity. And yet, for all of its beauty and imagination, this scene touched an odd chord in me. Some of my earliest television experiences were shaped not by watching *The Partridge Fam-ily* but instead programs like *Fat Albert and the Cosby Kids, The Harlem Globetrotters' Razzle Dazzle Popcorn Hour* (featuring Rodney Allen Rippy), *What's Happenin'?, That's My Mama, Sanford and Son, The Jeffersons,* and *Good Times.* As an adolescent who grew up in the relatively homogeneous, decentralized suburban sprawl of Miami, such programs seemed to offer some version of black "realism" that appealed to me infinitely more than the sanitized, white-bread antics of the Partridges or the Bradys. Perhaps I felt, at the time, that these programs — featuring the likes of Antonio Fargas, Redd Foxx, and Mabel King — constituted television's only sincere attempt to celebrate diversity or represent the bitter truths of racial inequity and social injustice in America. In retrospect, I now think that the producers of these programs were trying to exploit the cultural legacy of black anger generated during the decade. With professional skill and artifice, they were able to reconfigure this anger as something akin to "soul" — that sassy, "authentic" version of urban black *Weltanschauung* — and consequently market it, for mass cultural consumption, to naïve white kids like me.

This anecdotal tour through my personal television experience belongs, I think, to a much richer historical context for looking at the multiple, and important, connections between black popular culture and the consumption of soul images by young people. As many scholars and critics have already argued, in this volume and elsewhere, mainstream American culture during the late 1960s and early 1970s witnessed an efflorescence of sounds and images directly associated with, and rooted in, the postdiasporic consciousness of Afro-American experience. But whatever its status as an internationally recognized style, or set of visual, musical, or sartorial cues, soul might also be seen as a specifically American variant of a much larger globalization of black culture that occurred during the same historical period, or at least since the late 1940s with the first triumphs of African and West Indian political independence. From the work of Amiri Baraka, Nikki Giovanni, Ntozake Shange, Gil Scott-Heron and the Last Poets, and the Black Arts Movement to more commercially driven projects such as blaxploitation films and the "Philadelphia Sound," soul crystallized after the civil rights activism of the 1950s and 1960s as a readily identified reference point specific to black American experience. In this sense, I want to distinguish between soul as it was generated by an international cadre of black cultural activists, and the variations or permutations of American soul that formed a core vocabulary of commercial black images that were seized upon, marketed, and internationalized within the United States and throughout the world.[2]

By the late 1960s, many progressive educational institutions such as PBS's Children's Television Workshop and the Bank Street College of

Education began to develop songs and, eventually, short cartoon vignettes for elementary school curricula that self-consciously utilized soul music and iconography rooted in a northern, urban, inner-city aesthetic. Soul's status as a familiar genre with a hip cachet may help explain its popularity on American network television, especially in urban crime dramas such as *The Mod Squad, Baretta, Kojak, and Starsky and Hutch.* But why progressive teachers who wanted to reinvent the tenets of inner-city education chose soul in the first place is another question altogether, especially since educational television programs were never intended for outright commercial gain. By looking at a few soulful examples—in particular, moments from ABC's *Schoolhouse Rock* and PBS's *Sesame Street* and *Electric Company*—I hope to demonstrate the dialectical relationship between educational television and black popular culture during the 1970s. These musical ideas, visual images, and cultural symbols not only taught children fundamental skills, but they transformed young viewers into savvy consumers of a black American soul aesthetic.

■ ■ ■

In order to understand the political and cultural milieu from which this children's garden of soul evolved, we need some historical background for urban educational reform, which started in the late 1950s and early 1960s in older northeastern industrial cities with large minority constituencies. The unprecedented growth of suburbia after World War II and the accelerated depopulation of whites from congested inner-city areas lured many skilled educators and sympathetic administrators away from urban school districts. By the early 1960s, research universities began to ask how and why education had failed for urban minorities when it obviously had been more successful for their white suburban counterparts. As early as 1961, Harvard University's president, James B. Conant, outlined the specific needs of urban education for inner-city youth: "Big cities need decentralized administration in order to bring the schools closer to the needs of the people in each neighborhood and to make each school fit the local situation." [3] By 1969, such varied institutions as the Center for Urban Education, the Bank Street College of Education, and the Children's Television Workshop—all of which were located in New York City—symbolized the critical liaisons forged between the practical concerns of the public school system and the theoretical pedagogy that was to subsume urban educators throughout the decade.

Riding the political momentum of *Brown v. Board of Education*, many theorists declared that improved race relations were absolutely essential for rehabilitating urban education. Indeed, as Sol Gordon asserted, the inadequate attention paid to race relations within the public school system was "expressive and symptomatic of, rather than intrinsic to, the urban condition."[4] Gordon's use of the phrase "urban condition" suggested that urbanists could no longer explain the material circumstances of segregation or socioeconomic inequality as "natural" or "organic" conditions indigenous to metropolitan areas, as the influential Chicago School of urban sociologists had done for two generations.[5] Throughout the 1960s and early 1970s, liberal organizations began to recognize educational reform as a potential ticket to community empowerment and individual agency, which educators and grassroots activists alike wanted to instill in minority urban youth.[6]

Consequently, educational reformers proposed to invent useful pedagogical methods that would bring about new opportunities for learning, thinking, and synthesizing information. But they were also painfully aware that, despite their efforts, students in inner-city school systems exhibited a disparate range of skills and abilities. This was the period during which special education researchers began to address the psychological needs of the inner-city child, focusing their attention as much on "maladjusted, brain-injured, and retarded" children as on kids from urban settings who were identified, in the parlance of the time, as "disadvantaged" or "socially handicapped."[7] Gordon, for example, argued that, according to diagnostic tests, urban kids tended to respond better to verbs or "action" words than to adjectives or "descriptive" words, and he cited the verbal dexterity among black inner-city youth as evidence of this trend. Therefore, educators encouraged teachers and schools to develop new strategies that would incorporate the physical and social landscape of the urban environment: apartments and tenements, neighborhood institutions, public transportation, and representatives from different racial and ethnic groups and economic strata.[8] This position was perhaps best exemplified by the "Schoolhouse in the City" conference, organized in 1968 at Stanford University by future Third Wave impresario Alvin Toffler.[9]

Following these educational epiphanies, the Children's Television Workshop created its cornerstone program *Sesame Street*, first broadcast in 1969. *Sesame Street* presented a chaotic, multiracial, polyglot urban neighborhood comprised of adults, children, and the Muppets, Jim Henson's pre-Lapsarian mutant puppets. Though its radical vision of a proactive, pluralistic neighborhood has softened over the years, *Sesame Street*'s aesthetic sensibility still seems drawn from the early 1970s. Even today, the show remains part Robert Rauschenberg, part Marlo Thomas, part Stephen Sondheim, and part *Laugh-In*. But *Sesame Street* was also revolutionary television programming, not least of all for its sophisticated appropriation of popular genres deeply entrenched in the political and cultural milieu of the period. Much was made, for example, of Henson's commitment to using pastel-hued puppets whose racial identities were conspicuously abstract, especially in relation to the human actors with whom they worked. Roosevelt Franklin, an early Muppet character whose name played implicitly with the tradition of post-Emancipation black surnames, was clearly delineated as the program's ghetto Muppet. In 1974, the Children's Television Workshop released funky, upbeat children's records with self-affirming titles like "My Name Is Roosevelt Franklin" and "Just Because," on which the orphaned Muppet innocently declared, "I would never hurt anybody, just because you told me to." [10] Other innovations on *Sesame Street* included psychedelic animation, sophisticated (and extremely tongue-in-cheek) parodies of familiar rock, pop, and soul hits, diverse, working-class neighborhood characters, and compelling animated and musical segments that aspired to the status of "relevant TV," an early 1970s catchphrase equivalent to "multiculturalism." [11] If cynics challenged *Sesame Street* for being too gimmicky, it *was,* with gusto. *Sesame Street* was a commercial and critical success for PBS. If it didn't teach children reading or math skills, it did teach them a core vocabulary of generic cues that would enable them to express themselves fluently in the cultural capital of popular music, film, and television.

In 1971, the Bank Street College of Education—a private, progressive training institution in Manhattan—wanted to create a series of contemporary pop songs through which elementary school instructors could teach math skills. Conceptually speaking, the impulse was to tap the same urban-identified cultural resources as *Sesame Street*. Bank Street solicited George Newall, David McCall, and Tom Yohe, all of whom had worked in the corporate corridors of Madison Avenue for years, to act as professional advisors to the project. Newall—who invented the campaign for Hai Karate aftershave in the late 1960s—introduced McCall and Yohe to a composer, Bob Dorough, whom Newall knew from his days as a jazz pianist. [12] Bank Street adopted a number of Dorough's songs and tested them through trial sessions in the college's education courses. In time, Dorough composed a group of twelve songs henceforth known as "Multiplication Rock," which became the first installment in the *Schoolhouse Rock* canon.[13] About this time, McCall began to work with a young executive at ABC named Michael Eisner—who had not yet hitched his star to the Disney empire—on producing the educational equivalent of the public service announcement. ABC wanted to create short cartoons that they could intersperse with commercials and regular programming, and that also would be competitive with the Children's Television Workshop's hegemony over "relevant" programming for kids. The idea passed muster with Eisner and ABC. Since 1973, McCall, Newall, Yohe, and Dorough—along with composers Lynn Ahrens and David Frishberg and singers Blossom Dearie, Ezzra Mohawk, Zachary Sanders, Jack Sheldon, and Grady Tate—have created a body of work that has been immortalized in a recent wave of *Schoolhouse Rock* nostalgia, the substance of which has revealed the cartoons to constitute something of an ur-text for American kids who grew up during the 1970s.[14]

■　■　■

Born in 1923 and raised in northwest Texas, Dorough was intimately schooled in a number of musical genres indigenous to the Texarkana region. Through his experiences in his hometown marching band and as an aspiring jazz musician, Dorough absorbed traditional and experimental musics from the surrounding environs: Mississippi Delta blues, Kansas City swing, New Orleans jazz, Kentucky bluegrass, Nashville R&B, Memphis soul, and what he calls "boogaloo," a vernacular hybrid of southern soul, boogie-woogie, and funk. When Dorough arrived in New York City in 1949 to enter a graduate program in music theory at Columbia University, he fell headfirst into a thriving bop scene, where he had the honor of trading jams with Charlie Parker and Dizzy Gillespie.[15] Dorough remained a session musician and club player for many years, accumulating a long list of credentials that included arranging the score for the Broadway musical *Stuff* and producing hits for the mid-1960s band Spanky and the Our Gang. But the symbiotic relationship between Dorough's deep southern roots and his professional northern training and session work provides the real connection between him and the soul images ultimately borne out in *Schoolhouse Rock*.

Schoolhouse Rock songs were almost always composed and recorded before animators created storyboards or designed any other visual imagery. The bulk of the inspiration for the finished product therefore relied heavily on a given song's genre-driven musical cues. For Dorough, each song was "dictated by its own rhythm," which meant that his goal was to generate "as many different beats" or rhythmic configurations as possible. As a consequence—although Dorough cheerily denies any direct influence—every song he composed for *Schoolhouse Rock* pays exceptionally authentic homage to whatever genre of music Dorough's musical imagination investigated: from the gospel-inflected "Elementary, My Dear," to the Dylanesque "Three Is a Magic Number," to the Louis Jordan–meets–Ray Charles bounce of "Conjunction Junction," to the Brill Building bubblegum of "Lolly, Lolly, Lolly (Get Your Adverbs Here)."

One of the best-remembered moments from *Schoolhouse Rock* remains "Verb: That's What's Happening," the second cartoon created for the "Grammar Rock" series (the first was "Conjunction Junction") beginning in 1975. From the outset, the recording history of "Verb" exemplifies many of the impulses that characterize the appropriation of soul by mainstream commercial interests during the 1970s (though the commercial success of "Verb" has come some twenty-five years later). Dorough typically recorded his own demo versions of his songs, and often the final product as well, both of which feature his trademark Texan drawl. But when Dorough went in to record "Verb," he recalls that Newall and Yohe told him, "Let's get a different singer,' " a suggestion Dorough interpreted to mean "Let's get someone black." Indeed, Dorough admitted that "Verb" pushed him and the studio band "further out into the black area of music," with a desire to replicate a soul-funk fusion that did not rely on "long, drawn-out melodies" for inspiration. Dorough enlisted the vocal talents of Zachary Sanders, a great session singer, as well as a "ladies' staff" of female backup singers who Dorough imagined would be comparable to Ray Charles's Raylettes.

Structurally, the concept for "Verb" was to create a superhero whose grammatical adventures would allow for a vivid panoply of action scenarios: as Verb announces, "I can take a noun and bend it / Give me a noun ... I don't know my own power."[16] Drawn with the classic stylistic hallmarks of the hypermasculine comic book hero—enormous chest, tiny waist, tight red bodysuit and cape, elongated face, and chiseled jawline—Verb also sports slick, proto-Jheri curls and sunglasses, which ultimately mark him not just as a superhero, but a specifically *black* superhero. Since musical arrangements were written to suit the rhythmic dimensions of the song, casting Verb as a black superhero almost involuntarily "pinned [Verb] down," as Dorough explained, "into a more soulful bag." Musically, "Verb" was arranged as a cut-time, three-note jam that sounds like a cross between horn-driven Memphis soul and that genre of action-film music often described as the blaxploitation soundtrack.[17]

The uncanny resemblance between "Verb" and blaxpoitation film music is hardly coincidental. After the enormous success of independent black film scores such as Isaac Hayes's *Shaft* (1971), Curtis Mayfield's *Superfly* (1971), Marvin Gaye's *Trouble Man* (1972), and James Brown's *Black Caesar* (1973), slickly produced, bass-driven commercial funk was the theme music of choice for film and television producers looking to reproduce the inner city's grit and danger for their audiences.[18] The zeal with which television producers sought out "soul" music as theme or incidental music—coded repeatedly as the unofficial soundtrack for inner-city black experience—permanently calcified the relationship between inner-city images and "soul" culture. This trend may have reached its most absurd nadir when ABC commissioned Henry "Moon River" Mancini to write the theme music for *What's Happenin'?*, the sitcom reconstitution of the network's dramatic social realist telefilm *Cooley High* (1975).

The aesthetic links generated between Verb, Shaft, Superfly, and other black male icons demonstrates how commercial soul images were almost always derived in part from a palimpsest of popular icons and historical figures marked by their public political activity. For example, about the same time that *Schoolhouse Rock* and *Sesame Street* gained wide circulation and critical acclaim, the Children's Television Workshop produced its successful and controversial program *The Electric Company* (1971–78).[19] The program featured an urbane adjunct to the black superhero in the guise of Easy Reader, played by a young, laconic, and fabulously ironic Morgan Freeman.[20] Freeman's Easy Reader openly wore the ice-cold accoutrements of beatnik beatitude: turtleneck, goatee, sunglasses, brown leather overcoat, and poetic rap. A 1974 recording captures Easy Reader reciting the terms of his professional vocation— "Top to bottom, left to right / That reading stuff is out of sight!"— before he turns the ingredients on a can of "Dr. Delight" soda into an object of literary exegesis.[21] Freeman's rap is layered over an incredibly slick but crass vulgarization of an Isaac Hayes–style arrangement that is far too tongue-in-cheek to be taken seriously, and that makes Freeman sound like Slim Harpo held captive by Van McCoy. But in the end, Freeman's Easy Reader could only serve as a complicit caricature of the inner-city soul brother. Easy Reader may have drawn his inspiration from Amiri Baraka, Gil Scott-Heron, and Richard Roundtree, but the political significance of his character was utterly neutralized in the commercialization process.

Clearly, both "Verb" and Easy Reader exploited the generic familiarity associated with soul music and iconography. In retrospect, they also reveal infinitely more about the aesthetic and cultural presumptions behind urban educational reform than they do about the minority constituencies to whom such soul icons were pitched. Yet, educators in the late 1960 and early 1970s who conferred such didactic power upon soul gravitated toward its music, language, fashion, and images for many of the same reasons that postdiasporic black culture generated it. Far from being merely an aesthetic posture or generic convention, soul could also strategically embody a type of social realism that not only could inspire self-empowerment and self-identification but could provide a lucid, immediate, and polemical cultural form through which one could imagine and articulate political change.

One of Dorough's lesser-known tunes from 1973, "I Got Six," remains an impressive and enduring artifact of the transformative possibilities of soul music and visual imagery. More than any other *Schoolhouse Rock* selection, "I Got Six" ambitiously explores the complex roots of soul on a number of levels. Dorough created an easy four-beat, two-chord riff undergirded by call-and-response female vocals, horns, and a walking bassline—consequently, the song sounds like a nursery rhyme set to King Curtis's "Memphis Soul Stew." Dorough brought on his pal, drummer Grady Tate—"a cat who gives you what you want"—to sing lead vocals on the recording, a choice that was expected to produce a certain "authenticity" since, on the track, Tate sounds like a young Joe Tex. (Later, at the same recording session, Tate lent his vocal talents to the superb "Naughty Number Nine," an exemplary Chicago-style blues.)

The resemblance of "I Got Six" to a nursery rhyme is not an accidental component of the song. In fact, the song's graceful simplicity belies what is essentially a funky version of a child's rhythm game: "I got six, you got six, she got six." The song's arrangement as a self-aware soul tune transforms the rhyme into a cool, familiar, recognizable format that remains a clever parody of a hit single straight out of Memphis or Muscle Shoals. Indeed, even the song's title puts a self-consciously inner-city twist on "proper" white English. On the other hand, the song also resonates with the tradition of Christian gospel songs that are built on counting games. One thinks, for example, of Nina Simone's cocktail-hip allegory, "Children Go Where I Send You," or any number of postwar gospel outfits such as the Dixie Hummingbirds who blurred the lines between big band swing, doo-wop, R&B, and early rock and roll. Like Dorough's own "Elementary, My Dear," "I Got Six" invokes the undulating rhyming pattern of the black church spiritual precisely be-cause it is the very genre that informs the aesthetic roots of soul music.

For the first few stanzas, Tate maintains an effortless call-and-re-sponse structure with his backup singers. The intentionally childlike lyrics move from the playground to the candy store and are punctuated visually by black-and-white illustrations of black and white kids playing counting games together. About halfway through, however, the song expands outward from the antics of neighborhood children toward a kind of sociological reportage:

Nine hungry men had six dollars each.
Now that's fifty-four bucks, but they were out of luck
'Cos fifty-four bucks won't buy dinner downtown, not for nine;
And there were six hungry men, they had nine dollars each.
And they went downtown and the waiter said, "Sit down!"
Oh, it makes a big difference how you spread it around.[22]

Dorough explained that his use of nine/six hungry men was lifted from his "New Math" classes at Columbia. According to the communa-tive property of multiplication, two numbers multiplied together will always result in the same product, no matter in what order you "spread" the numbers "around." But despite the coy reference, "spread it around" also communicates a very prescient truth about the unequal distribution of wealth in the city as it might have been imagined, especially by urban minorities in large metropolitan centers like New York, during the 1970s.[23] Indeed, the animation plays this out: nine hungry men (of color) move aggressively toward the restaurant in construction hats, work shirts, and facial stubble. By contrast, the six hungry (mostly white) men march haughtily in top hats and tails and smoking cigars, and clearly represent a core urban elite.

The animation in "I Got Six" brilliantly manipulates a simple mathematical principle in order to tap the residual and often inarticulated anger of urban social dissent. But it is the music, self-consciously constructed to embody soul's "authentic" essence, that consolidates the cartoon's power and, indeed, the oppositional potential of soul culture itself. In the last twenty seconds of "I Got Six," the melody ascends one whole key to introduce the consummate example of a figure whose brief appearance suggests the full extent to which early 1970s soul iconography had saturated the cultural imaginary:

See that prince over there, the one with the fuzzy hair?
He's got six rings on every finger,
He don't wash no dishes, not with sixty diamonds.

In a swirling, psychedelic injunction of Billy Preston–esque Hammond B-3 organ, the song shifts from the communative property to the image of "The prince . . . with the fuzzy hair." The prince is sketched alone in his own padded restaurant booth, wearing an Angela Davis–style afro, dashiki, sunglasses, sixty diamond rings, and other gold jewelry.[24] The prince is aligned neither with the dissenting voices of the "nine hungry men" nor with the downtown elite. In addition, the prince is clearly from a space above and beyond the "ghetto," expressed both through his regal indifference and through subsequent images from the song: eleven camels "loaded down with oil and spice" and twelve veiled wives. This blurry mélange of international and domestic black symbolism does more than merely provide an interesting conclusion to the cartoon. The suggestive composite of the prince as both Soul Brother and quasi-Muslim nationalist also demonstrates how commercial soul of the 1960s and 1970s relied on powerful visual images and musical cues culled directly from Pan-Africanism and proletarian social realism. In this deceptively complex two-minute cartoon narrative, the prince not only serves as the imaginary apex of schoolyard counting games, but becomes the ideological conduit between two complementary threads of postdiasporic black political consciousness.

■ ■ ■

In his excellent history *Sweet Soul Music* (1986), Peter Guralnick argues that, as much now as during the 1960s and 1970s, soul is nourished and ultimately kept alive by musicians and singers who are only second- or third-tier figures.[25] Aretha, Marvin, and Otis may define certain familiar aspects of soul's institutional character and commercial flavor. But on some level, Guralnick suggests, the real work of remembering soul is done through cult favorites, local celebrities, music festivals, manic record collectors, obsessive DJs, reissue companies, and those who simply fell—by default or fate—through the cracks of soul's ever-replenished collected history.

Programs such as *Sesame Street, Electric Company,* and *Schoolhouse Rock* furnished an entire generation of young people during the 1970s with many of the most familiar characteristics of soul—and perhaps even, for some, the first (and only) images with which they engaged black culture. Like the ephemeral afterglow of *Crooklyn*'s muted colors and bittersweet nostalgia, soul sounds and images in educational television of the period helped to give an aesthetic, moral, and spiritual shape to the lives of inner-city residents who, typically understood only through "objective" statistics, were routinely deprived of a shared, experiential history. If nothing else, these educational cartoons also marked a particular historical moment in our collective national memory: a moment that legitimated a very public, very politicized black cultural vanguard whose power was exercised through its overt and sustained confrontation with mainstream American society. In this sense, soul remains one of the critical and multivalent engines that drives black history and black cultural identity in the late twentieth century.

NOTES

1. An earlier version of this chapter was presented at the *Soul: Black Power, Politics, and Pleasure* conference in April 1995 at New York University. Megathanks to the following folks who helped to make this production possible: Bob Dorough, Robyn Dutra, Richard Green, Monique Guillory, Wayne Hoffman, Joan Saab, and Richard Simon. This essay is dedicated to Carol Magary, with love and fond memories of our childhood.

2. It also might be worth distinguishing between the down-home southern "soul" of postemancipation rural black culture and the street-smart northern "soul" or urban, inner-city culture. Of course, I do not mean to imply that such conceptions of soul are meant to be mutually exclusive. As the site of the "authentic" geographical source of soul continues to shift—one thinks, for example, of Arrested Development's brand of hip hop–as–rural ethnography— the interplay between these two competing soul "ideologies" becomes ever more

clear. In my estimation, the soul images that were most perniciously exploited by commercial interests during the 1970s were of the northern urban variety.

3. James B. Conant, *Slums and Suburbs* (New York: McGraw-Hill, 1961), 147. See also the proceedings of the Conference on Integration in the New York City Public Schools at Teacher's College, Columbia University, *Integrating the Urban School* (New York: Teacher's College Press, 1963).

4. Sol Gordon, "Primary Education in Urban Slums," in Robert Dentler et al., eds., *The Urban R's: Race Relations as the Problem in Urban Education* (New York: Center for Urban Education/Praeger, 1967), 108. See also "Challenging the Myths: The Schools, the Blacks, and the Poor," *Harvard Educational Review* (1971); and Larry Cuban, *To Make a Difference: Teaching in the Inner City* (New York: Free Press, 1970).

5. See the influential study by Robert E. Park, Ernest W. Burgess, and Roderick D. McKenzie, *The City* (Chicago: University of Chicago Press, 1925); and Robert E. Park, *Human Communities: The City and Human Ecology* (Chicago: University of Chicago Press, 1952). The myth of the "urban condition" as some irredeemable and fixed urban ecology ignores the ways that groups or institutions have been politicized against each other for the economic security of the state—a myth, one might argue, whose exposure helped to foment the inevitable wave of riots, protests, and civil disobedience in inner-city areas throughout the late 1960s and early 1970s.

6. The studies produced by the Center for Urban Education in New York City were roughly concurrent with the revolutionary sociological work of Manuel Castells, who created tremors throughout the field of urban studies by challenging the authority of the Chicago School in his book *The Urban Question* (Cambridge: MIT Press, 1977 [1972]). See also Stuart Lowe, *Urban Social Movements: The City after Castells* (New York: St. Martin's Press, 1986).

7. See Frank Reissman, *The Inner City Child* (New York: Harper and Row, 1976), 32. See also Ruth Hamlin, Rose Mukerji, and Margaret Yonemura, *Schools for Young Disadvantaged Children* (New York: Teacher's College Press, 1967); and Everett T. Keach, Robert Fulton, and William Gardner, eds., *Education and Social Crisis: Perspectives on Teaching Disadvantaged Youth* (New York: Wiley, 1967).

8. Gordon, "Primary Education in Urban Slums," 54. Gordon's findings corroborate similar accounts by researchers at Teacher's College. See, for example, Ruth Fedder and Jacqueline Gabaldon, *No Longer Deprived: The Use of Minority Cultures and Languages in the Education of Disadvantaged Children and Their Teachers* (New York: Teacher's College Press, 1967).

9. See Alvin Toffler, ed., *The Schoolhouse in the City* (New York: Educational Facilities Laboratories/Praeger, 1968). It is especially ironic, though perhaps par for the course, that Toffler would have helped to organize a conference for restructuring urban education. Alvin and Heidi Toffler's Third Wave theory

uses the promise of information technologies to justify the systematic removal of skilled jobs in industry and manufacturing, which traditionally sustained minority populations in metropolitan areas. So, in retrospect, Toffler's later work attempts to provide "historical" explanation for the very conditions that necessitated conferences like the one he organized in 1968.

10. Transcribed by the author from "Just Because" (New York: Children's Television Workshop/Children's Records of America, 1974). Many commercial soul productions tapped the exaggerated features of what Daniel Patrick Moynihan invented as the "pathological" black family. Within children's popular culture of the period, social realism about urban life for kids, such as Alice Childress's *A Hero Ain't Nothin' But a Sandwich* (New York: Coward, McCann, and Geoghegan, 1973) or the ABC telefilm *Cooley High* (1975) mobilized many of the tragic discourses about urban poverty, crime, drug use, and the collapse of the black family unit.

11. For more about "relevant" TV, see Andrew J. Edelstein and Kevin McDonough, *The Seventies: From Hot Pants to Hot Tubs* (New York: Dutton, 1990), esp. 182–98.

12. Author interview with Bob Dorough, October 23, 1995. He still tours! You can get on his mailing list, just like a real groupie. Along with show tunes and standards, Dorough will sing, upon request, your favorite Saturday morning tunes. For more background information about the evolution of *Schoolhouse Rock,* see George Newall and Tom Yohe, *Schoolhouse Rock! The Official Guide* (New York: Hyperion, 1996).

13. Dorough recorded and released the first twelve songs as an LP, *Multiplication Rock* (Capitol Records, 1973). Following the cartoons' early success, ABC made 16mm film versions of *Schoolhouse Rock* cartoons, as well as teachers' guides, available for educational distribution.

14. De La Soul's *Three Feet High and Rising* (Tommy Boy Records, 1989) samples "Three Is a Magic Number" and may be one of the first coups in the scramble to honor the enduring influence of *Schoolhouse Rock* among twentysomethings. In 1994, the Chicago-based Theatre BAM created *Schoolhouse Rock Live!,* a revue that includes many of the best-remembered tunes from the series. Also, in one of its less insipid scenes, Ben Stiller's *Reality Bites* (1994) features an ensemble tribute to "Conjunction Junction." In May 1995, the Museum of Television and Radio in New York City sponsored a seminar, "Reading, Writing, and Rock 'n' Roll: A Look at Schoolhouse Rock," for which Dorough, Newall, and Yohe served as panelists.

15. Dorough arrived at Columbia just months after Allen Ginsberg graduated and took up his longtime residence in the bohemian hinterlands of the Lower East Side. A decade or so later Dorough, along with Hoagy Carmichael, followed the lead of his beat forbears and recorded *Jazz Canto,*

Vol. I (World Pacific Records, 1958), which featured spoken-word renditions of poems by Lawrence Ferlinghetti, Langston Hughes, Philip Whalen, and Walt Whitman.

16. Transcribed by author from "Verb: That's What's Happening," music and lyrics by Bob Dorough (1975) in *Schoolhouse Rock: Grammar Rock* (Racine, Wis.: Western Publishing Company/Golden Book Video, 1987)

17. For a discussion of blaxploitation films, gender, and genre, see Richard Simon's chapter in this anthology. For more about blaxploitation film scores, see Darius James's *That's Blaxploitation! Roots of the Baadasssss 'Tude* (New York: St. Martin's/Griffin, 1995).

18. While male-centered urban crime dramas such as *Hawaii Five-O, S.W.A.T.,* or *Kojak* appropriated the aesthetic legacy of black film soundtracks, theme music concocted for female cop shops such as *Police Woman, Get Christy Love,* and *Charlie's Angels* were often subdued, with string orchestrations that came closer to Barry White's aural sex soundscapes than the hard-nosed, masculine funk of their male contemporaries.

19. See Samuel Ball and Gerry Ann Bogatz, *Reading with Television: An Evaluation of "The Electric Company"* (Princeton, N.J.: Educational Testing Service, 1972); and Richard Bale, "Organizational Change and Innovation in American Elementary Schools: The Case of 'The Electric Company' " (Ph.D. dissertation, Florida State University, 1976).

20. Since the show regularly played on ethnic and cultural stereotypes—Rita Moreno's feisty bilingual caricature of the wacky Latina was lifted almost verbatim from her roles in *West Side Story* (1962) and *The Ritz* (1976)—*The Electric Company* knew quite well how to tap the heritage of vaudeville, burlesque, experimental theatre, and early television to create complex, multilayered parody figures.

21. Transcribed by author from "Easy Reader," music and lyrics by Joe Raposo, on *The Electric Company* (Children's Television Workshop/Children's Records of America, 1974).

22. All references to "I Got Six," music and lyrics by Bob Dorough (1973), in *Schoolhouse Rock: Multiplication Rock* (Racine, Wis.: Western Publishing/Golden Book Video, 1987), author's transcription.

23. In New York City, the lyric's distinction between "uptown" (i.e., Harlem) and "downtown" speaks explicitly to racial and economic polarization, and implicitly to the radical urban dislocation that occurred during the 1950s and 1960s, when the city displaced hundreds of thousands of black and Hispanic residents for elite, Rockefeller-sponsored projects like Lincoln Center.

24. True to form, the visual image that accompanies the lines "Each camel was loaded down with six casks of oil and spice / They brought quite a price" depicts the prince shuffling an enormous wad of cash and bearing a smile that

combines blaxploitation pimp with the minstrel-like exaggerations of Jimmy Walker in the late Marlon Rigg's *Color Adjustment*.

25. See Peter Guralnick, *Sweet Soul Music: Rhythm and Blues and the Southern Dream of Freedom* (New York: Harper Perennial, 1986).

9

A Sexual Revolution

From Punk Rock to Soul

ELENA GEORGIOU

I was 16 in 1977
when the young, British working class
opened their legs wide
under the guidance of Malcolm McClaren
and gave birth to Punk Rock
giving me the excuse to disrobe
from a flower power purple theory of peace
and re/dress myself in the bright red
political theories of a revolution
I didn't fully understand
except I knew my socialist tendencies
and being able to quote the Clash lyrics
would always get a smile
and a proverbial pat on my back from the other 16-year-old pothead, wannabe radicals
disguised by the ripped jeans, guitars and U.B. 40's
they wore like badges of working-class honor
and when we sang
beat the drum tonight, alfonso
spread the news all over the world
the big meeting has decided on total war
instead of wondering where I was gonna find a machete
and how was I gonna run with the dog pack to survive I was still back on
   the first line

wondering who the hell Alfonso was

because I hadn't seen any sugar fields

or cotton plantations in London

and I'd never seen the Sandinistas wandering around the flowery suburb
    we lived in
but I knew if the Clash was singing about this man
I could relax long enough for the music to push me forward
until we both lost our voices from shouting their songs

over the engine of your tin can

roaring down the highway like the inflated ego
of a Renault 5 thinking it was a brand new BMW
on our way back from our middle-class trip to France
where I'd let you go further than your fingers
discovering full-fledged sex for the first time and so
we didn't leave our hotel room for the whole 2 weeks
making a holiday out of sexual positions blended together with the French
    cream cheese
you spread over my no longer private parts

and ever since that day

cream cheese has never looked the same to me

and Sinead sings
its been 7 hours and [2,920] days
since you took your love away
but that's alright
because our love wasn't really passion
but brother and sisterly
we even had the same last name,
we even had the same skin color,
hair texture, culture and class
but you changed from a 4 year old
who watched bread turning
into toast for entertainment
into a 23 year old who now had full
membership to the British Film Theater

and I changed from a 4 year old
who preferred books to dolls
into a 23 year old who wanted someone
to get nasty with on the dance floor
so you traded me in for a couple of our friends
on your way to a new girlfriend
and I traded Punk Rock in for Soul
but I—a former teenage revolutionary—
knew George Michael was really a Smokey Robinson rip-off

and the radicals we knew would never have given him
the award as the best R&B male vocalist
and we were quick to turn up our noses
at those politically "ignorant" Americans who managed to give birth to the
    Black Panthers
but still didn't know who Tommy Smith was
and even though we were only 7
at the time of the 1968 Olympic games
we grew into teenagers with pictures
taped to our bedroom walls of Tommy Smith
clutching his gold medal in one hand and holding his black power fist high
    with the other
but it was much safer to play George Michael
than Smokey Robinson in '82
because the sound of Smokey was dangerously close
to that flower power shit we were trying to run away from
and I bet you were glad when George Michael became famous
because now people could stop telling you
you looked like Tony Curtis
and besides you, George Michael and me
all had the same last name
You, George Michael and me
3 Cypriots from Finchley—
Cypriots from Finchley
how much more ordinary can you get?
George Michael escaped the ordinary by becoming famous
and I escaped by coming to America where
"god save [steve mc]queen"
—and this [capitalist] regime

is the 1992 version of the Sex Pistol's lyrics and I hold onto my socialism
    for dear life
because it's so much easier to be corrupted
when you've lost your virginity
and talking about phallus-like pistols and virgins
I was 23 before I made love by candlelight—
and literally knocking into the flame
I made the sheets catch fire and I still have the scorch mark on my duvet to
    prove it
And I was 25 before I took my first bubble bath with a lover & Teddy Pend-
    ergrass singing
lets take a shower—
—a shower together

another lover making my day and night merge
making me lie down on a larger than queen-size bed
naked with the floor looking
like the inside of an expensive lingerie store
at the end of a one-day sale
making my body slide underneath your thighs
with my back arching in your palms turning me on my stomach while you
    kneel by my side
tracing the length of my spine with your tongue
while slipping your hand in between my legs
hoping I will ask you for more
but instead I remember Sinead again
and realize I can never make love
to a revolutionary song saying
england's not the mythical land
of madam george and roses
it's the home of police who kill
black boys on mopeds
and the only revolution I ever got close to
was sexual and here I am singing with a new lover
a lover who loves my love
but because of history
hates herself for loving me
because I don't know if I could kill
my grandmother if she was a racist

because I don't know if I could pack a gun in the name of a war against
  white people
because sometimes I want to make love
instead of talking about The Revolution
and because sometimes I want to make love
instead of talking about The Revolution
I had to end the relationship
with my new lover
but not before we sang

if this world were mine

and even though we made love
to the velvet voice of Luther
I knew the song belonged to the 60s
and I shake my head at myself
as I realize making love and love songs
go together so well
yes, making love and love songs
go together so well
because they're both
fortunate enough
to share the same soul
because they're both
fortunate enough
to have and to hold
from this day forward
as long as they both
shall live
SOUL.

10

Soul, Transnationalism, and Imaginings of Revolution

Tanzanian Ujamaa and the Politics of Enjoyment

MAY JOSEPH

Commodities of African Socialism and Transnational Desires for Soul

Revisiting seventies socialism and soul culture from the vantage point of the United States in the nineties raises important questions about the structures of enjoyment embedded in the anticapitalist stance of many emergent socialist states, such as Tanzania during that turbulent time. Most critiques of seventies socialist cultures readily dismiss socialism as having no soul. The inherent assumption of such critiques is that capitalism is the sole arbiter of enjoyment through free and ideologically un-contaminated flow of consumption. Such binary critiques oversimplify the relationship between state formations and citizens as consumers. These critiques further elide the intricate and nuanced strategies through which state ideologies such as capitalism and socialism, and cultural commodities such as soul culture, mediate and blur the boundaries of political rhetorics through transnational economies of consumption.

The disparate diasporic sites of soul culture allow for a more nuanced reading of the connections and slippages between citizenship and transnational state ideologies and their relationship to cultural commodities. Soul culture during the seventies converged conflicting ideologies, international capital, transnational affiliations within Cold War politics, and the proliferation of a Pan-African popular culture. Its international dissemination question of how cultural commodities from the United States were deployed as state propaganda to counter the rising fear of socialism within and beyond its borders. The export of U.S. entertainment industries through the State Department as part of its international foreign policy during the Cold War blurred the ideological boundaries of consumption.[1] The propaganda against socialism launched during the Cold War locates socialism as a de-racinating, de-eroticizing politics of scarcity. Socialism becomes an undifferentiated blank space with a functionalist understanding of need. What drops out is the whole spectrum of cultural forms generated through ideologically contradicting strategies of production and reception. This circulation of cultural commodities via official and unofficial spheres of consumption opens out the subtler areas of enjoyment through which a socialist youth culture emerges. Such circuits of exchange demand a more inflected reading of enjoyment under international socialism.[2]

This chapter will unpack some of the ambivalent and contradicting sites of enjoyment produced within Tanzanian notions of Ujamaa, or Self-Reliance. Afro-American soul culture of the seventies opens up sites of socialist longing through its dispersals into Tanzanian socialism. It operates ambivalently within the seductive, exploitative boundaries of U.S. imperialism, with consumerism being the new face of imperial expansion. Soul creates an international as well as local resurgence of Pan-African desire in Tanzanian popular culture during this time.

The simultaneous circulation of Afro-American popular culture through dramatically different ideological and geographical terrain beyond its national contexts foregrounds the complexities of transnationalism. Such circulation of culture accentuates the implications of transnationalism for contingent and specific nationalisms within the United States, such as Black nationalism, and within other nations such as Tanzania. The circulation of Afro-American pop culture of the seventies opens up the paradoxes inherent within a Pan-African aesthetic of political and rhetorical possibility under socialism. The mobile cultural capital and international repercussions of these cultural products during this period suggest a complex array of issues that drop out when viewed only within a national context. Mobile cultural capital complicates the more widely launched critiques of misogyny, masculinity, and blaxploitation as cop-out and the reductionist plot and character developments within many of these texts, whether they be films, music, or sports.

Soul culture was caught in the transnational economy of traveling commodities serving as ambassadors of official U.S. culture abroad during this time. Sports (through the Harlem Globetrotters and Muhammad Ali), Black music, blaxploitation cinema, and the struggle for visibility and visuality in Afro-American popular culture gets read and translated differently outside the domains of its national context. During the 1970s, the impact of soul culture far exceeded the domains of the United States, as the works of Paul Gilroy, Ngugi Wa Thiongo, Julius Nyerere, and Manthia Diawara, among others, have demonstrated.[3] In what follows, I will elaborate on some of these transnational circulations of soul culture in relation to Tanzanian socialist possibilities for enjoyment.

Tanzanian Socialism and the Social Regulation of Desire: Ujamaa and Soul

Tanzanian socialism was predicated on a conscious anticolonialist move to breakaway from the West's imperial obsessions. Beginning with independence in 1961, the rhetoric of postindependent Tanzania (whose name was itself was forged out of the violent struggle for independence, linking Tanganyika with Zanzibar to create Tanzania) was of an optimistic and self-conscious socialism that would create its own autonomous nation-state. This radical move toward progressively socialist state autonomy within neocolonial economies of dependencies was contingent upon the collaborative negotiations of Tanzania's neighbors, Uganda and Kenya. The fledgling state's move to decolonize education and the social imaginary at large was through the new ideology of Ujamaa, self-reliance.

Tanzania's move to invent an African socialism of self-reliance depended on the divergent ideologies of Uganda and Kenya in order to succeed. Ujamaa promised the utopian possibility of a self-reliant, self-contained state whose citizens would devote their services in the interests of the sovereign nation with the greater good of the Federation of East Africa in mind. This sacrifice of individuated desire in the interest of the greater public good was aimed at achieving a decisive break with imperialism in the short term, with the hope that a more egalitarian and self-reliant society would emerge in the long term. The ideology of self-reliance implicitly assumed that short-term radical conservatism would allow for a form of liberal socialism in the long run.[4]

The rhetoric of the unified state that Tanzanian socialism produced generated many regulative logics in the interests of an emerging egalitarian and educated civil society. One such logic was the production of citizens as agents. The Arusha Declaration of 1967 sought to animate citizenship as a pedagogical exercise in the nation's performance as a newly independent state. The Declaration's philosophy of governance and economics of self-reliance would redefine the participation of indigenous peoples as actors within their own state. The Arusha Declaration produced a system of state control whose rhetoric was a radical realignment of private interests as state interests, through policies that voiced the redistribution of wealth, land, and international dependency relationships. The Declaration was an elaborate philosophical argument in favor of breaking from the systems of capital that would lead to neocolonial dependency economies with former colonial and imperial powers. By the late 1960s, the nationalizing of property, businesses, and education created a monolithic state-regulated economy through which cultural work could emerge, but on radically nationalist and socialist terms, which very often were at odds with each other.[5]

State socialism in Tanzania struggled to articulate a progressive socialist possibility while setting up state apparatuses for the social regulation of desire. Consequently all forms of consumption had to be legitimated, funded, controlled, and regulated by the state. Cultural production and distribution were extensions of state ideology, though without the extreme forms of policing that such regulative logics took in China or the Soviet Union, for instance. Under Tanzanian socialism, self-reliance allowed more leeway within state-regulated structures such as education, entertainment, leisure, and political organizations to create an elaborate and multilayered society yet to be articulated as civil society. The negotiation of cultural citizenship in such a newly independent state would have to play out in the interstices of formal and informal popular culture, such as Tanzanian soul culture.[6]

Transnational Circuits and Pan-African Longing: Socialism and Soul

Tanzania's sympathies with Leninist and Maoist ideologies were in tension with the ideological agendas of the United States. Blaxploitation film and other Afro-American cultural production circulated ironically in such a transnational economy as commodities of socialism embodying capitalism's mobility. The transnational circulation of commodities from the United States during this period is significant because of the ideological tensions embodied by Cold War politics. Afro-American cultural production circulated independently of mainstream U.S. ideology. It inflected local articulations of Pan-Africanism, being internationalist in its appeal and resonance for struggling emergent economies such as Tanzania.

Afro-American commodities influenced local Tanzanian youth culture and style, generating an internationalist patina of modernity experienced by local Tanzanian youth as a transnational desire for Pan-African belonging. This Pan-African youth style activated resistance to forms of state authoritarianism created through a homogenizing Tanzanian youth culture, opening up contingent modernities that explode Western and non-Western narratives of both the Cold War and state socialism. Afro-American culture, both legitimate and boot-legged, permeated Tanzanian youth culture, circumventing the social regulation of political desire through the contradictory identification of "Americanness" as Blackness.[7]

The transnational commodification of soul raises difficult questions about consumption as it travels, translates, and is reinvented through its localized receptions and circulations of meaning. These formal and informal circulations of soul in the West, as well as in what were referred to as developing nations and newly emergent African states such as Tanzania, created a complex and rich conglomeration of imagined readings. The cooptations, evocative linkages, and rhetorical connections generated in Tanzanian popular culture through these commodities elaborated on the tensions, promises, and betrayals of modernity. They invoked the black feminist radicalism of June Jordan, Maya Angelou, and Angela Davis; the struggle for rights of *Cleopatra Jones;* the urban decay and class politics in James Brown's 1974 albums *Hell, Payback,* and *Reality;* the anticolonial strategies of *Superfly TNT;* the cosmopolitan extravagance of Grace Jones; and the Pan-African longings of Aretha Franklin, Muhammad Ali, and Miriam Makeba.

This sphere of ideological contestations, where Blackness signifying Americanness blurs the boundaries between the state regulation of desire and spectatorial seduction by capitalist consumption, demonstrates the antagonistic sites of enjoyment as agency. Enjoyment becomes crucial to expressing forms of cultural citizenship. As consumers of commodities, citizens negotiate contradicting identifications as free agents within authoritarian states. In this site of pleasurable social antagonism, Ron O'Neal, Tamara Dobson, James Brown, Angela Davis, and Muhammad Ali all embody the struggles against state exploitation, whether capitalist or socialist. They embody the appeal of capitalist self-fashioning signified by their lifestyle and the intoxicating promise of a fully democratic, capitalist state. Through their free and open performance of dissent and insurgency within the international imaginary as Black feminists, Black communists, Black guerrillas, Black Muslims, or international Black popular icons, they realize a transnational sense of Black radicalism. They perform a modernity that disrupts the economic rhetorics of scarcity and dependency by proposing transnational links of solidarity and struggle.

The question of cultural capital is another avenue around which the international repercussions of soul congeal. The cultural capital embedded in these commodities needs to be read in conjunction with the anti-imperial, anticapitalist sentiment of Tanzanian Ujamaa as expounded by Julius Nyerere. Nyerere's experiments in African socialism marked a radically utopian struggle to break free from the West's economic grip. Tanzanian socialism combined an eclectic and nonpartisan attitude of cultural open-mindedness toward both East and West, while limiting the avenues of consumption in the interests of the nation's greater good. The limitations placed upon imports and exports homogenized the avenues for consumption in unprecedented ways. Chinese stationery, shoes, and books and Soviet-sponsored machines, railway technology, teachers, and books became the visible representations of this homogenization. So, even when commodities such as sugar, milk, or luxury items (except locally produced fabrics and other goods) were unavailable, one could buy rubber-soled Bata shoes, or yellow HB pencils, or notebooks with Marxist slogans stamped "Made in China."

In this climate of considerably narrowed sense of the international public sphere, the possible imagined spaces more immediately invoked Castro's Cuba, Tito's Yugoslavia, Maoist socialism, or Brezhnev's Soviet solidarity. Imaginings of alternative modernities were mainly possible through the proliferation of music—specifically, Afro-American music—through the Tanzanian Broadcasting Service, as well as the new glut of Hollywood films geared for Third World countries, such as blaxploitation films and Westerns. The Kung Fu Movies of Bruce Lee, Jim Kelly, Richard Roundtree, and Ron O'Neal competed for attention in a market flooded by cheap Italian spaghetti Westerns; Sergio Leone, Russian,

Hong Kong, and Chinese Kung-Fu movies; Hindi melodramas; and John Wayne and Clint Eastwood films. Films like *Shaft in Africa, Cleopatra Jones, Superfly TNT,* and *Sheba Baby* created an eclectic audience of Kung Fu–loving, Hindi "flim"–acquainted, Western genre–immersed Tanzanians whose Pan-African imaginings most immediately resonated with the gun-toting, six-foot-two, Afro-haired heroine in platform shoes, taller than any white man around, and too tough though always cool with her Blackness. This was the early seventies—killing Native American Indians was not cool, but it was less cool to kill Blacks on-screen. Here was an imagining of democratic possibility that appealed to Tanzanian socialist youth dreaming about a more seductive kind of social transformation than that promised by Ujamaa: one that would incorporate red wetlook jackets, fabulous bell-bottomed trousers, and bad Lamborghinis with even more soulful revolutionaries like Superfly driving down the disappearing highways of economic modernity. I would swap my kangas and kitenges for your crimplene, or terrylene, or blue jeans—if only you crossed my path. Okay, only a seven-shilling fantasy of a few hours in complete contradiction with one's socialist sympathies and convictions, but benign because one has the Pan-African thread to legitimate the fantasy.

About Sex Machine, Black Moses, and Soulful States: East African Asians Got Soul

- James Brown, Isaac Hayes, Aretha Franklin, the Temptations, Marvin Gaye, the Jackson Five

In the early 1970s, Tanzanians drew upon a broad range of Pan-African styles to fabricate a local and specifically Tanzanian cool, and the Godfather of Soul, Mr. James Brown himself, was very much part of this screeching, screaming, and evocative culture of emergent nationalisms and their dissonant resistances. Ujamaa's powerful rhetoric of a coherent, homogeneous African state had to confront the nagging and volatile question of Tanzania's heterogeneous citizenry of Arab, Chinese, Indian, Persian, and African extraction, who practice Muslim, Christian, Sikh, Ismaili, Hindu, and indigenous religions. The rise of fascism in Uganda, resulting in the expulsion of its Asian citizens in 1972 by Idi Amin Dada, further exacerbated a climate of fear and anxiety within East Africa's remaining Asian populations, many of whom were second- and third-generation citizens of African states.

The implicit question that hung loosely around the politics of Tanzanian belonging during the 1970s, like a bui-bui in the afternoon light just before the four o'clock rains, was—Could Tanzanian Asians have soul? At the level of style and visibility politics this question was crucial because soul style politics, like soul music, was tied to a distinct and inarticulable soulness of contemporary Tanzanian modernity. Beginning with Nyerere's own production of a certain cosmopolitan and urban style politics—the Tanzanian collarless safari suits, the collarless kitenge shirt, the organic intellectual as self-styled pedagogue or "Mwalimu" of the newly independent state—soul style permeated national fashion. Following a longer international tradition of black radical intellectuals as self-styled revolutionaries/presidents/ leaders, such as Malcolm X, C. L. R. James, Martin Luther King Jr., Kwame Nkrumah, Léopold-Sédar Senghor, Jomo Kenyatta, and W. E. B. Du Bois, Nyerere practiced a soulful socialism, emancipatory in its vision. Socialist-style politics for Nyerere was first and foremost internationalist in its organizing metaphors of revolution, proleterian radicalism, and Black and Third World solidarity, while materially located firmly in myths about soil, roots, and national as well as Pan-African philosophies of belonging.

For a generation of Tanzanian Asians growing up under Ujamaa, caught between Nyerere's vision and the parochiality of various ethnic and religious identities, self-fashioning an aesthetic of cool became crucial. As new subjects of the socialist experiment, their struggle for cultural citizenship and belonging was linked to a Pan-African utopia and the fabrication of an East African Asian cool. They might have donned Afros, shades, and platforms shoes, á la Shaft, Nyerere, Angela Davis, Miriam Makeba, Fred Williamson, James Brown, and Diana Ross. But East Asian African cool had to be negotiated on ethnically particular terms, mediated by Hindi films and Muslim cultural practices of everyday life. The would have to create a shifting space of being Tanzanian Asian, a continuous struggle of signs and simulations reproduced in the microcosm of the state's citizenry. Tanzanian Asian youth of the late sixties and seventies were self-conscious about assimilation, integration, and acquiring soul in the eyes of the nation at large. They would be the critical mass that could create the difference, if East Africa was to come to terms with the Pakistani, Indian, and Chinese communities whose migrations to the East African coast were as old as the slave trade.

A broader questions attached to this situation was, Could teen Asians boogie or do the bump? Or if they did, why did they only perform within their segregated ghettos and enclaves of petit-bourgeois fiefdom? The arena of youth and education provided the crucible for the new nation's self-invention as a confident and self-reliant state. The streets, parks, roads, and parade grounds became the public spaces of youth education, within which much soul had to be negotiated for Asians. At a time of large-scale youth mobilization through sports, drills, *ngomas,* marches, and public addresses by Nyerere and other TANU apparatchiks, the formal and informal circulations of soul carried no small effect. For Asian youth, this was a time of the recovery of a certain kind of soul for themselves as citizens. Asians had participated in the articulation of Black consciousness. They had struggled alongside other Tanzanians against imperialism. But under a resurgent nationalism, the submerged history of this tenuous minority had dissappeared. Tanzanian Asians were precariously perched as undesirable citizens. Though ambivalently situated, Hindu, Muslim, Sikh, Ismaili, Confucian, Buddhist, Jain, Zoroastrian, and Christian (largely Goan) populations of Asian Tanzanians were simultaneously transformed by soulful socialism.

Many of these communities already bore complex migration histories coming from South Asia, Mauritius, or African countries such as Uganda and South Africa, and had been subject to persecution, grinding poverty, and antiminority sentiment within troubled nationalisms. In this context, funky self-invention was a site of great social antagonism for Asian youth in Tanzania. Urban Asian youth subculture, located primarily in Dar es Salaam, drew upon James Brown, Angela Davis, the Black Panthers, soul music, and the masculinist discourse of Black American radicalism, which was translated into locally particular terms. "Soul" showed up in public spaces: James Brown's "sex machine" was scribbled on high-school walls, motor bikes, and necklaces. Isaac Hayes's gold chain and shades had its very local Hindi movie versions. Phrases like "dig," "soul sister," and "soul brother" slowly shaped a nascent discourse of Asian-cool in its interpretive reinventions of Black cool, which mingled with Tanzanian socialism's mandatory *ndugu,* or comrade.

For Tanzanian Asian youth of the seventies, soul raised possibility of "integrating" through a certain international Black cool. When Asians were forced out of East Africa in the early 1970s, their ambivalent relationship to the production of a certain East African soul became imbricated. Did Asians not have enough soul to pass for local? Why did they live in ambivalence within East African social life for many generations, while rearticulating it in the process? Always sojourners in their political stakes with East Africa, Asians both constructed themselves and were read as being ambivalent about East African citizenship during the early seventies. Soul embodied a certain Tanzanian essentialism that would continuously produce its minority citizens as not having enough soul for Tanzanian socialism. For East Africans during the seventies, Asians would never have soul enough for the new nation-state.

Traveling Internationalists and People Who Never Move: Pan-Africanism and the Mystique of Mobility

For Tanzanians nurtured within a socialist internationalism articulated through the state's founding rhetoric of freedom and unity, *uhura na umoja*, travel was crucial to a Pan-African imagining. The African National Congress used Dar es Salaam as its headquarters through all its turbulent years, and exiled South African nationalists, writers, and intellectuals continuously traveled to and from Tanzania, using it as a mediating place for future revolutions. Nyerere's support of Frelimo and the struggle for the liberation of Angola, Namibia, Mozambique, and South Africa situated Tanzania in complex ways to other African states. In turn, the idea of a certain Black internationalism shaped the ideology of the Tanzanian state.

Miriam Makeba, the "soul" of South African music of that period, had a Tanzanian passport, and her marriage to Stokely Carmichael linked East Africa indirectly to the Black Power Movement in the United States. The continuous front-page coverage of Angela Davis, George Jackson, and images of the Black Panthers, along with the emergence in Tanzania of a style politics that simulated Afro-American hairstyle and fashion, blurred the boundaries between a distant reality supposedly shaped by opposite ideological investments of capitalism, and the broader rhetorics of empowerment and revolution that Black American visuality and music made possible. Here was a Black modernity that imagined and fashioned new agents of history, both in film and in music, for postcolonial Tanzania. These ideologies, encountered at the level of the visual, aural, and fantasmatic, escaped the rigid boundaries of state control, where the rhetoric of class and labor made it difficult to articulate gender, transnational desire, consumption as a form of cultural citizenship, and Blackness as a traveling aesthetic.[8]

Colonialism and its economic aftermath had set up travel as a class-determined space. Postindependence scarcity created the promise that everyone was equal, but not all could afford to travel. The proleteriat, in other words, did not move in the national imaginary. They did not travel, in spite of the massive mobilization of people in the agrarian restructuring and economic restrategizing that was going on between the capital, Dar es Salaam, and the rest of the country. On the one hand was a strong invocation of groundedness to land and agriculture that gave a renewed sense of rootedness; on the other were the dramatic changes of industrialization and expansion shaping this modernity of self-reliance, locked between utopian visions of economic independence and large-scale help from various transnational companies from China and the Eastern Bloc countries. In such a space, a cosmopolitan character like Ron O'Neal's Youngblood Priest in *Superfly TNT* has more in common with Tanzanian popular imagination than the rhetoric of state socialism, while both coexist in their contradictory pleasurability. In *Superfly TNT* (script by Alex Haley, directed by Ron O'Neal, music by Osibisa), Priest is a nomad in Europe. He drives coupes in Rome, speaks Italian, has lived in France, England, and Norway, and is chased by paparazzi photographers. Priest travels to Senegal and helps a West African Francophone revolutionary (played by Roscoe Lee Brown) overthrow colonialism in a West African nation called Umbia.

While the possible negative critiques of *Superfly* (directed by Gordon Parks, Jr., soundtrack by Curtis Mayfield) and its sequel *Superfly TNT* are numerous and valid, I want to point out the contradictory and radical spectatorial pleasures for an urban Tanzanian audience in Priest's development from nihilism to hope and active agency. *Superfly TNT* provides the imaginative terrain of agency for a kind of popular hero who was politically and visually allowed a modernity that was otherwise not available for the average Tanzanian citizen. The translation of Priest as a traveling hero is linked to his being an Afro-American. Priest's cultural and economic capital is distinctly translatable in specific ways for a local Tanzanian as a mobile and seductively insurgent agency, both Western and anti-imperial at the same time. There is simultaneously style, radicalism, a critique of capital and real dollar value, around the historic visibility of Afro-American visual modernity in seventies

136

Tanzanian popular imagination (gestured toward) by the president of Umbia to be Roscoe Lee Brown. Brown acknowledges the value of Superfly's Afro-American modernity as an African-Amercan playing a cultured African revolutionary in Europe role.

Tanzanian soul culture in the early seventies shaped the structural feel of urban youth socialism and its Pan-African imaginings. Next to film, radio was the primary disseminator of international popular culture, as there was no television and scant availability of visual representations of pop icons. All official forms of entertainment were mediated by the state and hence bore the signs of its legitimacy. As the most popular and versatile site of mass consumption, the radio generated disparate and heterogeneous audiences. Seventies Tanzanian nationalism deployed the popular appeal of soul music, among other forms of popular music, to fill the material vacuum in times of economic hardship. As records were largely unavailable and certainly unaffordable, funk operated as an inventive terrain of scarcity, where very little goes a long way, in the interests of self-reliance. Aretha Franklin's numerous hairstyles and fashions, Isaac Hayes's style politics, James Brown's closing gestures with the mike, and the Jackson Five's spectacles were encounters to be had on travel or in exile, new but familiar resonances experienced as a dislocation from the specificity of the United States. Invoking a specific time (the seventies), a specific place (Dar es Salaam), a specific context (radical socialism), and a particular technology (radio and spool tape), these texts would be revisited on new terms, on different terrain in the diaspora.[9]

NOTES

1. My thanks to Gitanjali Maharaj for pointing this out to me.

2. I am greatly indebted to Fred Moten for his insightful and astute suggestions, which have fueled this paper.

3. See Paul Gilroy, *There Ain't No Black in the Union Jack* (London: Century Hutchinson, 1987), Manthia Diawara, "Afro-Kitsch," in Black Popular Culture, edited by Gina Dent (Seattle: Bay Press, 1992) Julius K. Nyerere, *Crusade for Liberation* (Dar es Salaam, Tanzania: Oxford University Press, 1978).

4. Juluis K Nyerere, *Freedom and Unity; Uhuru na Umuja* Dar es Salaam, Tanzania: Oxford University Press 1968, 85.

5. Julius K. Nyerere, *Freedom and Socialism, Uhuru na Ujamaa* (Dar es Salaam, Tanzania: Oxford University Press, 1968), 231.

6. Ibid., 179–410.

7. See Nyerere, Crusade for Liberation; for further elaboration of Afro-American and African alliances.

8. Miriam Makeba, *Makeba; My Story* (New York: Penguin Books, 1987), 163.

9. Many thanks are owed to Professor Ngugi Wa Thiongo for encouraging me to write about Tanzania. To Toby Miller, Richard Green, Radhika Subramanium, Abdul Karim Mustapha, and Gitanjali Maharaj, I owe much for the soulful discussions and generous editorial comments that I greatly benefited from.

11

Soul's Revival

White Soul, Nostalgia, and the Culturally Constructed Past

GAYLE WALD

In May 1988, English singer George Michael became the first white solo artist ever to have a number one album on *Billboard*'s Top Black Albums chart. Having dethroned the debut of another British soul import, self-proclaimed *wunderkind* Terence Trent D'Arby, Michael's album *Faith* held on to its number one ranking for six weeks, until New Jack artist Al B. Sure! precipitated its gradual slide down the charts and out of musical memory. *Faith* represented a sharp departure—artistically and commercially—for Michael, who achieved international fame as the more musically ambitious half of Wham!, an English pop duo known for playing upbeat, if sometimes vapid, versions of 1950s and 1960s rhythm and blues. Featuring explicit lyrics—most famously in "I Want Your Sex" (a song that was banned in some markets)—and accompanied by videos that played heavily off of Michael's heartthrob physical appeal (so much so that the TV show *Saturday Night Live* saw fit to parody Michael's dance routines in a well-known skit about his love affair with his "arse"), *Faith* was the vehicle for Michael's emergence as a legitimate singer, songwriter, and producer. With *Faith,* or so the story goes, Michael was transformed from a pop sensation of limited credibility into a talented performer who won industry acclaim for his ability to attract a demographically diverse audience.

Although musically speaking *Faith* holds little of enduring interest, the trajectory of Michael's career nevertheless raises a number of important questions about the place of white musicians within what was formerly, or primarily, a black domain. Issues of white artists' attraction to and appropriation of black musical styles are, of course, hardly new within studies of popular musical culture, having been explored at great length and with great intelligence by cultural critics such as Coco Fusco, Paul Gilroy, George Lipsitz, Richard Fung, Eric Lott, Dick Hebdige, and bell hooks, among others.[1] Although these writers approach the question of appropriation differently, in general they demonstrate that struggle over cultural symbols is not and has never been strictly limited to the realm of culture. Lipsitz, for example, coins the term "strategic anti-essentialism" to describe how white performers transcode "minority" styles for the expression of their own needs, fears, and desires, a process that ironically often affirms the very ethnocentric biases these performers set out to contest.[2] In her critique of formalist analyses of cultural style, Fusco notes that although hybridity has always been the condition of cultural production in the Americas, the glib celebration of hybridity that sometimes emerges under the banner of postmodernism threatens to erase the complex history of struggle that informs the cultural practices of marginalized populations.[3]

In addition to raising the sorts of questions that these writers explore—questions about the complex political, economic, and ideological stakes of allocating cultural symbols across unevenly constructed lines of social and cultural identities—Michael's success in styling himself a white soul singer for the 1990s prompts concerns about the stakes of what I will call "cultural revivalism," or the retroactive and frequently nostalgic appropriation of symbols associated with an earlier (and in this case privileged) era of black cultural history. Cross-cultural revivalism of the sort exemplified by Michael's career conflates two previously separated sets of issues: those pertaining to traversing cultural boundaries; and those concerning negotiating temporality, or the crossing of lines that distinguish past and present. Michael's success in resurrecting a black cultural practice (soul) associated with asserting black difference and expressing black resistance thus raises issues not only of what it means to revive or recall the past, but of what it means to do so within the highly charged context of cultural "borrowing." The trajectory of Michael's career illustrates the complex intersection of various postmodernist cultural practices: the "flow" of cultural symbols within an increasingly centralized and corporatized global music industry; the appearance of fluidity in the construction of racial identities; and the flattening out of temporalities within capitalist narratives of perpetual resurrection and renewal.

A number of music industry trends of the late 1980s and early 1990s enabled Michael's unprecedented success as a blue-eyed soul singer for the MTV generation. Most importantly, Michael's revival of a vocal style reminiscent of black artists such as Aretha Franklin and Stevie Wonder (both of whom he has acknowledged as influences) is part of a larger trend, dubbed "retronuevo" by cultural critic Nelson George, in which contemporary musicians creatively update and reinterpret past musical styles in order to create "new" sounds—in the best cases, music that recalls an earlier era without blandly recycling or nostalgically recreating it.[4] In the United States, retronuevo produced such notable "Quiet Storm" vocalists as Anita Baker, whose 1986 breakthrough album *Rapture* featured well-crafted ballads that drew upon jazz, gospel, and soul, and Luther Vandross, whose soulful, if sometimes sentimental, singing and lush production attracted a fervent and devoted audience. In Britain, retronuevo took a slightly different turn, most notably in the much-touted British "soul revival" (sometimes called "Brit-soul" or the British "soul invasion"), in which artists such as Soul II Soul, Lisa Stansfield, Culture Club, Seal, Paul Weller, Sade, Simply Red, and George Michael churned out sleek r&b with a 1990s sensibility. With few exceptions, Brit-soul musicians were critically praised for their innovative appropriation of soul music traditions. Reviewing Stansfield's album *Affection* in 1990, for example, George applauded the maturity and emotional depth of her vocals, calling Stansfield "the best white soul singer since Teena Marie."[5] Surveying the field of black and white artists, a celebratory 1992 article in *Time* magazine found that "soul with a British accent" sometimes actually improved upon the music of its predecessors.[6]

Although no easy generalizations can be made about Brit-soul, nevertheless the very metaphor of a "soul invasion," with its connotations of cultural infringement and symbolic violence (who or what is being invaded, and with what weapons?), suggests the need for a critical discourse about white artists' participation in such a movement. Insofar as it recalls the original British invasion of the 1960s, when rock groups such as the Beatles, the Who, and the Kinks crossed the Atlantic with interpretations of American r&b that appealed primarily to white teenagers whose tastes did not embrace the "blacker" sounds of soul, the

British "soul invasion" raises the specter of history repeating itself. Just as the British invasion reflected the triumph of white supremacist sensibilities even as it affirmed the universality of black music, so we might ask whether the success of someone like George Michael represents the return of the racial repressed in the guise of the fluidity of "black" style.[7] Or we might ask whether Michael's reverse crossover success signifies the erosion of such sensibilities, keeping in mind that white artists' translation of black American music into a countercultural language for white youth actually helped to facilitate the growth of a highly politicized white counterculture that contested racism, sexism, and militarism. What exactly is being revived when a white artist such as Michael revives soul? To the degree that soul music is a black cultural formation whose primary audience is black (think of James Brown exhorting his audience, "Say it loud, I'm black and I'm proud!"), what is the role of the white subject who revives and reworks its practices, not only as a matter of artistic inspiration but as a matter of cultural self-fashioning and economic resurrection?

Michael was among the first to assert the significance of his "invasion" of *Billboard*'s Top Black Albums chart. In interviews given around the time that *Faith* crowned both the Pop and Black charts, he repeatedly remarked that he regarded his rank on the Black charts as the more personally meaningful of the two career landmarks, despite the fact that record sales to black consumers accounted for a significantly smaller share of his profits. "I was much happier with [*Faith*] being the No. 1 Black album than I was when it became the No. 1 Pop album," he told reporters from magazines as different as *Jet* and *Rolling Stone*. "There was much more of a sense of achievement."[8]

The implications of such a statement are varied. Michael's expression of gratification at black consumers' "faith" in him indicates a desire for black approval that is common to white artists working within black musical traditions. This desire functions both as an oblique acknowledgment of white musicians' indebtedness to black artists and as a sign of anxiety at their appropriation of black idioms. Michael's comment, which establishes black audiences as the privileged arbiters of his musical legitimacy, recalls the sentiments of earlier white musicians such as jazz clarinetist Mezz Mezzrow, who devoted his entire career (even when serving time on Riker's Island) to seeking the blessing of his musical heroes, Sidney Bechet and Louis Armstrong. By expressing his happiness that *Faith* attracted black fans, Michael also implicitly acknowledges the crucial function of "urban contemporary" radio in promoting his work. This practice dates back to the late 1970s (ironically also the dawn of narrowcasting), when radio stations oriented toward black consumers began playing disco acts such as the Bee Gees, an Australian group whose trademark falsetto tones (themselves clearly influenced by soul singer Marvin Gaye) propelled the *Saturday Night Fever* soundtrack to similar heights of popularity among black record buyers.[9]

If Michael's comments suggest that he views his success as an indication of the capacity of artistry to triumph over parochial categories of race and genre (the notion of "black music" here uneasily straddling ethnographic and artistic categories), then a slightly different interpretation of his success was offered by *Jet* magazine, a mainstay of the black middle-class press, in the fall of 1988, after Michael performed at Detroit's Palace Arena on the U.S. leg of his critically acclaimed "Faith" world tour. Titled "White Singers Cross Over to Soul Music and Find Success," this warily upbeat feature article spotlights "I Knew You Were Waiting for Me," Michael's popular duet with Aretha Franklin, and includes a photograph of the two performing their song together at the Detroit gig. Like Michael Bolton, whose frankly imitative cover version of Otis Redding's "(Sittin' On) The Dock of the Bay" received praise from Redding's widow Zelma as her "all-time favorite version" of her husband's classic, Michael receives accolades from black fans, the article suggests, in part because his music is associated with an era that continues to occupy a special place within black popular memory.[10] Appealing to the nostalgia of its readers, the *Jet* article touts Michael's childhood attraction to Motown—an enduring symbol of black achievement within the music industry—and recalls a long list of white performers (including John Lennon, Elton John, Joe Cocker, Darryl Hall, Mick Jagger, and Janis Joplin) who have acknowledged their indebtedness to 1960s black music. Although the article perfunctorily notes the difficulties black soul singers have faced in crossing over to white audiences, in general it paints a rosy picture of soul as a rich and enduring musical vocabulary that can be imitated by white musicians as long as they possess the requisite vocal skills. As Eddie Levert of the O'Jays explains, "If a White act is good enough, Blacks will accept them." Labeling Michael a "perfectionist" and attesting to the "great chemistry" between them, Franklin lends her support to the notion that Michael is not only a legitimate performer, but a legitimate heir of the music she helped to innovate.[11]

Six months later *Jet* abruptly changed its tune, so to speak, this time with a feature article titled "Are White Soul Singers Taking Over Blues and Soul?"—a question that in this instance *Jet*'s readers clearly are to understand as rhetorical.[12] The apparent catalyst for the magazine's change of heart was Michael's success at the American Music Awards, where he walked away with trophies for Favorite Male Vocalist in the rhythm and blues category and Favorite Rhythm and Blues Album, beating out more likely recipients such as Keith Sweat and Glady's Knight and the Pips. This article includes the same photograph of Michael and Franklin performing "I Knew You Were Waiting for Me," but the caption differs in certain noteworthy respects. Instead of emphasizing collaboration, the caption emphasizes the instrumentality of Franklin's reputation to Michael's success. Instead of being portrayed as Franklin's partner, Michael is depicted as a performer who quite literally capitalizes upon the Queen of Soul's cachet—her reputation not only as a musical icon but also as a powerful political symbol, the woman who made the immortal musical demand for "R-E-S-P-E-C-T." Moreover, instead of calling Michael a soul singer, the caption remarks rather dryly upon his "pop music appeal," thus explicitly demoting him to a less privileged mode of artistic expression.[13]

Jet's initial cautious interest in and subsequent uneasiness at Michael's success attest to the legitimacy of the argument, cited earlier, that white performers' appropriation of black musical vernaculars has never been a matter of simple flattery or imitation. Indeed, the simultaneous fragility and durability of the very *Billboard* categories through which success in the music industry is measured confirm Fusco's critique of the apparent fluidity of socially constructed identities. In terms of form and influence, there is often very little that distinguishes "Pop" music from "Black" music, but the persistence of such categories speaks volumes about the industry's desire to sustain multiple markets and hence maximize profits. While the impetus behind such categories is not, in any obvious or simplistic sense, racism among music industry officials, nevertheless the endurance of these categories has the effect of bolstering the public imagination of distinct racial identities ("Black" music for black people; "Pop" for those others who are apparently racially "unmarked") and encouraging segregated patterns of consumption.

Although certain black musicians may cross and recross these lines, nevertheless their mobility is often predicated upon their ability to overcome what Reebee Garafolo identifies as two deeply unsatisfactory options: absolute exclusion from, or radical incorporation within, a commercial "mainstream" defined by the music industry and the society as a whole.[14] By contrast, the very mobility of white artists such as Michael hinges on the stability of musical markets and genres, as well as on the preservation of white privilege, broadly speaking. For example, the year of Michael's debut as a soul singer also saw important album debuts by Tracy Chapman (*Tracy Chapman*) and Living Colour (*Vivid*), artists who helped to redefine the possibilities for black performance by challenging the marginality of black voices within folk and rock musical traditions. In the case of Living Colour, led by Black Rock Coalition co-founder Vernon Reid, the visibility of a black rock group on MTV (where Living Colour's video for the single "Cult of Personality" was in high rotation in 1988) was more than a symbolic affront to the notion that rock was primarily, if not exclusively, a white domain; it also represented the possibility that black artists might reclaim a position of commercial strength within a musical genre originated by black musicians. The achievement of Chapman, a former Barnard student whose acoustic single "Fast Car" established her as an important new voice in the female singer-songwriter tradition, lay not only in overcoming stereotypes about the proper form of musical expression for black women, but also in bringing to popular music a critical discourse of poverty and racism.[15] By contrast, as long as social distinctions of race are upheld, white artists are furnished the "right" (whether or not they exercise it) to invade and colonize the musical traditions of subordinated groups. The race of white musicians, in other words, determines their agency within the music industry and hence the ease with which they negotiate artistic, economic, and racial boundaries relative to their black peers.

Such observations go a long way in explaining *Jet's* less optimistic appraisal of the trajectory of Michael's career after his unanticipated triumph at the 1989 American Music Awards. While it was relatively easy for *Jet* to incorporate Michael's number one *Billboard* ranking within a narrative of black cultural and economic agency (insofar as his success on the Black Music chart largely reflected the buying habits and tastes of black consumers), the American Music Awards emblematized precisely the kind of erasure of cultural and economic agency to which Fusco and others refer (economic in the sense that record purchases inevitably follow such mainstream recognition). Reinterpreted within the context of such erasures, the proliferation of white soul singers in the late 1980s no longer embodies the integrationist hopes and desires of early soul music (as in the first article), but instead epitomizes the repeated displacement of black artists from their rightful station as the owners and preeminent practitioners of soul. In the second article, it is not just Michael's identity that is in question, but his ability to profit from the consumer support of black and white listeners as a "Black" music artist.[16] As the second article is well aware, Michael's recognition has the potential to impact the visibility and commercial viability of contemporary black artists, a fact that has implications for the place of soul music within popular memory.

The second *Jet* article relegates aesthetic concerns—such as whether Michael is a great or even a good soul singer—to a secondary status, marking a shift from questions of artistry and a focus on individual expression to questions of integrity and a focus on collective cultural expression. Soul music, in this analysis, is not primarily a musical style that Michael emulates, but is instead a complex cultural practice that mediates his attainment of success. In fact, the transition to a more soulful sound inspired by the likes of Franklin and Wonder paid off for Michael (born Georgios Kyriacos Panayiotou in North London) in a variety of ways. Becoming a soul/solo artist, for example, enabled Michael to assert a more conventionally masculine image that may have helped to deflect associations between Wham!'s campy pop music and "teenybopper" and/or homosexual desire. Moreover, such a career shift allowed Michael to showcase his talents as a songwriter who had evolved beyond lightweight compositions such as "Wake Me Up before You Go-Go." If he had previously "sold his soul" for commercial success in Wham!, then with *Faith* Michael recuperated his reputation by styling himself as a newly "soulful" white artist.

Although *Jet* is not known for its political outspokenness or its musical expertise, I dwell upon these articles because they demonstrate that the status of "white soul" is irreducible to aesthetic questions, even when, as in the earlier of the two articles, aesthetic criteria are invoked as a primary tool of interpretation. In both articles, the question of whether George Michael is a talented singer, a usurper of black cultural tradition, or some combination of both reflects material realities such as chart rankings, record sales (*Faith* went platinum at least five times over), and promotional opportunities in the form of concerts and highly publicized awards ceremonies. In addition, both articles imply two distinct ways of positing soul: as a black cultural practice in which the occasional white performer may participate, and as the object of the white performer's cultural and economic conquest.

The *Jet* articles suggest a critical reappraisal of two terms I have used more or less unproblematically thus far in this discussion: *soul* and *revival*. *Revival* is in many ways the easier of the two terms to understand, and yet even in the context of the Brit-soul movement of which Michael is but one voice, it is misleading. For one, although they evoke familiar soul tropes and traditions, the various Brit-soul artists, influenced by punk, reggae, ska, house, and hip hop, diverge from the soul music of the 1960s and 1970s in their instrumentation, vocal presentation, and production values. Formally, the singing of smooth soul chanteuses such as Sade or Stansfield recalls and yet diverges from that of Franklin or Carla Thomas, singers whose vocal styles emerge more directly from gospel. Like all revivals, Brit-soul is not a simple, unmediated, or disinterested re-presentation of the past. As demonstrated in the *Jet* articles on Michael, his "soul revival" is a discourse that both actively and passively interprets—and through this interpretation constructs—soul music antecedents, and thereby does not occupy a position of ideological neutrality with respect to the cultural past. Just as all historical narratives illuminate present needs and desires, so too is Michael's soul revival a potentially quite meaningful intervention within broader cultural wars of position.

Soul is potentially a more troublesome term, subject even in the *Jet* articles to differing interpretations. That one can *have* soul, *be* soulful and play *soul music* demonstrates soul's compass over varied terrains of style, politics, ideology, subjectivity, and spirituality. Indeed, although my interests here lie primarily with music, soul has not been understood as only—or even primarily—an artistic practice, unless one understands art as something that overlaps and interacts with commerce, politics, and ways of being. Instead, soul exemplifies what Paul Gilroy calls "dissident forms of black expressive culture"—forms which, he explains, occupy the crossroads between "black cultural practice and black political aspirations," and which dissolve "the discrete fixity of culture and politics."[17] Along the same lines, and on a continuum with other diasporic black cultural practices, soul erodes Western distinctions between realms of secular and sacred, deriving its "rapturous style" from the dynamic, devotional energy of gospel, which it translates and transforms.[18]

Soul's rootedness in the black church is central, rather than incidental, to its cultural and political practice. Unlike most popular black vocal music of 1950s (as exemplified by Nat King Cole, the first major black crossover artist), soul music prizes black vocal difference, deriving inspiration from gospel's vocal vocabulary. While earlier black popular music sought to conceal the distinctness of black voices, soul music celebrates individual vocal personality, from Sam Cooke's smooth melisma to James Brown's percussive groans, grunts, and shouts. This emphasis upon individual vocal styling gave rise, in the 1960s, to a new popular musical sensibility, defining a newly dynamic relationship between performer and audience that hearkens back to blues. Soul required the singer to touch his or her audience through the performance of emotional authenticity, and it likewise encouraged the listener to express his or her investment in an individual singer's performance. As a result soul music, like blues, is characterized by its ability to articulate the needs and aspirations, both spiritual and profane, of its audience.[19]

While the two *Jet* articles provide insight into the framing of white soul within the popular black press, it may be instructive to pursue the line of inquiry opened up by the case of Michael's soul revival a bit further, with an eye toward examining the cultural construction of white soul within other texts of mainstream popular culture. Although Hollywood comedies are hardly known for their introspection, nevertheless two recent films provide useful examples of such contemporary white "soul revivals": Alan Parker's 1991 movie *The Commitments,* which tells the story of the brief flowering of a white Irish soul band, and John Landis's 1980 film *The Blues Brothers,* a cinematic vehicle for characters developed on *Saturday Night Live* by comedians Dan Aykroyd and John Belushi. Both films appropriate soul music as a way of exploring aspects of white identity, illustrating the argument (made by Lipsitz and others) that white performers have used black popular culture for their own self-expression, economic conquest, and cultural self-aggrandizement. To a certain degree, this tendency describes my own relation, as a white academic, to the narratives that I construct through my professional work on issues of race and identity and through my teaching of black literature. Yet, just as academics bring different ideological investments to their scholarship, so these films propose ideologically divergent narratives of "white soul." Landis's loose and fast comedy explores how, under cover of "black style" (a look that Belushi once described as part FBI agent, part businessman, and part hitman),[20] two white male losers manage to evade the law and save an orphanage. In a different but related vein, Parker's affectionate film posits a social homology between working-class black Americans and working-class Irish youth as it traces the adventures of a sometimes hapless, but always committed, white soul band.

Early on in *The Commitments*, Jimmy Rabbitte, an unemployed Irish youth living in the economically depressed Northside section of Dublin, places an advertisement in a local newspaper inviting anyone who can answer the question "Have you got soul?" in the affirmative to audition for the group he is putting together. If soul music were a religion, then Jimmy would be its most devoted Dublin acolyte; like his Northside peers, Jimmy knows that his future has already been forsaken, but for him soul music holds out an elusive promise of socioeconomic salvation, or at least a promise of spiritual sustenance amid hard times. As Jimmy soon comes to realize, however, he is nearly alone in his devotion to a black American musical style that was in its heyday when he was still a child. When he administers a simple litmus test of soulfulness to the young hopefuls who answer the newspaper ad, asking them to describe their musical influences, he finds that they are likely to cite local boys-made-good U2. Most of them, Jimmy discovers after enduring some painfully unsoulful auditions, have never even heard of his heroes Otis Redding and Wilson Pickett.

Jimmy's hard work results in the Commitments, a group of mostly amateur musicians and singers (whose roles are acted, incidentally, primarily by nonactors whom Parker discovered playing in various local Dublin bands). Fronted by Deco, whom Jimmy discovers singing drunkenly but tunefully at a mutual friend's wedding, the band manages to learn how to play spirited covers of 1960s southern soul, enjoys small-scale celebrity after an enthusiastic if somewhat accident-prone debut in a local community center, and then breaks up, the promise of becoming the next U2 left unfulfilled. At the end of the film, as band members go their separate ways, the implication is that soul music will have furnished the Commitments an opportunity for diversion, a chance to hone musical talents, an outlet for sexual energies, and even a moment or two of notoriety, but not a solution to their collective economic marginality. The Irish may be the "blacks of Europe" and the Northsiders the dispossessed of the dispossessed, as Jimmy proselytizes, but the film makes it clear that 1960s black American music does not therefore lead the

Commitments to discover their own symbolic language of resistance. Given more pressing concerns such as work and child care, no one even has the time to lose herself in the "ecstasy" of being a "white Negro."[21]

As I have been implicitly suggesting through this selective redaction of the film, *The Commitments* raises questions of the similarity between the socially conditioned experiences of two oppressed populations in order to probe the limits of cross-cultural "translation." At times, as when Jimmy exhorts the bewildered band members to proclaim "Oy'm black and Oy'm proud," the film is disingenuously coy on this score, but generally speaking, its narrative of "white soul" is deliberately antiro-mantic, suggesting that while the styles associated with soul may be imitable, the particular experiences and cultural traditions that gave rise to black American soul music are not so easily transposible. This re-straint in *The Commitments* is to the credit of Alan Parker, whose earlier movies include *The Big Chill*, a film that uncritically celebrates the most unctuous sort of white middle-class and middle-age nostalgia for black music, as well as the more notorious *Mississippi Burning*, a film chiefly remembered for its reckless and wholesale revision of the history of 1960s black political struggle.[22]

In *The Commitments*, however, Parker seems wary of allowing the audience to walk away embracing Jimmy Rabbitte's redemptive and recuperative narrative of white soul. It is particularly telling, for exam-ple, that even after the members of the Commitments come to feel "at home" playing 1960s American soul music covers, they seem perfectly content to play it straight. Never once, for example, do they consider ways in which the music may be transformed into something they might more properly call their "own," through the sort of musical innovation modeled by many of the "real" Brit-soul musicians. Rather, it is as if their failure to work changes on the music were a metaphor for the ways that the characters themselves feel immobilized, unable to work changes upon their environment and hence their lives. They receive their soul "education" in the School of Hard Knocks, their lack of luck as perform-ers mirroring their lack of opportunities in general. However, if black music fails to provide a source of transcendence, it is not because the Commitments are "inauthentic" in any obvious sense; indeed, one of the film's unexplored ironies concerns the proximity of soul, in ways both acknowledged and unacknowledged, to their musical and cultural expe-rience. Instead, because they are unable or unwilling to transform the music into something more personal and hence more durable, their soul community is more transitory than lasting, more existential than political.

At its best moments, *The Commitments* suggests a succinct critique of appropriation. Generally speaking, the film works hard not to confuse the proficiency of its amateur cast's performances—or the obvious pleasure they manifest while they're playing—with the characters' relations to black music or black people (although this is hardly surprising in a movie whose only black American character is the elusive Wilson Pickett's limousine driver).[23] In this respect, *The Commitments* avoids making too much of the band members' affection for black music, an affection that would, in any case, be ideologically irrelevant. In a context where the flipside of patronizing attitudes (e.g., beliefs about the "natural excellence" of black performers) is the very patronization of these performers, there is little to be said for the redemptive potentialities of musical appreciation.[24] Historically speaking, an attraction to black culture has not necessarily translated into concern for the actual welfare of black people, just as the tremendous popularity of black American popular music on a national and international scale does not portend the disappearance of white supremacy.

I make no apologies for genuinely liking *The Commitments* and for appreciating its self-critical narrative of "white soul." But by the same token, I do not want to offer a too hastily sanguine reading, one that applauds the film's content while dismissing or overlooking its actual material practice. (To do so, I am suggesting, would be to repeat the shallow if well-intentioned analysis of the first of the two *Jet* articles about George Michael.) It is far from irrelevant, for example, that Parker's film adaptation of Roddy Doyle's novel about a Dublin soul band was produced to coincide with the Brit-soul phenomenon, just as *The Big Chill* was calculated to take advantage of baby-boomer nostalgia for a racially harmonious 1960s that exists only in popular myth. *The Commitments* resulted in a successful a film soundtrack recorded by the cast of Irish musicians whom Parker recruited for the movie, and it actually led, in the case of the sixteen-year-old actor/singer who played Deco, to a major-label recording contract.

Successful soundtracks being a dime a dozen these days, it is perhaps more remarkable and more telling of the ways that black culture circulates on the global marketplace that *The Commitments* was directly responsible for initiating a "craze" for black American soul music among Australian consumers. By January 1992, the MCA soundtrack had climbed to number three on the Australian charts, quickly selling more than 75,000 copies and sending record buyers to stores searching for contemporary soul cover albums, such as *Soul Deep* by white rocker Jimmy Barnes, as well as expensive soul reissues of the work of black performers. A three-volume, forty-dollar Ray Charles compact disc reissue, which may otherwise have languished on record store shelves as a collector's item, sold 20,000 copies and made it into the Australian top twenty by virtue of aggressive television promotion that took advantage of momentum generated by the film. Live performers also benefited from the Australian soul revival. Not only did the movie result in the formation of a cottage industry of soul tribute bands, including one called (what else?) the Soul Commitments, but the Neville Brothers sold out a twelve-date tour of Australia and New Zealand, playing to thirty thousand people "entranced by a music that was virtually unknown a year before."[25] A *Billboard* reporter put the Australian soul revival in historical context: "During the '60s," he observed, "a number of conservative pop radio programmers did their best to keep most soul music off the airwaves, reasoning that Australians—being predominantly white—were not at all interested in black music. Apart from a handful of hits by such mainstream Motown acts as the Supremes and the Four Tops, and the odd Atlantic or Stax hit . . . black music came Down Under via cover version by local pop sensations."[26] In sum, the film *The Commitments* accomplished the very global soul revival that the Commitments band could not even sustain in the local pub scene in Dublin. And not surprisingly, although some black artists profited from renewed (or rather, new) interest in their music, the chief beneficiaries of this revival were the multinational corporations that supported the promotion of soul music in commercials on Australian television and radio, and in displays set up in Australian record stores.

Impressive though it may be, the marketing bonanza launched by *The Commitments* pales next to the orgy of consumption set in motion by Landis's *Blues Brothers,* a film in the venerated white-fraternity-boy tradition of Landis's earlier hit *Animal House.* Best remembered by fans for its plethora of car crashes and for its destruction of an entire shopping mall in an elaborately conceived chase scene, the film cost an unprecedented $38 million, setting a record at the time for most expensive comedy. *The Blues Brothers* stars Belushi and Aykroyd as Jake and Elwood Blues, who upon Jake's release from Joliet State Penitentiary resurrect their defunct Blues Brothers band in order to raise money to save a Catholic orphanage. Eventually pursued by the Chicago police force, Illinois state troopers, a local branch of the American Nazi Party, Jake's estranged girlfriend, and an enraged country-and-western band, Jake and Elwood wreck cars and incite general mayhem, their ability to come through with a triumphant musical performance and enough cash to rescue the orphanage never seriously in question.

If *The Commitments* used soul as the cultural landscape in which to explore economic anxieties among youthful members of the Irish working class (the *Village Voice* reviewer noted that the actual proliferation of Dublin bands in 1991 was a sure indication of the lack of opportunities for young people there),[27] then *The Blues Brothers* uses soul music as the cultural landscape upon which to stage an elaborate fantasy of gratified adolescent white male desire. The film revels in particular in a string of cameo appearances by instantly recognizable black soul legends. Within the stated logic of the film, the comic significance of these brief and sometimes scene-stealing performances originates in their very absurdity: Cab Calloway is the orphanage cleaning man who nurtures the brothers' early musical sensibilities; James Brown is the Rev. Cleophus James, whose charismatic preaching infuses them with the "spirit" to perform; Aretha Franklin is the saucy lunch-counter waitress who takes their order before bursting into a rendition of "Think" that provides film's most memorable performance; and Ray Charles is the music store owner who provides the brothers with equipment for their fundraising gig. Although the film implicitly attempts to disavow charges of racism by making the Blues Brothers the object of pursuit by Nazis and various uniformed agents of the state, the conceit of white guys (even white orphans and former convicts) as the primary objects of police persecution wears a little thin. Similarly, no amount of kidding around on the part of Belushi and Aykroyd, and no amount of footage highlighting the "good clean fun" of the integrated Blues Brothers house band, can convincingly dispel the impression left by the images of black soul icons playing an array of enabling, subordinate functions (janitor, waitress, stereotypically impassioned black preacher) that hearken back to Hollywood film of an earlier era.

Generically, *The Blues Brothers* may be a comedy, but under any other terms the band and the film were no joke. As a quasi-serious r&b act, the Blues Brothers (featuring Belushi on lead vocals, Aykroyd on blues harp, and a band including noteworthy musicians Matt Murphy, Steve Cropper, Duck Dunn, and Paul Schafer) took their *Saturday Night*

Live act on the road for the first time in 1978, when they opened for comedian and frequent *SNL* host Steve Martin at Los Angeles's Universal Amphitheatre. *Briefcase Full of Blues,* a live recording of the L.A. concerts, followed shortly thereafter, receiving from *Rolling Stone* the kind of ecstatic review usually reserved for artists who produce original material, or who at least project a modicum of authenticity in their performance. One of the truly telling aspects of their reception in the most established organ of the rock music press was that Belushi and Aykroyd's musical amateurism was seen as a virtue. The Blues Brothers' "genius," wrote Timothy White, "lies not in an ability to surpass or even rival the classic material they choose to cover, but rather in the unpretentious sense of fun with which they imbue each song."[28] Needless to say, no one has ever bothered to contemplate whether black musicians in similar circumstances could get by on their unpretentious sense of fun.

Less a strictly blues act than an r&b and soul cover band who made the song "Soul Man" their trademark, the Blues Brothers eventually produced four more albums, including *Made in America* and *The Original Movie Soundtrack,* both released by Atlantic, the label responsible for nurturing soul both through its own releases and through its affiliation with independent labels such as Stax. In the 1990s, Aykroyd and Jim Belushi, who began touring with the band after his brother John's death, became coinvestors with Isaac Tigrett, founder of the global restaurant chain Hard Rock Cafe, in a new venture: a chain of restaurant/clubs called House of Blues, complete with wooden floors, authentic blues memorabilia, and gift shops hawking products emblazoned with the Blues Brothers logo.[29] Despite the posh location of the premier House of Blues on West Hollywood's Sunset Boulevard, *People* magazine enthused that it "promises all the danger and high-voltage excitement of an old-time juke joint."[30] "I think the thrust of the Blues Brothers' popularity is their coolness," Aykroyd told the reporter who had come to see him perform with James Brown. "A little on the shady side, they aren't materialistic. Their whole pursuit is to play and sing their music at any cost."[31] More successful of late as a musician than as a comic actor, Aykroyd reportedly plans to start his own record label.

Aykroyd's remarks about playing at any cost notwithstanding, the Blues Brothers' pretense of comic nonchalance has consistently masked the seriousness and purposefulness of their economic endeavor. In fact, the plot of *The Blues Brothers* movie neatly sums up the trajectory of

Aykroyd's and Belushi's musical career: they assemble a backing band of well-respected studio musicians, legitimize and support the endeavor by showcasing their connections to authentic black music legends, and end up winning the adulation of white audiences. Moreover, the very ahistorical manner in which Blues Brothers mix together blues, "hip," and soul recalls colonialist entitlement to mine the archives of "native" tradition.

Given the kind of symbolic violence exemplified by Aykroyd's and Belushi's pillaging of the "soul archives"—committed under the aegis and with the blessing of the music industry—it is hardly surprising that cultural theorists of late have focused a great deal of attention on the question of the circulation of cultural symbols across lines of nation and culture. Not all such instances of cultural revivalism are as blatantly opportunist as *The Blues Brothers,* however. In *Dangerous Crossroads,* for example, Lipsitz brilliantly explores the emergence of various "diasporic dialogues" that coalesce around the import and export of local music cultures. Within this multilingual, multivocal conversation, local identities interact with, transform, and are transformed by cultural symbols circulating within the global marketplace, in effect producing a new set of relations between the local and the global, as well as between what were previously imagined as the separate spheres of the "margins" and the "mainstream."[32] Lipsitz's notion of diasporic dialogue does not cancel out the relevance of critiques of cultural appropriation; rather, it makes it possible to historicize and localize these critiques, allowing for subtle and important distinctions between modes of cultural borrowing that seek to erase difference and modes that seek to complicate and extend difference along lines of shared experience.

Using diasporic dialogue as the lens for examining the work of black British musicians such as Jazzie B of the group Soul II Soul, for example, Lipsitz demonstrates how certain Brit-soul artists attempted to translate the "unity and spirit" they heard in black American r&b into music that would express the unity, spirit, and struggle of their own complex diasporic communities. This artistic dialogue between black British and black American popular musicians grew out of, was reinforced by, and, in effect, enhanced a perception of shared "black" experience. In the case of Jazzie B, who has acknowledged American soul singer Curtis Mayfield as a formative influence upon his musical and political sensibilities, the diasporic dialogue between black British and black American soul attests to related struggles against racism, poverty, labor exploitation, cultural imperialism, and political subordination. As the name of Jazzie B's group suggests, this musical dialogue is one that connects black populations, soul to soul, without promiscuously abrogating their differences.

The notion of a diasporic dialogue facilitated by a global music industry whose primary export is black American music complements earlier ways of understanding black musical practices as the products of creative appropriation. Moreover, it provides a context for understanding the differences between these and other approriations (including differences among white appropriations), so that the notion of "appropriation" does not itself become the object of critical fetishization or reification. What the foregoing analysis of white soul "cultural revivalism" suggests is that we need such distinctions, especially in an era in which, encouraged by the emergence of widely available sampling technologies, recycling has becomes so central a part of the *dominant* musical aesthetic. Hip hop is only the most obvious and musically influential example of this aesthetic/ethic of revival, which encompasses everything from Brit-soul to the emergence of "1970s" radio stations (which, tellingly, tend to erase funk and disco from musical history) to the phenomenal recent popularity of the group Ace of Base, which was nothing if not an unabashed ripoff of the 1970s Swedish supergroup Abba (not that it mattered to fans). One of the dangers of "white soul" that revives black musical traditions outside of their original cultural context is that the cultural past may be resurrected not to be celebrated or reworked, but to be replaced by new narratives that enshrine white experience and benefit white musicians.

The Blues Brothers' central contradiction—that black music can be the "fun" and "unpretentious" antidote for a "soul-less" consumer culture even as white capitalism reaps the profits—is also a central contradiction of "white soul" as I have been examining it here. Although the Americans Belushi and Aykroyd profess the same emotional affinity for soul averred by Jimmy Rabbitte in *The Commitments*, nevertheless it is more "real" for dispossessed kids in Dublin, a place with its own histories of cultural oppression, to call a black performer such as Pickett "brother." As *The Blues Brothers* film demonstrates, narcissism is the only possible outcome of white cultural mimicry that fails to interrogate the infrastructure of white privilege upon which such crossing of lines depends. Revivals of soul that do not question white mobility and white agency can only replay white middle-class experience, albeit in a new and different form. Whether or not black style fronts for it, maybe that is as "soulful" as white capitalism gets.

NOTES

1. Coco Fusco, *English Is Broken Here: Notes on Cultural Fusion in the Americas* (New York: New Press, 1995); Paul Gilroy, *Small Acts: Thoughts on the Politics of Black Culture* (London: Serpent's Tail, 1993), and " 'To Be Real': The Dissident Forms of Black Expressive Culture," in Catherine Ugwu, ed., *Let's Get It On: The Politics of Black Performance* (Seattle: Bay Press, 1995); George Lipsitz, *Dangerous Crossroads: Popular Music, Postmodernism and the Poetics of Place* (London: Verso, 1994); Richard Fung, "Working through Cultural Appropriation," *Fuse* 16, nos. 5–6 (summer 1993): 16–24; Eric Lott, *Love and Theft: Blackface Minstrelsy and the American Working Class* (New York: Oxford University Press, 1993); Dick Hebdige, *Subculture: The Meaning of Style* (London: Methuen, 1979); bell hooks, "Madonna: Plantation Mistress of White Soul Sister?" in Evelyn McDonnell and Ann Powers, eds., *Rock She Wrote* (New York: Delta, 1995).

2. Lipsitz, *Dangerous Crossroads*, 49–68.

3. Fusco, *English Is Broken Here*, 28–29.

4. See Nelson George, *Buppies, B-Boys, Baps and Bohos: Notes on Post-Soul Black Culture* (New York: HarperCollins, 1992).

5. Ibid., 189.

6. David E. Thigpen, "Soul with a British Accent," *Time*, November 23, 1992, 68–69.

7. My observations about the original British invasion are informed by comments made by Reebee Garafolo at the "A to the K" Conference, New York University, spring 1994.

8. "White Singers Cross Over to Soul Music and Find Success," *Jet*, September 26, 1988; 54.

9. The *Saturday Night Fever* soundtrack reached number one on what was then *Billboard*'s Top Soul Music chart in 1978, about a decade before Michael topped the charts with *Faith*. The only other white group to approach number one on the Black Music chart was the rap-rock fusion group the Beastie Boys, whose album *Licesed to Ill* went to number two in 1987. See Adam White, "George's *Faith* Rewarded," *Rolling Stone*, June 30, 1988; 21.

10. "White Singers Cross Over," 58.

11. Ibid.

12. "Are White Singers Taking Over Blues and Soul?" *Jet*, March 6, 1989, 60–63.

13. In the earlier piece, the caption under the photograph is descriptive: "Aretha Franklin and George Michael sing their hit, 'I Knew You Were Waiting for Me' at recent concert at the Palace arena near Detroit." In the later article, the caption to the same photo reads " 'I Knew You Were Waiting' [sic], Aretha Franklin's duet with George Michael, helped him win over many Black fans and broaden his pop music appeal."

14. I draw here from comments made by Garafolo at the "A to the K" Conference, New York University, spring 1994.

15. See George, *Buppies, B-Boys, Baps and Bohos*, 31–34.

16. I owe this observation to Rona Peligal, from personal correspondence.

17. Gilroy, "To Be Real," 12.

18. See Arnold Shaw, *Black Popular Music in America* (New York: Schirmer Books, 1986).

19. Peter Guralnick, *Sweet Soul Music: Rhythm and Blues and the Southern Dream of Freedom* (New York: HarperCollins, 1986), 3. Guralnick's book has shaped much of my understanding of 1960s soul music.

20. Chris Hodenfield, "Saturday Night's Soul Fever," *Rolling Stone*, November 2, 1978; 18.

21. See Norman Mailer, *The White Negro* (San Francisco: City Lights Books, 1957).

22. See Julian Dibbell, "Straight Outta Dublin," *Village Voice*, August 20, 1991; 55–56.

23. The film's restraint is no guarantee, of course, that white American movie-goers left the theater with the same respectful distance.

24. As Guralnick notes in *Sweet Soul Music*, his comprehensive and affectionate tribute to southern soul and its/his "dream of freedom," the southern white fraternity circuit provided an important source of sustenance for many 1960s soul bands.

25. Glenn A. Baker, "Aussies 'Commit' to Soul Music; Boom Attributed to Film's Soundtrack," *Billboard*, January 1, 1992; 12.

26. Ibid., 18.

27. See Dibbell, "Straight Outta Dublin," 55.

28. Timothy White, "The Blues Brothers' Funky Family Reunion," *Rolling Stone*, January 25, 1979; 98.

29. Dana Wechsler Linden, "Spread the Blues," *Fortune*, September 13, 1993; 90, 94. The first House of Blues cost $3 million and opened in November 1992; it was expected to gross $5 million in 1993. Additional House of Blues clubs are in Cambridge, Massachusetts, New Orleans, and New York.

30. Todd Gold, "Turnin' It Loose with . . . Dan Aykroyd," *People Weekly,* May 16, 1994; 122.

31. Ibid., 124.

32. Lipsitz, *Dangerous Crossroads*, 4, 42.

"Soul": A Photo Essay

It seems to me that soul is not so much in the heart or the mind, but in the hands. The gestures.

Maybe soul is a language of power that we speak with our hands.

MARILYN NANCE

12.1. "*Marching Band* at the St. Anthony's Day Parade, Super Sunday," New Orleans, La. 1991

All photos © 1997 Marilyn Nance. All rights reserved.

12.2 *"The Tailor,"* Benin City, Nigeria. 1977

12.3 *"Walkin'*," Lagos, Nigeria. 1977

12.4 *"Altar Call,"* Brooklyn, N.Y. 1988

12.5 *"House of Kumba Street Festival,* Harlem," New York, N.Y. 1973

12.6 "*Moore's Bar-B-Q,* 125th Street, Harlem," New York, N.Y. 1973

12.7 *"Afrikan Street Festival,"* Brooklyn, N.Y. 1987

12.8 *"Lil' Bit Braiding Michael's Hair"* Brooklyn, N.Y. 1986

Part Three

BLACK PLEASURE

INTRODUCTION: BLACK PLEASURE—AN OXYMORON

Ishmael Reed

By writing about black pleasure, I risk being chastised by universalists for even positing that there might be such a thing. For the rigorous-minded, the notion of black pleasure might be problematic, since, technically, those we designate as "African American" are transracial, having DNA from Asia and Europe. This is a murky area that serious intellectuals will have to deal with sooner or later.

Moreover, with the grim statistics confronting African Americans, what is there to take pleasure in? Why does this topic even come up? One thinks of those didactic cartoons, printed in *The Final Call,* showing African Americans finger-popping while everything is going to pieces all around them.

I think that I'm a serious person. I don't engage in trifles. But I seem to need my hip hop stations in order to do my daily walking exercises. If I forget my earphones, I sometimes return home to recover them before proceeding with my schedule. And so there's more to black pleasure than merely fun. Take work songs, for example. Those songs weren't created under pleasurable circumstances. Working on a chain gang isn't my idea of pleasure. But certainly, singing songs while pounding rocks made life easier. And so, one form of black pleasure is that which makes life easier, no matter how difficult the circumstances under which this pleasure is experienced. Take dance. African American dance is used not only as a form of pleasure, but in African American religion throughout the hemisphere. Indeed, some of those religious dances have invaded American dance clubs, rendering Yoruba a pervasive, persistent cultural influence throughout most of the Western hemisphere.

But is there something that distinguishes black pleasure from white pleasure or yellow or brown pleasure? Can pleasure be defined and discerned according to race? Is there something about black pleasure that attracts members of other races? Do members of other races see something unique about black pleasure, something that can't be found in their own origins?

Why is it that 70 percent of the hip hop market is dominated by white suburban teenagers? Why did whites take such pleasure from minstrel shows, and why did they enjoy getting up in blackface? Why do millions of whites and yellows enjoy blackfaced interlopers like Elvis Presley, whose imitation of the black style brought him millions of dollars. And why is jazz so revered in Japan? Is it merely a perverse racist thrill for the exotic?

I remember a photo I saw at the University of Kansas Museum. In the photo stood about twenty-five white pioneers. They seemed gloomy. In another photo, there were done up in blackface. They were smiling.

I once asked a group of Frankfurt intellectuals why they were so devoted to African American music and literature. They replied that their own culture, the warrior mythology, celebrated in German music and lore, had gotten them into trouble. They needed something more soothing. A few years ago, I shared an elevator with some businessmen in Den Haag. It was morning and they were on their way to work. The music hovering in the elevator was something by Louis Armstrong. Everybody was smiling. A few months ago, I visited the African American collection at a library in Minneapolis and ran across a book, written in the 1930s, in which the white author claimed that the African Americans' contribution to American culture was "passion."

It's easy for African American intellectuals, who've been trained in a European educational system, to believe in such a thing as "omni-Americaness" and denounce any notion of an African heritage with crowd-pleasing invective. It takes an extraordinary individual to wander beyond a curriculum that rewards and coddles those who remain within its boundaries. Maybe that's why the exploration of the African past has often been launched by off-campus, extracurricular intellectuals. For example, I recently appeared on a panel with a well-known African American intellectual who was arguing with other members of the panel that African Americans were a Western people. As proof, he pointed to the Western references in Martin Luther King Jr.'s speeches. But this intellectual was unable to trace Martin Luther King Jr.'s preaching style, which, like the African American form of worship, is derived from West African religion. One doesn't have to be a Columbia-trained anthropologist to see the obvious parallels.

The mainstream talented tenth intellectuals of the right and left, whose quarrel seems to be over which white male authors one should read and for whom the Enlightenment (an off-campus movement, incidentally), which introduced scientific racism, is an intellectual model, would argue that the African memory was wiped out during the Atlantic crossing, so that what some would call black pleasure is really a style that's occurring in the Latino and Asian American intellectual circles. In Asian American literary circles, writers are arguing over the interpretation of literature written in Kanji, hundreds of years ago, and whether Asians forgot this literature during the Pacific crossing to the West Coast. Frank Chin, who is on the cultural nationalist side of the argument, says that Asians no more forgot this literature than the English forgot Shakespeare. I believe the same holds true of African Americans. I think that there's enough evidence throughout this hemisphere that West African ideas of culture are still present in the day-to-day practices of Africans in the Americas, and if they mixed in Western styles with those when they arrived, it's because West African culture is absorptive.

The African American idea of pleasure, whether it be in cuisine (some of which is West African derived, like blackeye peas and okra), music, or storytelling, is African derived, and the Africans have a warning about the dangers of excessive pleasure—one doesn't have to go to Aristotle to find this.

In Yoruba, the language that most Africans spoke when arriving in the Americas, the word for pleasure is similar to the word for pain— *Dun.* Too much pleasure, our ancestors are telling us, is not a good thing. That's not the only wisdom that they've imparted to us, but it will take a new generation of scholars to uncover more of this ancestral gold, much of which still awaits translation.

13

Ethnophysicality, or An Ethnography of Some Body

JOHN L. JACKSON JR.

Big-butted Bodies

"That boy can flat-out sing," seventeen-year-old Shanita says to me as she ever so carefully drapes a just-ironed pair of Boss jeans over a wire hanger. And who am I? I'm AnthroMan®, the anthropologist-in-training who is superscientifically stretched out across Shanita's pecan-sandy colored comforter.[1] I'm engaged in fieldwork on this day (that rite of passage called participant observation) and one of my first tasks as an ethnographer is to discursively render my environment. So I simply sit on the comforter, take in my surroundings, and jot down notes.

Shanita's living room is the same size as my mother's, but the layout is quite different. Mom's apartment is on the southern side of the building, windows glaring out over cemented sidewalk space on a little corner of King's Highway in Brooklyn. Shanita's place, along the same building's northern end, boasts windows that peep surreptitiously into a backlot of garbage cans, bricks, beer bottles, and sometimes worse— like when "this motherfucker was like wailing and crying and shit and wasn't nobody doing nothing' except sayin' shit like be 'be quiet and shit cause some folk got jobs to go to in the moring' and come to find out the next day that his ass is lying dead back there." But that was a while ago, Shanita assures me, "and ain't much happen back there since then."

It is a spring evening, and my AnthroMan® Notepad© is once again being scribbled upon by my AnthroMan® Pen© (due to force applied by my AnthroMan® hands and head). I am trying to jot down exactly what it is about Tyrone (the aforementioned boy who can "flat-out sing") that makes his story seem so fascinating to me—so much so, in fact, that my special SocioSense is tingling (which means, of course, that there is valuable sociological data in the air). I am brimming with ethnographic expectation.

"Flat out sing?" I quip back, the inflections in my voice purposefully projecting something less than unequivocal agreement. "He's awwiight! I mean, if it is that boy who I saw at your school's last gospel concert, the one with the foot-high fade, lookin' like Lord-knows-what, then he ain't all that."

"I don't know how you muster up the nerve to talk about someone else's singing when you can't even Sing Sing prison," she responds.

"Don't make prison jokes like every black man has to relate," I warn. "I'm just saying, he's good, but you biguppin him like he's the brothuh from another planet."

"Anyway Luther Vandrone, that wasn't him. David was at the concert before. That is the person you seen. Tyrone wasn't even there last time. He is gonna be the one everyone can't wait to see this time around though, with his big-butt self. You know what? A friend of mine from school was playing around and shit saying that she did a survey and found that every black person knows at least one person from the neighborhood where they grew up who had a big butt. And that usually the person was named Tyrone. And I was like oh shit, there was a boy that used to live in 9308, and he sure did have a huge butt—like a woman's. We would all clown on him when he did stupid shit, too. Those were the good old days."

"Damn, you all may be on to something," I say of her joke-making, thinking back to when I spent my earlier years in a Canarsie neighborhood that was home to at least one big-butted Tyrone. Maybe two.

"And there was always at least one big-headed person, too," Shanita continues. "I don't know if they all have the same name, but we always called them watermelon heads. We got one in the choir now, but he is quiet. He can sing too, but it is Tyrone we wanna see on Thursday night."

Shanita starts to laugh.

"Why?" I ask.

"Cause we gonna see some drama."

"Drama like what?"

"Well, the principal said that no one can catch the Holy Spirit or anything like that on stage, and that as soon as anyone did he would stop the concert and the person would get suspended. And even when we just practicing, Tyrone be looking like he about to break down and faint or something."

"From the Holy Spirit?" I ask again.

"I don't know, but Tyrone, when he starts getting into a song, especially 'Firmament'—which we will be singing by the way—he be really getting into it."

"Getting into it like how?"

"Like body shaking and stuff. He be like crying and . . ."

"And the school told you all that they would not allow that?"

"Mmhmm."

"And what did you all say?"

"Nothin'. What we gonna say? We just all wanna see what happens with Tyrone Thursday night at the concert. You comin', right?"

My only reply is an exaggerated and emphatic "Hell Yeah!" Anthro-Man® could hardly miss such an occasion!

Dead Bodies

When discussing bodies and souls and whatnot, it is quite understand-able for one to eventually begin waxing eschatological, musing over fleeting souls and rotting bodies.[2] And where do the souls of those dead bodies go? Well, hell or heaven of course, depending on the moral histories lived by the decomposing bodies in question. But first, what about the living bodies, those still musing over their fates after death? Where do they go? To church services of course, so that the translation from "body" to "spirit" means eternal life for the "soul" involved. Of the churches I have visited, some are more "into" the body (in varying ways) than others. My most recent attempts at fieldwork would lead me to believe that at least part of this difference may be (partially, but not totally) generational.

The rather conservative congregation I was brought up in seemed accustomed to a very particular articulation of individual bodies in the sanctuary and never wanted new converts to rechoreograph church motion (be that motion in the pews, behind the pulpit, or on the choir loft). As one church member argued, "God is one, infinite and perfect; he doesn't change, so why change church doctrine, making church more worldly, with all the heavy drum music and the hand clapping?" And I guess he has a point, right? And some members get even more particular: "If God didn't want women to talk in his church when the Bible was written," a seventy-seven-year-old deacon tells me, "then that mean he don't want them talking in it now as preachers and stuff. And he surely don't want no heavy music and hip hop dancin' in it. All that stuff got to go." But the deacon's arguments are not persuading many of the younger members, who, for the most part, feel that the church must stay up to speed with the times (and get over its masculinist hang-ups) if it hopes to win black souls and bodies to the Lord. During one Crown Heights congregation's weekly meeting about youth-outreach, I listened to several members debate the implications of musical innovation (and its embodied accompaniment, dancing) on the sanctity and reverentiality of their church services.

"Young folk need to be in the church," says Sister Daley, a twenty-seven-year-old Jamaican-born nurse who is addressing the small group of church members assigned by the pastor to increase the number of young people in the congregation. "They aren't here, and we got to bring them in. Cater the message to them. Give them good music and a welcoming spirit, and they will come."

"The church has good music," responds Sister Rosalind, who has been a deaconess in the church for over twenty-five years. "You are talkin' bout that drumming, drumming and all that worldly sounding music. Them things promote a certain kind of feeling in the church that doesn't lead to understanding the serenity of God."

"I'm not trying to say that we got to have only an organ in the sanctuary," Sister Madeline, a newly baptized member from Trinidad, chimes in. "We just can't be bringin' all that bup, bup, bup, into God's house. Once you start wit de tump, tump, tump, your mind move from God and your head start moving to the beat—then your backside sure to follow. Save all dat fa' Saturday night. Dis here ain't no nightclub to be wiggling, wigglin' ya bamsy."

"You can move your backside to the lord, though," is Sister Daley's quick response. "King David's Psalms tells us to play all our instruments to the glory of the lord. And summa y'all should be tankful you still got bamsies ta wiggle."

But the movement of bamsies, backsides, and behinds for the Lord has been going on for centuries now.[3] It is dance's potential connections to the sinful world, to the carnal lust of Saturday night-dance clubs, that is protested by Sister Madeline. It is not that bodies shouldn't move at all; she is not Medusa trying to turn flesh into stone. The body can do all the movin' it wants, she maintains, those movements just shouldn't be reminiscent of a dance hall. Those members who argue against Sister Madeline place the dancing and gyrating church-attending body in a more generous light. They reclaim the expressive meaning of dancing bodies from exclusive coalescence with the bacchanalian (from some kind of direct or implied correlation with sin and transgression) and dress them in new robes of heavenly white. These dancing bodies, accompanied by strings, drums, and the like, are identified as heaven-bound bodies, part of the Christian Jubilee. The path to the pearly gates can almost be seen lined with speakers, and God, the DJ, is cutting and scratching and mixing souls to a celestial beat tapped out with a finger on the Book of Life. Well, maybe not quite, but someone I know very well, my great aunt Agnes, understands first-hand about God and dance, about God and the body. You see, she's been grooving to that Godly beat for quite a while now.

"Every time the preacher say something in church, she get up to do the fox trot." Her husband Rudy chuckles as he says this.

"And give me time I'll do the Buggaloo and the Charleston, too," she replies.

Sanctified Bodies

In discussions of the mind, the spirit, the soul, and their connectedness to the human body, the complexity of that confluence almost appears indescribable. It is talk of the impossible and the inevitable all in one fell swoop. Like the rest of the academic world, I too am into "the body" — literally and otherwise, my own and others'. It is the body, is it not, which holds and houses its aforementioned cohorts: soul, spirit, mind? The soul resides within the body, or, even better, is the body in a different dimension—on a different plane. The spirit permeates the body, informs and coats its physicality like magic mist or some celestial paint job. And the mind is quite inside the body, a part of the physicality of one's very body, the electrical cognitivity of all utterly liquid bodies.[4] Bodies, bodies everywhere and not a drop to drink![5]

But what are the high school administrators saying about human souls, bodies, spirits, and minds by attempting to ban "catching the holy spirit"? How do they hope to outlaw a phenomenon like that? Are they calling it fake, phony, forced, or illicit? Do they just not understand? Maybe they don't want to understand. If not, why not? 'Cause it is a black thang? Maybe a ghetto thang? How about a seventeenth-century Quaker thing?[6] Whatever the case, the Lord sure do work his spirit work in mysterious ways. And yes, AnthroMan® knows from experience.

When a godmother of mine took me to her church for the first time some twenty years ago, the black bodies there all freaked me out because of just how emphatically they were performing some "holy spirit–catching" activities of their own. But that wasn't the only thing that made me uncomfortable. First of all, there wasn't no church bulletin for me to doodle on. There wasn't even no church really, just the second floor of her friend's private house lined with rows of fold-out chairs facing some kind of makeshift wanna-be podium. No pews, no organ. Just an electronic keyboard and a microphone both hooked up to a small speaker on an oval-shaped, bright-red mat placed at the front of the room. To someone who grew up in a huge Seventh Day Adventist church with a conventional edifice, a four-tier choir loft, a carpeted rostrum, and a built-in baptismal pool, my godmother's attic-turned-sanctuary seemed, at the time, more than lacking. It was profane! But, as I've said, that was hardly the worst of it. Even more horrifying than architectual concerns were the bodies of the some twenty or so people that made up the collective church body. These bodies were doing things that seemed, at least to my young Adventist sensibilities, anything but spiritual. They were moving like they were insane. Sure, I had long considered my mom's church far too tame and uninteresting, but this alternative seemed an even greater extreme in the other direction. It seemed rather sinister.

The preacher's message began by sounding quite usual to me— periodically seconded by the collective punctuation marks of his congregation. That was very familiar. So was the occasional arm flying up into the air with an open-palmed handshake to the Lord at the end of it. None of this was new. I even felt at home in it. My mom's Seventh

Day Adventist church, with all its middle-class aspirations and its six-hundred-seat sanctuary, was used to a moving sermon or two. But my godmother's preacher brought on my horror, quite simply and succinctly, by saying something to the effect of, "Move spirit of God, and move in me," and then chanting something like "humdumalumla, hummunnala."[7] Then there was the man with the big, fat burgundy tie sitting to my right who began saying something close to "nobononlacasa." And the preacher was still going and now the man was going, and then a woman on my left chimed in "oohhlooloonahsun." So all three could be heard. Then another. Then another. Slowly, what seemed like the entire congregation had joined in—each playing his or her respective tune.

And then the burgundy-tied man's hands began moving. First just the right one. It was more like twitching initially, then the twitches got bigger and grander. Around and around. Here, there and everywhere. For a long time after that, the man with the burgundy tie around his neck plagued me in nightmares, his gesticulating hands often appearing as five-fingered tormentors detached from their wrists of origin—flexing and unflexing, clenching and unclenching.

Did I think these folks were faking the spiritual funk? Not in the least bit. It all seemed legit, but I still would have pleaded for them to stop if my ten-year-old self could have worked up the nerve. Amid all this movement, however, I (ironically enough) was utterly paralyzed—as though the sheer force of their movements precluded my own. These gesticulating bodies became hideous beasts capable of jailing me within the motionless prison of my own fear. They did not fit into my notions of what bodies did anywhere (let alone at church). Their unintelligible words were like swords at my throat.

But I was horrified to an exponentially greater degree when I inched my eyeballs around to see what was happening three seats diagonally in front of me: Tears flowing down a silent, godmotherial cheek. Her body was rock-hard, utterly still. She looked as paralyzed as I felt. And that is when I figured that if her spirit possession came upon her so silently, so motionlessly, then maybe I too was, at the selfsame moment, also being possessed. Only I didn't even know it. So I simply stared at my godmother, who stared, it seemed, right through me. Her body's only conspicuous movement—some liquid escaping from her insides by way of her eyes. The spirit and/or soul of the body oozing out from within her? Bodies, bodies everywhere, and not a drop to drink!

Relative Bodies

I am driving in my mother's recently paid-off light blue Mazda 323 with my great-aunt, Agnes, and her husband, Rudy. They are keeping me company and telling me stories as we drive to Shanita's gospel concert. Aunt Agnes loves three things unequivocally: gospel music, Reverend Frederick Price's syndicated TV worship service, and the workings of the spirit. And let me tell you, she understands the power of gospel music on the body and has at least one rather vivid experience with that very power.

I have heard the story, with different emphases and inflections, several times. She tells it with awe and thanksgiving: "Back when I was real sick, you weren't even born yet," she'd say, "I was on my way to the grave; I was surely gonna die." She was lying up sick in a hospital bed and Death himself tiptoed by her, she says. It snuck passed the twenty-four-hour nurse at her bedside and pinched her shoulder blade talking 'bout "time to go. You just about done." That is what the voice said. Her nurse-attendant had been daydreaming or sleeping or something when Death made its entrance, but was pulled from her trance by my great-aunt's mammoth-sized wail. "On cue, seeing the shade of Death cover her patient's face, the nurse moved from the windowsill to the bedside, preparing to sing me into God's open arms. And I heard her voice, and it sounded so beautiful, so warm and loving, that I decided to sing along. Nothing too strenuous—I didn't have the strength. I didn't even sing really; it was more like humming. But I tell you, as God is my witness (along with Mrs. Covington, that nurse by my side), I began to sing along with her in a way that made ol' Death wait just a little while longer. Ssshhhheeeee, if not for that singin', I wouldn't be talkin' now."

Ahh, the miracle of music on the body! She retells that story as we drive.

The concert is about twenty minutes away and the three of us look for a place to park the Mazda. We are in Manhattan, so finding a parking space will take vehicular cunning and an all-eyes-involved collective procedure. After a few minutes of futile searching, I decide to pay the million or so dollars for a two-hour stay in a garage, so we park and make our way to the auditorium. Shanita's mom is already there, standing in the lobby reading a copy of "the eyes, the ears, the honest voice of New York, the *Daily News*." She came straight from work, so her light blue dietary aide's uniform with the white stripes boldly peeks out from underneath a dark brown overcoat. I introduce my great-aunt and -uncle to her, the three exchange pleasant smiles, and we all move toward the auditorium entrance.

In the lobby, vendors sell flowers and posters commemorating the event. Merchants flank the auditorium doors hawking goodies of all sorts: bits of chocolate, whole pies and cakes, novelty candies, long-stemmed roses wrapped in colored foil. "Oh my God, look at the prices of these things," my aunt says. "Between that and the tickets, they wanna take all our money." I ask her if she'd like something. "Oh no, that is too, too expensive," she responds. "Ain't no cake worth that. The sweetness of the music gonna have to fill me tonight."

Shanita's mother bumps into one of her friends, Denise, the mother of a pair of twins in the choir, and introduces her to us. We all exchange pleasantries, smile at one another, talk about the pending performance, and begin to usher ourselves into the auditorium for the show. We are right on time. The theater house is just about packed, and we struggle to find a spot where we can all sit together. Bodies, bodies everywhere!

Resurrected Bodies

Surely what could be called my great-aunt Agnes's musically induced resuscitation is not the only example of black bodies moving toward the great beyond and then back again. It is not even her only one. And some bodies even cross completely over the living/dead divide—only to scuttle on back to this world of mortals. Maybe you've seen the newspaper advertisements placed by people who have come back from the dead with supernatural abilities. One of Agnes's favorite tales is a story of her decision to consult one of them.

"It was when I was much younger, more silly," she says. She found out about him from some friend of hers. "He works good," her friend told her. At first she was spooked ("You know," she says, "being a Christian and all"), but she got desperate. So she went to visit him: the great man of all the many mysteries that were revealed to him from beyond the grave. The man who removed stumbling blocks from path-ways and brought loved ones back from the dead and removed the demons from around you and made many shattered lives whole—and took out ads in local black weeklies. She had taken the newspaper advertisement with her, to make sure she didn't forget the address and to keep reading it to herself, to keep convincing herself of the powers that this man claimed to have. If he could do half of what he said, she thought, he'd be able to help her. So this Christian woman passed up prayers to Christ for this, or rather (as she explains it) did both. "I figured that I might as well cover all my bases," she says. But why? Why was she calling on the services of the great beyond? She gives her reasons better than I could ever hope to summarize:

"Rudy was lookin' deathly sick, and I didn't know what to do. At first, when Alicia, that's my friend who told me 'bout this fellah, gave me the ripped-out ad from the paper—or maybe it wasn't a newspaper at all, it might've just been a flyer—anyway, I didn't want to hear nothin' about some man who says he's come back from some grave. I figured that some crazy dead man didn't know nothin' that could help me. But I always kept hearing my mother talkin' 'bout miracles. And I had tried everything, so I asked God if it would be *okay* to go to this man to try to save Rudy's life (cause he was real sick, folks thought he was sure to die), and I asked that if it ain't okay he should tell me so (cause, you know, I just wanted an excuse to do it), I was young. I was desperate. And I went into his place, it was in Harlem, and I didn't even tell Rudy I was goin'. I didn't tell anybody. I knew most of my friends would think I was crazy, so I didn't tell no one. And Rudy was so far gone that he wouldn't have known what I was talkin' 'bout anyway. Now, I'll tell you something, some of these folks are just fakers. Others really do be conjuring. Like those Haitians who be messin' with Voodoo. And this guy was Haitian, so I figured he probably knew some of what he said he did. And I was just so scared for Rudy.

"The place was not too far from where your Aunt Sandra used to live, her first house. So there was something consoling about being so close to someplace I knew. And the place looked so regular from the outside, like any other house on that block, nothing different or odd about it. I think I would've missed it if I didn't keep the number of the house in my brain: 462. You know, Alicia played that number a little while after that and won her a little something, like five hundred dollars. Number 462. I don't know, I think I expected the house's number to be burning in fire on the door or something, just burning and burning. But it wasn't. The place looked normal. The only way I even knew it was the right place was by the small black numbering partially hidden behind a row of potted plants.

"When I got inside, drawings and stuff were all over the place, monster-looking things, crazy-lookin'. And a small little woman asked me some questions and told me to go wait for a couple of seconds while she went upstairs to see about the guy. Long John was his name, or at least something close to it. The place was big, but it felt small 'cause of all the little dolls and pictures and trinkets crowding around one another and around me. The young woman who met me as I entered, she had a name like Rita or Linda or something, came down and told me that I could go into the next room and wait there for Long John to have council with me. My heart was beatin' so fast I tell you. I shook my head as if to say *okay* and walked toward the closed doors she had gestured for me to use. The walls, lined with dolls and strange pictures, gave me the feeling that something was gonna jump out at me. But I kept singing 'Precious Jesus' in my head and holding onto Rudy's old fishing hat I had brought with me, clutching that tired little brown thing as hard as I could, reminding myself that I was doing this all for him. I remember opening the door, a very heavy door, and thinking that I was glad I had chosen this place over some of the other ones I had heard about. The woman in the front seemed so nice. It was at least in a neighborhood I knew. It was right near where your Aunt Sandra used to live, so it wasn't even too far from home."

Hairy Bodies

... and on that great judgment day, I hope to be there. *Praisejesus. Yeslord. Thankyoufather.* Bodies and souls reunited in full. I got to be there. *Amen. Yeslord. Takeitslownowpastor.* But do you all want to be there? *Yeslord, Yesjesus. Thankyoujesus.* I said, I want to be in that chosen number, do you want to be there? *Amen. Yessir. Teachpastor. Preachit. Amenthankyoujesus.* Does anybody, uhh, does anyone remember the story of Samson? *Amen. Yessir.* You remember the story of Samson? *Yessir. Preachitpastor. Goheadnow.* You can never read the story of Samson enough. *Youright. Goheadpastor. Amennow.* Samson with the long, flowing hair. *Praisegod. Thankyoujesus.* Samson with the heavenly strength. *Yeslord. Thankyousaviour.* Oh, but Samson put a lady before the Lord. *Yeslord. Wellnow.* Uh-oh, I'm hittin' too close to home for some of ya'll now. *Youpreachitpastor. Yessiramen. Preachthe-truthpastor.* Ya'll sayin' amen now but some of you got stung by that last one. *Thatsalrightnow. Preachpastor.* Samson with the long, flowing hair put something else before sweet Jesus. *Preachit. Amennow.* And that something else took away all that Samson had in this world, took away God's gift of strength. *Wellwellwell. Preachpastor. Amennowpastor.* See, his body lost its strength cause his spirit lost its strength. *Yessir. Preachpastor.* It was Delilah, in case you don't know, who took his manhood from him. *Youbetterpreach. Goheadsir. Amen.* And God let that happen because Samson let the flesh, his love for the body, come before the Lord, before his love for the Lord, so the Lord took that body back. *Yessir. Amen.* God took it back. *Amenlord. Yes.* But you know what? *Bringithomenowpastor.* On judgment day God has the power to give it all back. *Amenamenamen. Thankyoulord, Yesjesus, Yeslord.* On the day, *yeslord, thankyoujesus,* you bet Samson will have his hair, his long flowing hair. *Praisejesus, Thankyoulord.* Rapunzel ain't got nothing on Samson. *Yeslord.* On that day the lord will be able to cry out, "Samson, Samson let down your hair!" *Amen!*

Cummerbunded Bodies

The auditorium is large, and, like I said before, packed. My great-aunt has been talking about the expensive goodies outside for the past ten minutes. The lights fade to half, and the crowd gets antsy and excited as the curtains part to reveal four rows of young high school faces and bodies draped in blue choir uniforms. The conductor is a light-skinned man with a large midsection (pronounced, it seems, by the red cummerbund around it) who takes slow and careful steps to the center of the stage. He takes his place in front of the choir, his back to the audience, his hands raised the baton poised. His steady head gives a nod to the instruments in the pit, and in a flash his arms drop. A huge, collective "Yes Looord," short, hard, staccato, all in unison, shoots out from the otherwise motionless and expressionless choir. Bits of the crowd begin to shout, clap, and "Thank you Lord" in the silent spatial comma left after the choir's outburst. In a flash his hands are up again. Then down. "Yes Loooord." More of the crowd responds. This is a teaser, and it goes on for about forty-five seconds before the choir allowed the school's orchestra to join them. The room becomes charged with an energy one only connects to through music. The songs continue and my mind is catapulted to tended fields and slave ships.[8] Tyrone, butt and all, is going through tunes without a hitch. He is controlling it—his body, that is. After an hour, the audience is up, waving hands and singing along. A young woman in the choir named Jackie begins to cry during her solo. But her body is held steady, calm. If any gesticulations are welling up inside her, they are being repressed, dammed up within, able to spill out only in tiny droplets from her eye sockets. The cummerbunded man steps aside, and Tyrone starts conducting with long, strong arm movements. Agnes faintly mirrors his motions from her seat. Hands up and out, up and up and out. "What does the conductor really have to do?" Rudy asks her. "Cause that boy ain't conductin' nothin' but himself wildly." But he wasn't that wild, just moving to the melody of the music. There was control there. Could he catch the spirit as he conducted? I waited, but nothing. My notepad and pen are ready, resting in my coat pocket. The choir continues on. When the last song begins, Tyrone takes his place at the microphone, and by this time he has already been teary-eyed for some time—along with a good deal of the crowd and choir. The evening has been emotionally draining for most, wonderful but taxing. Tyrone is sniffling a bit, trying to hold back his tears now. Maybe even fighting back the encroaching spirit:"Don't come in my body. I could get suspended and get in trouble." Like signing a fake hall pass would get him detention. Or like fighting in the lunchroom would get his parents called. Shanita's microphone is on the other side of the choir, and she is on fire in a solo of her own. Her mother has told me many times that she feels Shanita could be a professional singer if she wanted to, "but she is just as good at so many other things that she hasn't devoted as much time as she could to this natural singing gift of hers." Shanita wows the crowd, and as she finishes Tyrone piggybacks on her last note and takes the audience over from there.

Everyone is still clapping for Shanita when Tyrone begins. I look over at my great-aunt, and she is clearly enjoying herself, so I am glad that I dragged her along. By this time, however, my uncle is fighting sleep, slap-boxing with it and losing, his head bopping up and down from blows—up then down, his red eyes open for a second and then shut. The entire crowd is standing now, and my aunt and I have to stretch our necks just to catch a glimpse of the singing bodies before us. And then it starts. Tyrone's body begins breaking the high school principal's decree. First his legs twitch jerkily—then his arms. The light-skinned choir conductor with the red-satin cummerbunded midsection looks behind the stage and runs his right index finger across the front of his neck, left to right. That was to be it. Tyrone's legs and arms are jerking and flexing. The conductor calmly and slowly walks to the front of the auditorium as Tyrone is beginning to flail his arms. What was once twitches are now swings; Tyrone almost falls but catches himself. "Thank you Jesus," he is singsaying. The choir is finishing up the song, and a few of the other members begin to shake. The conductor is still walking to the backstage area. The crowd is clapping and moving with the choir. My great-aunt complains about dizziness. My uncle is clearly awake now because of all the adrenaline pumping through bodies around him.

The huge maroon curtains are being drawn together. Several members of the choir are crying now. Suddenly, the curtains stop. They give two or three jerky movements. One curtain seems to be stuck on something. The musicians are still playing; some of them are crying. Tyrone has almost fallen again, but recaptures his footing. The conductor is now completely out of sight behind the stage. The music is still going and coming through the audience. The choir is still singing and crying to the Lord; the crowd is still standing and appreciating it all. Everyone is clapping already, many are crying, and most are singing along. The curtains are unstuck, but wait, Tyrone is too far downstage. He is out of its reach, and it will close behind him and leave his spirit-catching body uncovered and exposed to our collective gaze. The music feels louder. The choir is still singing. Tyrone appears to have absolutely no control over his body now, bending, falling, and wailing "Thank you Jesus. Thank you Jesus." One of the women in the front row takes his hand and draws him upstage, safely behind the closing curtain's plane. The crowd, responding to the curtain's symbolic finality, reinvigorates its applause. The curtain shoots out at points where, undoubtedly, Tyrone's body is still uncontrollably hitting up against it—then that too subsides. And beside me, poor Uncle Rudy is trying to revive his wife who has just fainted and fallen back into her seat. Everybody's body is different, but each body can only take but so much spirit filling up its soul.

No Bodies

AnthroMan®, without hesitation, bolts for the backstage area, questions ricocheting back and forth in my head: Was Tyrone being reprimanded for his actions? Chastised for his bodily behavior? Would he be physically removed from the premises so that other fledgling spirit-catchers could take note of the swift and sure-footed justice such an infraction would meet? Not this day. Backstage, people simply hug and cry and thank the Lord. Even the cummerbunded choir director (who, only seconds earlier, made the "death" sign with his index finger across his neck) has only hugs and smiles for all, even Tyrone. No censures or criticism. He says nothing and embraces any and all within reach.

The following week, Tyrone is mildly scolded by the principal. "I would have been suspended, they said," he tells me, "but since my grades are good and I am about to graduate, they said that they were letting me off the hook. They just said that I can't have another solo—which doesn't matter anyhow 'cause that was the final gospel concert of the year! So they ain't really do nothing. And if they did, I wouldn't have cared. The Holy Ghost can't be stopped."[9] Maybe not, but Anthro-Man's® question is, can it be measured, analyzed, or interviewed? And if so, when is the best time to come by?

NOTES

1. AnthroMan® is a caricatured (re)presentation of the methodological underpinnings that help form the foundations of the social sciences. He is used to articulate the need for social scientists to perform almost superhuman explanatory feats. One task taken on rather directly, though implicitly, in this piece, is "the telling of ethnographic time"—a discursively based struggle against the pull of ethnography's perennial past-present tense, which according to Johannes Fabian, fixes "the other" in a less complex and sophisticated time than "our" own. Of course, the very assumption about what "the other" entails—and just how "our" and "the other" connect—is also up for grabs here.

The ®© symbols mark the politico-economic issues involved in knowledge production in the late twentieth century, which that has almost reached the level of the absurd in its all-encompassingness. The commodification of knowledge (through high-priced book deals, six-figure salary negotiations, and academics with rock star followings) is almost better described as a kind of "comedyfication"—where the powers of a hyper and ludic capitalism reign supreme and the invisible hands of the marketplace grasp at its own belly in uncontrollable laughter.

2. *Bracketed Bodies:* This essay is really two, and I shall use the second part of it, these notes, to wrap my ideas around the body of work generated by

Ferdinand de Saussure's student body. I rehearse my thoughts with recourse to Saussure's not so much because of how he talks about the "thingness" of the human body, but rather because of how he would seek to talk "the body" away, to defer it from his linguistic analyses indefinitely. This engagement with Saussure may seem to some an unnecessary addition to the text. However, I believe it to be a vital ingredient in my own working out of the information presented.

When Saussure set up his linguistic sign, he was dealing with sound-images and concepts. He was not dealing with objects, not dealing with material bodies in the everyday world, not dealing with physical, frightening bodies singing, crying, and acting-out the Tower of Babel scene. Any notion of a "referent," that which exists beyond the sign (and which a "concept" stands in for) is outside the bounds of his analysis. The linguistic sign does not unite a "thing and a name." Signs are the things; they do not link up with any things outside of themselves. With this move, Saussure defers any and all talk about the referent/world/object, any talk about the Babellian body in motion. His linguistic system is self-contained and self-referential. Any changes in language, therefore, ultimately are not due to the actions of individual language users but to the internal dynamics of language as a sign system. The point here is not that Saussure's theory is inaccurate or unreal, but rather the merit of a conceptualization of a phenomenon that removes the phenomenon from the context within which it operates. One can't have language without language users, and an analysis that downplays the importance of that connection is not simply a closed system, it is a stifled and claustrophobic one. By "ethnographizing" Saussurean linguistics, I hope to think more generally about the relationship between a stilted system and a fluid one—while implicitly challenging conventional linkages between semiotic systems and material conditions/constraints.

Charles Sanders Peirce posits a more open system by incorporating the idea of the referent/world/thing into linguistics, arguing that some signs have a "physical connection" to the objects to which they relate. Peirce has several ways of looking at things he calls "signs." Peirce's sign differs from Saussure's signifier in that it can intrinsically resemble (iconicity) or adjoin spatio-temporally (indexicality) an "object" in the real world. So he sets up a system too, but it is markedly different from Saussure's. Indeed, every system is self-contained and self-referential, but how much is too much? Philosopher Paul Ricoeur would most certainly set out to challenge the degree of closure posited by the likes of Saussure. Ricoeur asks questions about the referent/outside/existence ignored by Saussure's system. Human beings and their existence, he would posit, come before language (a representation of that existence), and this is of utmost importance, he believes, in any analysis of language. Here he falls back on a kind of Heideggerian notion of a pre-existent Being. "Is it not philosophy's task," he asks, "to ceaselessly reopen, toward the being which is expressed, this discourse which linguistics, due to its methods, never ceases to confine within the closed universe of signs and within the purely internal play of their mutual relations?"

So Ricoeur wants to open language up into the being/world/referent/object/ practice/existence, and so on, to open up the study of language such that it no longer points within itself alone. It can be argued that part of what, say, Jacques Derrida does is just that: he opens up the sign. But he does not open it up into the world/thing/object/referent/being. Instead, he cracks it open into "text." There is no Being, for him, which pre-exists text. Text comes before being in that every text is, in a sense, tied to all those texts that came before it.

So now what? Well, we can look at Derridean notions of differance/trace/play/ absence/mark (not synonymous terms, but in cahoots and allied in integral ways) in light of their connection to his (or any) idea of violence—a sneaky rerouting of the discussion back to human bodies. For we can say that Derrida's differ- enced man is akin to the one, in those old-time gangster movies, who knew his days were numbered when the mobsters sent a package of wrapped fish to his home. We (the movie audience) and he knew that it was just a matter of time before the Mafia killed him. He was already ("always already") a walking corpse. With all its Derridean and Mafioso connotations, he was already a *marked* man. For some background, see Paul Ricoeur, *The Conflict of Interpre- tations: Essays in Hermeneutics,* ed. Don Indie (Evanston; Ill.: Northwestern University Press, 1974); Charles S. Peirce, *Pierce on Signs,* ed. James Hoopes (Chapel Hill: University of North Carolina Press, 1991); Roland Barthes, *Ele- ments of Semiology* (New York: Hill and Wang, 1967); Robert Innis, ed., *Semi- otics: An Introductory Anthology* (Bloomington: Indiana University Press, 1985).

3. The connections that link rituals, spirit worship, and dance are indeed interesting, and the literature on those linkages is quite vast. One of the best- known links is the pop-culturally familiar "rain dance."

4. Each of these assertions (about the connection among souls, bodies, and spirits) can be problematized or redescribed. For instance, the Michel Foucault of *Discipline and Punish* would reverse my articulation of the relationship between soul and body by stating that the body is imprisoned within the soul. I invoke my own mind-body-soul connections here not as final concretizations but rather partial articulations.

5. But what is "the body" for the likes of Saussure? It is none other than the phonological accumulation that amounts to the utterance "body"—flung from a speaker's tongue and crashing against a hearer's eardrum like a badass Elvin Jones solo. Saussure attempts to change/revolutionize the study of linguistics by looking at language structurally, a move that can be seen as creating an epistemological break between him and those who have been called his words- as-nomenclature predecessors. He wants to analyze language "as a system of distinct signs corresponding to distinct ideas." And that is reasonable enough.

Language is to be considered a schema/order/structure composed of interrelated parts. But to get at that structure, one of Saussure's initial moves is to bifurcate linguistic phenomena into the portion that is deferred/ignored/precluded (*parole*—the individual, chaotic, heterogeneous, performed speech acts) and the portion that he believes is scientifically analyzable and classifiable (*langue*—the "self contained whole" that rests behind those speech acts and anchors them). As a linguistic scientist, he is able to perform this metaphysical operation (a linguistic lobotomy, some would say), this privileging of *langue* over *parole*—this removal of *parole* from the linguistic body like a blighted organ—by arguing that *langue* "gives unity to speech." Therefore, he contends, without separating and isolating the analyzable/classifiable *langue* from the rest of language, linguistic phenomena would be beyond scientific analysis. For us, the almost supernatural implication of the term "disappears" supplies an important transformation of Saussure the theorist into Saussureo the linguistic magician with his trusty black tophat, into which he drops the chaos of individual speech acts. But the question can then be asked, what else is lost (disappears) in such a maneuver? Could an analysis of *parole* hold any keys to a competent understanding of language that does not seek to banish a large portion of the subject area beyond the bounds of understanding? Sticking with our rather overextended metaphor of the linguistic magician and his theoretical magic wands, could there not be something more compelling than that same old disappearing (speech) act? Like hacksawing *parole* into a thousand tiny pieces and recombining them before our very eyes?

To further highlight Saussure's vanishing of the linguistic body, it is important to incorporate into this discussion his belief in the arbitrariness of the basic components (organs) of that body, linguistic signs. He believes that any linguistic sign (the connection between the *signifier,* the written or spoken "n-i-g-g-e-r," and the *signified,* the concept of the brown-hued Homo sapien creature that actually makes its way in the world) is arbitrary and unmotivated, and he uses this idea to reinforce the importance of the *langue*/schema/structure in any understanding of language—for the value of the linguistic sign rests not in some natural and intrinsic bond between the sound-image and the concept, and especially not in some inherent link between the sign and the "referent" existing in some world beyond the linguistic one. For Saussure the linguistic sign can only ever have value when looked at in (and locked within) the context of the entire sign system within which it operates. The sign is a relational structure that only has meaning within a larger framework of which it is a part, and this is why "structure" is so important to Saussure. It allows for the privileging of *langue* over *parole*, system over speech acts, the social over the individual, the homogeneous over the heterogeneous, the ordered over the chaotic, form over content, head over heels—and on and on. This is one of the founding moves of both linguistics and its kissing-cousin, semiotics. Various theorists have expanded and commented upon Saussurean structuralism/linguistics. This kind of structuralism and its basic privileging maneuvers come up repeatedly in Western social theory. This is the same Saussurean structuralism that I am attempting to ethnographize by placing it squarely on the backs of some religified black bodies, hopefully allowing for an inelegant rematerialization of those things invisibilized by the great Saussureo.

6. Maybe "ghetto thing" misses the point completely by haphazardly dehistoricizing the phenomenon. We may have to take this motherload back to Africa, but now is not the time or place.

7. A bit on the subjectivity versus objectivity debate: It goes without saying that my own re-collections and rememberings of events (be they ethnographic or autobiographic) are quite subjective and distorting. Any and all such accounts are inherently partial—although an argument can always be marshaled around degrees of partiality. However, this partiality, in and of itself, is not the problem. Rather, it is the attempt to downplay, ignore, and underestimate that very partiality (through a rhetoric of objectivity that pretends to write it off into discursive oblivion) with which I take issue.

8. This reference to slave ships stems from my own work on the "middle passage" and its metaphorical and magical present-day (re)interpretations. A forthcoming article will discuss the different modern rememberings and/or reinventions of the Atlantic slave trade.

9. So picture Saussure as a high school principal chasing snotty-nosed teens around poorly lit hallways with a bullhorn. Imagine him checking out the chaotic movements of his school's gospel choir, their blue-clothed bodies careening and convoluting far away from any and all comprehensibility. Would he get it? Maybe, maybe not, but that is not where the heart, spleen, or torso of this argument rests. But why, you ask, are big-butted bodies and Christian-based spirit possession linked in any way to Saussure, Derrida, or any of the other theorists discussed in these notes? Well, because nothing could be finer than a locked-up body, a confined body, a big-butted Bataillian body out on parole and singing to the glory of God. And this essay only seeks to point out an interestingly analogous rehearsal of linguistic premises on other-than-linguistic terrains, on the big-butted bodies of would-be Winans and high school hottentots to ethnographize the theoretical. Think of this as a testing of "evidential truth" that tries to shift the terrain from epistemology to metaphoricity, or even farcicality. And no doubt, it is all a straining of parallels. But "no pain, no gain." So in this essay's corporeal light, one can at least empathize with Saussure's fear of chaos and his need to close off our language (or our analyses of language) from any discussion of actual bodies doing physical things in spatial realities.

14

Black Bodies Swingin'

Race, Gender, and Jazz

MONIQUE GUILLORY

At the end of the day, the seductiveness of artists like [Miles] Davis isn't
awe at their skill. It's the dangerous visions they unleash in others that
make them truly arresting and irresistible, their power as dreamers to decolonize their audience's dream spaces. Or to unlock their nightmares.
— Greg Tate, "Preface to a One-Hundred-and-Eighty Volume Patricide Note:
Yet Another Few Thousand Words on the Death of Miles Davis and the Problem of
the Black Male Genius"

This love of drums, of exciting rhythms, this naive delight in glowing color
that exists only in cloudless climes—this warm, sexual emotion, all these
were hers only through mental understanding . . . .
We are all savages, she repeated to herself, all apparently, but me!
— Mary Love in Carl Van Vechten, *Nigger Heaven*

It is a curious phenomenon of over-determinism and excess that the
largest flower in the world smells like rotting meat. On July 30, 1996,
when the *Titan arum* plant bloomed at Kew Gardens in London, throngs
of people filed past the unsightly blossom—a phallic monstrosity with a
yellow pistil towering ten feet above a mound of fleshy, deep-purple
petals. Apart from the botanical significance of the rare sprout, the
flower's appeal lies not in its anticipated beauty but rather in its vocifer-
ous odor, news of which has permeated the countryside like, well, a
putrid stench. People drawn to the plant explain they want to find out

for themselves just how bad the smell is, but they often leave a bit disappointed when the flower/phallus does not reek as badly as they imagined—somewhere between rancid meat and dead fish has been the general consensus.

I set the *Titan arum* at the head of this project to serve as a center-piece, a coda of contrast and irony. Left to its unbridled nature, a plant can exhaust the phenomenological matrix we use to identify those objects we understand to be "plants." In a most extreme and over-wrought state, a plant can mimic its conceptual counterpart, flesh, and to some extent evolve into a gross perversion of its sweat and pleasant perfume. For the design of this analysis, the pungent and remarkable flower provides an appropriate metaphor for those qualities of jazz culture I examine here. Without contest, jazz is the sweetest and most cherished flower in the garden of American culture. Organically culti-vated in the soil of the New World, it embodies the often contradictory forces that comprise America. An impressive hybrid, jazz sprouted from a conglomeration of African rhythms and European harmonies. It was pruned by racism, watered by the seas of the Middle Passage, fertilized by democracy. The last time the *Titan* plant at Kew Gardens bloomed was more than three decades ago in 1963—a watershed moment of social change in the United States. At that time, the assault of assassina-tions, the torrents of political and civil unrest eclipsed news of the plant's metamorphosis. But 1963 also marked the heyday of bebop, whose energy and dissonance reflected the dynamics of the times. In the garden of American fine art, jazz has evolved as both a pristine, white gardenia and strange fruit hangin' from poplar trees.

But like the flower that entices with its stench rather than its per-fume, there is a dark underside to jazz as complex and alluring as the music itself. This chapter examines how constructs of masculinity in jazz sought to correct and overwrite the history of slavery, lynchings, and discrimination that spawned the music. However, in the attempt to reclaim the masculinity that American history denied them for so long, black jazzmen fashioned a cloak of masculinity that reified the patriar-chy, misogyny, and sexism of the white mainstream. In backstage conver-sations and late night talks, in the musicians' own words and works, one finds a fresh canvas on which to reconfigure the overextended representations of black masculinity in the public sphere.

The political economy of jazz, the elitist venues that sustain and validate the music, imbibe it with an air of social propriety and high culture. However, historic chronicles and biographies elucidate how black, hyperheterosexual bravado circulates as a discursive construct within jazz communities. While America relishes its love affair with jazz, once a bastard child, this does not erase the common ties jazz shares with hip hop in the more contemptible side of the black vernacular tradition.[1] However, jazz has had the unparalleled good fortune of camouflaging itself in an array of tailored suits, articulate spokesmen, and intellectually sophisticated music—unlike its errant stepchild, hip hop, which seems to invade and overwhelm cities like a tangled mess of unruly weeds.

Boys Being Boys

Through the gossip grapevine that trails all musicians on the road, men fill long empty hours away from home with rather predictable conversations about women. They guesstimate the scores of sexual conquests, swap stories about particularly finessed victories and notably famous vixens. Lies may be told, but legends are born. Despite the hyperbolic nature of this backstage shoptalk, it nonetheless informs how younger musicians attempt to fashion themselves after the more seasoned veterans—both as musicians and as men. In the same way that Tony Williams recalls Miles Davis and Max Roach "speaking like men, acting like men . . . Miles showed you how to carry yourself," jazz music continues to operate according to an informal code of apprenticeship and tutelage.[2] Although the audience may never hear the stories told in these more intimate moments, the musicians, through their own self-fashioning and stylization, recreate and reinvent in themselves fragments of the mythological jazz heroes who came before them.

Having grown weary with baggy-jean brothers constantly being subjected to the critical eye of the academy, I feel that the jazz world—a hermetically sealed boy's club for nearly a century—provides an equally fecund, if not overgrown, plot of black masculine tropes. I have negotiated the social tides of being a woman who owns a "2 Live Crew" album. But in the same turn, I have also had to grapple with my appreciation for the creative spirit of jazz music in spite of its rampant misogyny and patriarchy. In "Mad at Miles," Pearle Cleage recounts the anger and ambivalence she felt at the death of Miles Davis. She fondly memorialized him for the sensuality his music brought to her life, yet she remained angered by Davis's "*self-confessed violent crimes against women such that we ought to break his records, burn his tapes and scratch up his CDs until he acknowledges and apologizes and agrees to rethink his position on The Woman Question.*"[3]

Jazz enthusiasts have fought diligently to earn the music its proper respect within the context of American high culture, and this has been a worthy and important battle. I thoroughly recognize how jazz graces the nation not only with an impressive testament of African-American ingenuity and survival, but with living, thriving proof of the great potential and promise of American democracy. These things remain true regardless of the imperfections woven into the fabric of the music's culture and traditions. I suspect that many other women would agree with me that the sexism in jazz is a well kept secret. Jazz is no less, and perhaps no more, sexist than other musical genres dominated by men. However, handling jazz with kid gloves or neglecting it entirely in critical assessments not only precludes mutual understanding from both sides of the bandstand but also leaves one of black America's greatest cultural traditions underexplored. If we are to look anywhere for how constructs of black masculinity operate within the popular market, jazz offers one of the earliest and perhaps most vital models for the interdependence between personal gender politics and larger social factors in creating a long-standing cultural and artistic tradition. The blanket acceptance and even praise for jazz music should not exempt it from constructive exercises of critical engagement. Stuart Hall urges us to be skeptical of such vapid visibility which ultimately amounts to a kind of difference that doesn't make a difference of any kind."[4]

Blacks Being Black

The notion of jazz as synonymous with "black" music extends so deep into the music's history that trumpeter Roy Eldridge once claimed that he could hear the difference between white and black players. This bold assertion hinted at the unlikely possibility that the quality and style of a musician's tone depend not upon training, skill, or natural talent but on an inherent physical feature manifested through the biological trait of race. When Eldridge took a blindfold test to prove his claim, he could not identify even half of the artists' racial identity correctly.[5] Like the

14.1. "Sweet Swing Blues on the Road," reprinted by courtesy of Frank Stewart.

racial misconceptions of the ninetieth century, which continued to prolif-
erate even after human genetics and biology proved them wrong, negative attitudes toward white musicianship in jazz persisted long after
Eldridge's fallacious proposition in the 1950s. Racism and discrimination have significantly shaped the history of jazz, leading one critic to
brazenly claim, "all white musicians could be eliminated from the history of the music without significantly altering its development." [6]
    Like Eldridge, many believe they can perceive a difference in black
performance; however, few would be able to define it. Certainly, this
distinction of black performativity, particularly in the area of music,
commands more than a specific, clearly distinguishable sound. Rather,
this difference rests in a far more complex understanding of the transac-
tional dynamics of performance—the interdependence of the audience
and the artist in creating the performance. Jazz, with its underground
tendencies and esoteric works, has been especially susceptible to the
whims of its audience, who tend to be overprotective of the art and its
origins. The music has been hounded by a pervasive attitude that real
jazz is black music that grew out of black experiences and is played by

black people. Any deviation from this formula simply will not make the grade. But Walter Benn Michaels proposes that notions of identity rooted in culture and practice can ultimately be no less essentialist than racial, biological distinctions: "The very idea of passing—whether it takes the form of looking like you belong to a different race or acting like you belong to a different race—requires an understanding of race as something separate from the way you look and the way you act."[7] Michaels suggests here that white musicians who hope to "pass" into a black-dominated art form will not succeed simply by trying to sound like black jazz musicians any more than we can succeed in "hearing" that they are white. Consequently, Eldridge cannot successfully designate that illusory quality of jazz music that he believes to be dictated by race. On the contrary, race alone lends itself to more complicated social constructs and consensus than Eldridge imagined, not to mention the intricate specificities of artistic expression that is presumed to be the exclusive domain of a particular, imagined racial community. LeRoi Jones attempts to theorize this difference in jazz music with a bit more finesse and insight than Eldridge. Neither judging nor critiquing white jazzmen, Jones posits that "jazz as played by white musicians was not the same as that played by black musicians, nor was there any reason for it to be. The music of the white jazz musician did not issue from the same cultural circumstance; it was, at its most profound instance, a learned art.[8] Although Jones maintains an essentialist distinction that white musicians "learn" jazz while blacks presumably have a more natural proclivity for it, he also identifies the palpable role culture plays in endowing a certain "feel" to the music. Miles Davis also asserted he could tell the difference between black and white bands, but he located the source of this distinction not in the subject but in himself, explaining "I could just tell. 'Cos it [the white band's music] wouldn't go into my body."[9]

The question of whether white music could enter Davis's body indicates a mystical experience similar to spiritual possession—a sentient essence of the music's relationship to and with the body that encompasses both Eldridge's and Jones's prescriptives, the physical and the cultural. In a literal and metaphoric sense, the inability of white jazz to penetrate Davis's black body implies a litany of historic, cultural, and symbolic configurations. Certainly, Davis's observation speaks to his inability to make the necessary metaphysical connection to the music through the medium of his own body—a black body posed in direct social and historic conflict with the body of the white jazzman. The sexual metaphor of the music "entering" Davis's body (or rather, *not* entering it) precisely iterates a shift in the dynamics of masculinity during the Black Power Movement that jazz music engendered. Robyn Wiegmann explains: "Black power discourses in the 1960s [turned] repeatedly to the historical legacy of race and gender in order to define and articulate a strident black masculinity, one that worked specifically to negate lynching and castration's cultural and corporeal effect ... Black power asserted the priority of the black phallus and thereby reclaimed the imposition of feminization that has historically attended power relations between black and white men." [10]

That quality about performances we recognize as somehow transcending the ordinary, and therefore "soulful," does not emerge definitively from the performance itself but rather from the entire matrix of discourse and ideology that envelops the performance. This framework anchors itself on the body of the performer—the visual spectacle of the artist or athlete at work. Andrew Ross notes how "sweat on the brow" operates as a standard trope for the jazzman at work, "a comforting reminder to a white audience that labor exists, and is elsewhere, in a black body." [11] This delineation of performativity within the popular market relies largely on considerations of black masculinity that operate in a manner unique to other racialized/gendered contructs. The black, male body that symbolizes an exceptional standard of performance in jazz, hip hop, and basketball rests largely on a particular construct of black masculinity that inscribes the performative nature of each activity. As bell hooks explains, "It is the young black male body that is seen as epitomizing this promise of wildness, of unlimited physical prowess and unbridled eroticism. It was this black body that was most 'desired' for its labor in slavery, and it is this body that is most represented in contemporary popular culture as the body to be watched, imitated, desired, possessed." [12]

If It Ain't Got That Swing

Throughout sports and music, an enhanced sense of rhythm looms as a precious gift that is as intrinsic to blacks as it is untenable to whites. Nike tried to tell us "it's in the shoes," but rhythm is presumed to be such a sidekick to blackness that it has become a long-standing cliché to imagine a black person without it. There may be plenty of armchair evidence for this claim, particularly in the racialized stereotypes of the mass market. But while high-jumping, fast-running, and music-playing brothers and sisters may appear to be ubiquitous, rhythm is, at best, a mixed blessing to blacks. In *Soul on Ice,* Eldridge Cleaver speculated that rhythm was a skill whites must have possessed at one time, "but which they abandoned for Puritanical dreams of escaping the corruption of the flesh by leaving the terrors of the body to the blacks."[13] In other words, while blacks may hold a monopoly in the rhythm market, this nonetheless relegates them to the socially subordinate domains of the physical.

But while whites graciously concede corporeal endowments to blacks, rhythm in its many guises, manifestations, and executions cannot easily be reduced to a mere reflexive, physical function. LeRoi Jones locates rhythm as one of the most significant traits linking African-American music to its African traditions. On a more individual level, Michael Jordan can throw down a fine dunk shot, but he cannot improvise in 6/8 time like Miles Davis could, and neither of them could dance like Michael Jackson. While each maneuver may be physical to some degree, and all encompass some facet of rhythm, they each unquestionably entail specific combinations of mental and physical accord. As musicologist Curt Sachs states, "Rhythm comes from the mind and not from the body. Man does not follow a body-made rhythm in blind passivity. He himself, on the contrary, creates the law of rhythm and forces it upon the motion of his body in walk and dance, in work and play. Music and poetry accept this law to a greater or lesser degree according to their greater or lesser nearness to bodily motion."[14]

Recognizing the myriad manifestations and manipulations of rhythm in the popular marketplace allows a broader understanding of the nuanced complexities of rhythm within a historical context. Dispelling the presumption of rhythm as a natural and unconsciously biological quality, like a heart beat, may elucidate how rhythm can communicate beyond its practical musical applications. For example, when Wynton Marsalis was asked to cite the most important innovation the bebop era made to jazz, he explained: "They played a different way. And the attitude was different, less tied to the entertainment industry. But the rhythm, not the harmony, is what stumped the older musicians. The emphasis is on the eighth note as the basic unit, instead of the quarter note of New Orleans music. The call and response is much quicker between the musicians, like the way Bird [Parker] and Max Roach played back and forth. And the call and response isn't prescribed, the way it was in big band." [15] Jones concurs that although there always remains an empirically structural component to jazz, "music, as paradoxical as it might seem, is the result of thought. It is the result of thought perfected at its most empirical, i.e. as *attitude* or *stance*. Thought is largely conditioned by reference; it is the result of consideration or speculation against reference, which is largely arbitrary. . . . The Negro's music changed as he changed." [16]

These changes in attitude, which Eldridge thought he could hear and Davis believed he could feel, drove the music, with the nation dragging behind it, into a new social era. Michele Wallace recalls the 1950s as the calm before the storm of the social upheaval heralded by the 1960s. It was a decade where black passivity was at an all-time high, with one significant exception: "Jazz, black music, was more resistant to the dominant culture than ever. Black musicians took to wearing strange and grungy-looking clothing, or turning their backs on audiences. Even their language, always a code to exclude whites, becomes more difficult to decipher. There was a definite rumbling in the slave quarters." [17] Musical historian Martin Williams dubbed this quality "attitude" upon recognizing it in Charlie Parker's combo. Williams recalled that the first time he saw Parker perform, "as a white Southerner, the thing that struck me even more than the music was the attitude coming off the bandstand—self confident, aggressive, it was something I'd never seen from black musicians before." [18]

The attitude Williams witnessed no doubt resembles what *Newsweek* recognized in rap culture when they dubbed it "The Culture of Attitude" in a 1993 article. The attitudes that marked Parker's band in the 1950s and hip hop in the 1990s share rhythm as their aesthetic impetus, and the rage and hostility that emerges from rap resonate with the same defiance and resistance that characterized jazz. Along with artistic qualities such as rhythm, dissonance, syncopation, and improvisation, jazz and hip hop share the unique feature of redefining black masculinity, each using music to "displace older forms of textuality and reference a terrain of cultural production that marks the body as a site of pleasure, resistance, domination and danger." [19]

Within the historic tradition of black artistic expression, both jazz and hip hop render the "black-identified imagination unsatisfied with white supremacist definition of modernity," which drew on emasculated and subordinated representations of blackness located in notions of the primitive.[20] After jazz had become identified with the grinning and sweetly singing gentility of Louis Armstrong or the highly commercialized big band swing of the Harlem Renaissance, the instatiation of a renewed masculinity through the apparently cold, stoic distance of the bebop men marked a disconcerting and palpable shift in how the public would come to imagine jazz musicians. But this new cadre of black music men would overcompensate for the androgyny embodied by the earlier jazz sect. They "enacted a black masculine that not only challenged whiteness but exiled it to the (cultural) margins of blackness—i.e., in their hands blackness was a powerful symbol of the masculine."[21]

Vibes

The sense of masculinity that emanated from the music not only rose through the musicians' presence on the bandstand, but was reflected as well in the structure and form of the music itself. As jazz developed, the gender cleft that birthed it in New Orleans' pleasure houses gradually widened. During the nascent years of jazz in this southern city, where more than two thousand prostitutes were registered at city hall, sporting women strongly colored the gender roles of musicians and other working-class males. The association of jazz music with licentiousness made it increasingly difficult for men to accept female musicians on the bandstand. New Orleans traditions castigated these women as lewd and of lax morals. In addition, many women who played music were thought to be aligned with voodoo practices and witchcraft.[22] Some male musicians were so superstitious that they felt it was unlucky to play with women on the bandstand, or even that it was unnatural for women to want to play jazz. As Neil Leonard notes, "One measure of the masculine tome of the jazz world is its fraternal argot, which is full of macho terms. And for many devotees, the music itself is by definition masculine. As one pianist asserted in 1973, 'Jazz is a male language. It's a matter of speaking that language and women just can't do it.' "[23]

Few women were able to transcend the sexual discrimination that barred them from the bandstand. Yet, women and sexuality continue to provide a vital cornerstone on which jazz now stands. Rather than the personal and professional struggles of women who have etched out a space for themselves in jazz, the second part of this piece traces the more subtle but no less complex ways women factor into jazz culture, through their presence as wives, lovers, mothers, and whores—or through their absence. In addition to the various roles women play in jazz culture, the rift in attitudes toward and treatment of white and black women will also factor prominently into this consideration of gender constructs in jazz. Given the intrinsic relationship of jazz to notions of black sexuality and pleasure, representations of masculinity (both black and white) provide a salient point of analysis to understand jazz culture in opposition to and in conjunction with the larger framework of American culture.

Robert Farris Thompson reminds us that the name *jazz* itself most likely evolved from *jizz* and *jism,* Creolized forms of the Kikongo word *dinza* (ejaculation).[24] Although jazz music and culture circulate according to typical constructs of sexuality, the jazz bandstand exudes a resolutely masculine feel. It is a battleground of male competition, an altar of sacrifice and initiation. Off the bandstand, however, the atmosphere is one of camaraderie. Musicians spend countless hours on the road together, often in cramped and compromising spaces. They place their confidence in one another and build lives and careers together, measuring their own ability and value as musicians according to the opinions of their peers. Leonard offers the scenario of one band that was on the road for 329 days out of the year. The band members developed such a strong family feeling that when the band leader invited the wives and girlfriends to accompany the band on a leg of the trip, many members resented the intrusion. Leonard explains, "The experiment had to be abandoned after complaints from unaccompanied bandsmen strenuously objecting to intrusions into the band's 'domestic' equilibrium."[25] While jazz operates according to visibly homosocial patterns, the acknowledged presence of homosexuality in jazz is negligible. There are a few legendary exceptions, Billy Strayhorne being the most renown, but the likely possibility of other homosexuals within jazz's tight-knit fraternity remains the fodder of speculation and rumor.

Despite the paucity of female musicians on the bandstand, jazzmen quibble over the negative and positive influences women have sparked in jazz's artistic innovations. Trumpeter Cootie Williams felt that the pursuit of women drove a positive motivation for the music: "All great jazz musicians, every one of them, have had many loves and girls in their lives. People don't read about these things in books, but a girl is jazz music. They throw something into the mind that makes you produce jazz." In turn, the music threw something into the minds of the women it touched, which aided in creating a cult of sexuality around the bandstand. One musician theorized that the charisma the woman witnessed on the stage could somehow translate into heightened sexual potency: "The woman feels that she must have this. The thing that he's projecting, it's coming from somewhere else, but it comes through him and projects the woman out there. She feels that the spirit is strong but she can't collect that thing where it's coming from, and so she has to collect the person it's coming through."[26] However, not all musicians appreciated the swarm of sexuality that circled the bandstand. Ornette Coleman once suggested that women at gigs only distracted the musicians from the seriousness of the music. According to Coleman, once a musician realizes a woman in the audience is interested in him, he "forgets what he's up there for. . . . You don't know how many times I've come off the bandstand and had girls come up to me and hand me a note with their address on it. . . . I'm telling you this whole sex thing has more of a negative effect on the music than drugs, I'm sure of it.[27]

Jazz's propensity for inciting the emotions and sensual natures of women sparked a wave of backlash against the music. In the southern bastion of jazz's conception, historian Stephen Longstreet once proposed that the perversion of the music made its way into the writings of the South's most celebrated authors—Truman Capote, William Faulkner, and Tennessee Williams. Longstreet suggested that the tormented relationships these authors chronicled were the result of sexual aberrations spawned by jazz: "White women of certain warped emotional drives had been attracted to Negro men, and the black jazz men had an even stronger draw for the unhappy white woman. She saw in him an image of forbidden passion, of animal drive. Women bored by their protecting legend, aware of their husband's desire for brothel and Negro women, were driven to their own adventures."[28]

Similarly, in 1926, the public outcry and hysteria that trailed jazz music led city councils to restrict this "devil" music to heavily policed parts of the urban metropoles, where it ultimately thrived. In some extreme cases of jazzphobia, magazines and journals urged people to "jazz-proof" their home and environs by adhering to a strict and modest notion of hyperdomesticity. As jazz continued to trickle into urban hubs like Chicago, New York, and New Orleans, it became an easy scapegoat for all of society's ills. Kathy Ogren notes that the *New York Times* cited "jazz emotions" for the demise of young women. The article was written to protest the construction of a music theater next to a rooming house for women. The editorial opinion of the piece feared that "babies born in the maternity hospital are to be legally subjected to the implanting of jazz emotions by such enforced proximity to a theater and a jazz place." [29]

By the Book

While there was a sense of hyperbole and excessiveness in the presumable fears of jazz music, jazzmen also posed some legitimate threats to the women in their midst. In addition to their musical careers, some band members also took up side gigs as hustlers and pimps. During jazz's nascent years in New Orleans, "all the musicians wanted to be pimps," Pops Foster claimed. Foster noted that this ambition resulted in part from the police department's strict enforcement of vagrancy laws: "You had to prove that you were doing some kind of work or they'd put you in jail." [30] The seemingly incongruous juxtaposition of jazz with prostitution remains perhaps one of the most striking and pervasive tropes throughout jazz biographies. The most notorious and legendary accounts are Charles Mingus's *Beneath the Underdog* and Miles Davis's self-titled autobiography with Quincy Troupe, *Miles*. Although these authorized accounts of the musicians' lives may contain some exaggeration and fabrication, they nonetheless contribute to the lore that circulates about these artists. We may not be able to discern which stories are true and which are not, but these narratives represent a facet of the musicians' representations of themselves and at least part of how they are remembered. These texts provide two of the most comprehensive records of how jazzmen construct their own sexuality within the parameters of white patriarchy and its concomitant misogyny. While the historical context of each biography could provide crucial insight into its social and external influences, these incomplete portraits offer glimpses into the private lives of these vastly public men. Perhaps more importantly, they also reveal much through what they conceal. Particularly with regards to Mingus and Davis, these texts are an essential part of a jazz legacy that is still nurtured in the contemporary jazz scene. Therefore, the manner in which these men projected themselves to an audience beyond the jazz world sheds light on how jazz musicians participate in the generation of jazz culture and myth—particularly in the domain of sexuality, where myths often prevail.

Although their relationships with women provide a salient feature of their own masculine identities, the narrative threads of both Mingus's and Davis's sexuality wind through an assortment of other personal factors and relationships, including childhood experiences, class status, and adult lifestyle. For Mingus and Davis, the domain of women in their lives is well charted and clear, with wives and lovers factoring into their narratives in fairly conventional, although problematic, ways. These authors try to evoke a traditional, heterosexual pattern of masculinity, but a closer reading of their lives illustrates how neither man defined his sexuality predominantly through his intimate encounters with women. Mingus's troubled childhood and strained relationship with his father haunted him throughout much of his life—a significant emotional stress that likely drove him to his sexual excesses. And in spite of Davis's numerous marriages and casual relationships with women, he constructs his own identity largely through his relationships with other musicians. In his desire to transcend the constraints and privilege of his bourgeois background, Davis found support and a sense of belonging in the jazz community that was missing from his childhood.

Since his death in 1979, Charles Mingus's legacy continues to be of monumental import in the American jazz scene. Widely recognized as a musician of incomparable talent and innovation, Mingus was among the first jazzmen to elevate the bass from a rhythmic sidepiece to a center-stage, solo instrument capable of melodic phrasing and harmony. In addition to his musical genius, which was a dynamic impetus in the development of bebop, Mingus's eccentric personality and character situates him in the domain of mythic jazz legends—Billie Holiday, Charlie Parker, and Miles Davis, to name a few—individuals whose personal lives came to mean as much to jazz as their professional contributions.

Even today, more than twenty years after its publication, Mingus's *Beneath the Underdog* is still revered as one of the most important chronicles of and from the American jazz scene. Touted as a masterpiece of both literary and musical expression, Mingus's construction of his life and times focuses heavily on personal reflection rather than his career and musicianship. Some critics cite this as the book's fundamental weakness, while others applaud Mingus's intelligent and insightful illustration of the complexities of black genius.

Mingus the musician and middleman surfaces as the stabilizing factor between Mingus's dual selves. The gentler, over-trusting side of

Mingus's nature evolves from his childhood innocence to his transcendent spirituality as an adult. As a young boy growing up in the rougher part of Watts, the overweight and awkward Mingus is tormented by neighborhood bullies. He learns Judo and, to his own amazement, beats up his arch-rival, Fiesty. Rather than savoring his victory, Mingus laments his own capacity for violence. He apologizes profusely to the boy and leaves the scene, deeply antagonized by his desire to prove his manhood—an urge that conflicts with his personal, nonconfrontational code of ethics: "One minute he believes his actions were soul saving . . . the next minute he's wishing he'd beaten the life out of the punk. Then he decides he could never do that under any circumstances and hates himself for having destructive thoughts about any human being. He figures he must be somewhere in between Jesus and the Devil—closer to the Devil but unable to perform a perfectly evil act." [31]

Throughout the book, Mingus describes himself as a devil, particularly in his problematic dealings with women. Through all his sexual exploits, Mingus does come to have several long-standing relationships, two of which go on simultaneously. Lee Marie, a childhood sweetheart from Watts, is one of the central women in Mingus's life. Lee Marie was the daughter of a respected policeman, and her family never approved of her relationship with Mingus. She suffers relentlessly, including an abortion, sterilization, and exile to Europe at the mercy of her family. When she is finally able to marry Mingus legitimately, she willingly shares him with Donna, a white woman Mingus is seeing when he is reconciled with Lee Marie. The women accept each other in Mingus's life and become partners in prostituting themselves to support him. The women are so controlled by Mingus that when they have sex with each other, their guilt metastasizes into an apparition of him in the room with them. When they relay this story to him, he comforts them, telling them not to worry and fusing them into one being, whom he calls "Donnalee" (279–80).

Mingus's sexual recklessness throughout the book is disturbing and distracting, but upon closer examination his behavior merely hides a deep sense of insecurity and self-doubt based largely on his social impotence as a black man and the looming cloud of his father's own misery. Mingus tries to justify his sexual irresponsibility by looking to other historic examples of musicians with reputations as pimps. But this move is an obvious attempt to escape the oppression of his race: "By my reckoning, a good jazz musician has got to turn to pimpdom in order to be free and keep his soul straight. Jelly Roll Morton had several girls I know of and that's the way he bought the time to write and study and incidentally got diamonds in his teeth and probably his asshole. He was saying, 'White man, you hate and fight and kill for riches, I get them from fucking. Who's better?' " (267–68).

This idea extends even further in Mingus's relationship to white women. Although he does not discriminate between white and black women as lovers, white women embody for Mingus a troubled space of weakness and empowerment. When a white girlfriend offers to let him drive her car, he snaps, "I'm not your chauffeur, bitch, especially on Central Avenue in front of all the cats." The woman chides him for being "corny," leading Mingus to question his helpless outburst: "Yeah, she's right, I came on square race-wise. I got to act older and hipper with this chick" (148). He then takes the wheel. In several instances, white women empower Mingus through sex but emasculate him by what they signify as white women. In one episode, Mingus loses a gig because he is sleeping with the club owner's wife, Nesa. She not only has sex with Mingus in her office at the club, where her husband could easily discover them, but also skims large amounts of cash from the club for Mingus. There is, at first, a strong tension between Mingus and Nesa because she calls him "Boy." But Mingus conquers her through sex: "Cholly Mingus, I hate you 'cause you hate me, you tried to kill me fucking! Take me, anything I got, just don't fuck me like that! I saw you just before I blacked out—your face looked like Satan. I know I pulled a dirty Southern thing on you but I tried to change when I realized I didn't even know why I called you names. Don't worry, you cured me for life" (169).

This scene clearly exemplifies a sexual phenomenon between black men and southern white women outlined in Calvin Hernton's *Sex and Racism in America*. Nesa holds some control over Mingus because of her power at the club (she books the bands), so he cannot deny her outright. But he also enjoys the money and the pleasure she gives him. Hernton explains, "The sad aspect of these situations is that the Negro is 'trapped.' It is as hazardous to 'go along' as it is to refuse, because throughout the duration of the affair there looms the possibility of being discovered or of the woman getting angry." [32] In addition to these social constraints, Mingus is in a triple bind attempting to live up to the tradition of hustler and ladies' man as established by Jelly Roll Morton's sexual exploits and consequential material gains.

Ironically, not for a single moment in the book is Mingus's sexual performance anything less than supernatural, in spite of the fact that he openly expresses concern about his aging and overweight body. Food is another indulgence. His large, graceless body, particularly in the company of women, painfully ties him to his father's failure:

Crossing my legs is a real drag, I'm getting too fat to cross them comfortable. Damn if I know why my father's flashing through my mind again. You know why, Charles. Your father used his hands to help him cross his legs in front of his bitch on Forty-eighth Street. You hate yourself for being fat and using your hands to cross your legs, like him—it makes you remember his philandering—and your own. You're fat and greedy. That was your father's escape too—food helped him forget for a while the misery he was creating. He suggested a pattern for you to live by. (142)

In an almost clinical, diagnostic manner, Mingus attributes his insecurities and indulgences to a pattern laid by his father. Not only is he fat like his father, he is also a philanderer—an element of Mingus's childhood that brought him much pain. Mingus's father was seldom there to support the family in a meaningful way, and when he was, he was a strap-happy disciplinarian. When a neighbor shoots Mingus's beloved dog, the father buries the animal in powerless silence. As a small boy, Mingus understands his father's beatings as incarnations of his frustrations and insecurities over his manhood and self-worth, "sick, frustrated at a life spent in the post office when he'd trained to be an architect, and confused in many ways" (26).

Mingus's mother offers little relief from the father's abuse and is more concerned with social pretense and respectability than with her son's well-being. Mingus replicates his father's misogynistic example by turning on his mother out of his own frustration, as well as his feelings about his father's powerlessness. By blaming his mother for the family's unhappiness, Mingus sets a doomed course for all subsequent relationships with women. His wanton sexual abandon, though excessive and overwhelming, merely conceals a more powerful rage and helplessness.

Although a master musician and composer, Mingus uses *Beneath the Underdog* to explore his personal and emotional life, ravished by childhood abuse and insecurity. He leaves his music as a given, a haven from the torrents of emotional turmoil that envelop him. Through everything, he continues to perform, but the incidents off the bandstand feed his anxiety—his father's impotent rage, his mother's passive aggression, and the always problematic place of women in his life. Mingus juggles all of these, usually with little success, and often succumbs to his weaknesses. In *Beneath the Underdog,* Mingus's pathological behavior sheds little light on his role as a jazz musician; rather, it illuminates his troubled soul as a black man in America whose fears and insecurities at times overshadow his talent and vision.

While critics and reviewers offer various opinions on Mingus's distracting and excessive sex life, they usually make no reference to Mingus's general mistreatment of women. In most instances, reviews dedicate more analysis to Mingus's self-proclaimed hypervirility than to the resultant abuse and exploitation his sexual appetite causes. In fact, one critic even takes to reassuring "all those allegedly inadequate white males" that Mingus's sexual exploits were "deliberately fantasized." [33] One interesting method through which the critics rationalize Mingus's sexual indulgences is to link his behavior specifically and ironically to his brilliance—a peculiar association in that his ability to craft these erotic and sensual episodes somehow attests to his reliability to convey his world honestly. As one reviewer put it, Mingus "thinks of himself as a legendary womanizer, and if 10 percent of his yarns are accurate, he is, believe me, he is. He is also an unusually gifted pornographer, in part because he is an innovative soul, in part because he chases his dreams of tail with astonishing single-mindedness." [34]

The review continues by suggesting that Mingus's sexuality is not only an embodiment of his genius but of his race as well, in that "*Beneath the Underdog,* despite its repetitious copulations and orgies, is important and should be added to the growing library of worthwhile books by black people about precisely what it feels like to be black." The conflation of Mingus's sexual forays with his talent or his race implies a type of reductivist racism whereby black genius must necessarily accompany excessive sexual empowerment, a basic trait of the black male.

A Man of His Peers

For man needs an instrument to touch himself: a hand, a woman or some substitute. The replacement of that apparatus is effected in and through language. Man produces language for self-affection. . . . An introjected, internalized mirror, in which the "subject" ensures, in the most subtle, most secret, manner possible, the immortal preservation of his auto-eroticism.[35]

In the essay "Volume without Contours," Luce Irigaray analyzes male and female sexuality through ideas of touch and stimulation mediated not only physically, but also through language. In the above passage, the "instrument" is a metaphor for a substitute through which the man replicates himself in representation and "affectation." Irigaray applies this idea of the instrument to science and mechanics as well as to women—all of which are relegated to the "affect(ta)ion" of the man. However, the metaphor can also be extended to its literal meaning—an actual instrument used by musicians in producing the language of music.

Like Mingus, Miles Davis's manhood also crystalizes through his mastery of music. Davis's biography, coauthored with Quincy Troupe, adheres to a conventional form and is written in a lucid and engaging manner. It is a linear narrative, beginning with Davis's privileged childhood in St. Louis and following his burgeoning music career to New York. Here, Davis matures as a musician and a man, two evolutions that are in many ways synonymous. He grounds his personal security in his mastery of the music and judges other men according to their abilities. As with other musicians, women play an important part in this construct, but they are by no means central; to a large degree, other musicians whom Davis respects are esteemed higher than the women in his life.

Davis begins his biography, "The greatest feeling I ever had in my life—with my clothes on—was when I first heard Diz and Bird together in St. Louis, Missouri, back in 1944."[36] Davis commences with the pleasure principle of jazz, underscoring the general association of jazz with sexual pleasure. But this does not supply the substance of the narrative nor the bulk of Davis's masculinity, as it does in Mingus's biography. Mingus and Davis are hardly coming from the same place. While Mingus was tortured with fear as a child, Davis grew up with relative privilege and comfort. He rode horses on his father's farm and could count on his father to support him in any circumstance, even at the height of his drug addiction. Therefore, Davis is not acting with the same desperation that Mingus presents. Instead, Davis's sheltered youth and his innocence and naiveté about the world ultimately lead him to the same destructive tendencies that Mingus developed out of fear.

By the time he is twelve years old, Davis is serious about his music.

Unlike Mingus, who studied jazz because it would gain him more clout with women, Davis is interested in music largely as a matter of pride and self-fulfillment. A natural on the trumpet even at an early age, he thrives on the attention and praise he receives through his music. When his school band goes to play in a competition in Illinois, Davis gets the opportunity to meet verteran trumpet player Clark Terry. Still clad in his band uniform, he eagerly begins to ask Terry about trumpet techniques. Terry snubs him and says, "I don't want to talk about no trumpet with all them pretty girls bouncing around out there" (33). For much of the early part of his career, Davis characterizes himself with this sort of aloofness about the crucial components of jazz culture, namely, women and drugs. He arrives in New York when he is eighteen years old, leaving his girlfriend and young daughter behind in St. Louis. For the first two weeks, he neglects his studies at Juilliard and looks for Charlie Parker with an obsessive determination. When he asks about Parker, many musicians urge him to leave Parker alone because he is so heavy into his addiction. But Davis will not be deterred. When he finally catches up with Parker, the moment is less than transcendent:

I turned around and there was Bird looking badder than a motherfucker. He was dressed in these baggy clothes that looked like he had been sleeping in them for days. His face was all puffed up and his eyes were swollen and red. But he was cool, with that hipness he could have about him even when he was drunk or fucked up. Plus, he had that confidence that all people have when they know their shit is bad. But no matter how he looked, bad or near death, he still looked good to me that night after spending all that time trying to find him; I was just glad to see him standing there. And when he remembered where he had met me, I was the happiest motherfucker on earth (57).

Parker will be Davis's first gauge of manhood in New York. He has idolized Parker as a musician, but now he must deal with him as a man and this presents a unique problem for Davis. Young and naive, Davis has not yet learned the ways of jazz life. He is committed to Irene, who later joins him in New York with their daughter, and still has faith in monogamous relationships. Despite Davis's admiration for Parker's musical genius, he is repulsed by Parker as a man. In one instance, Davis is in a cab with Parker and a white woman who performs fellatio on Parker. While she's doing this, Parker is casually eating fried chicken. Davis is deeply troubled to witness this and struggles with his love and abhorrence for Parker.

In light of Parker's often erratic behavior, Davis finds himself torn between Parker and another of his idols, Dizzy Gillespie. Although Gillespie and Parker were musical soulmates, Gillespie, like many other musicians at that time, resented Parker's addiction and his abuse of others. Parker was unreliable, and on more than one occasion Gillespie quit Parker's band and swore never to play with him again. Davis found himself caught in the middle of their disputes both personally and professionally.

No matter what attitude, values, or assumptions Davis brought with him as a young man from St. Louis, if he was to be a notable force in the New York jazz scene, he would have to play by the game of his masters—a game governed by drugs first and women second. In his book *Jazz Myth and Religion,* Neil Leonard examines the pseudoprophet role many jazz musicians assumed with their fans. In light of the charisma many of them possessed along with their remarkable talent, jazz musicians were models to emulate on the bandstand and off. But Leonard points out how tragic this was with a figure as self-destructive as Parker: "For many neophytes there seemed little reason to stay straight when all the hip people were high. What inducement was there for the anxious novice not to indulge? And if Charlie Parker could illuminate the jazz world with the help of, or despite, his habit, why couldn't his eager admirers?" [37]

However, Davis's christening into the world of drugs is not initiated by Parker. Rather, Davis is driven to it after he is forced to leave Paris and Juliette Greco, a French girl who hardly speaks English but is the first woman Davis feels he ever really loves: "I was so depressed when I got back, that before I knew it, I had a heroin habit that took me four years to kick and I found myself for the first time out of control" (127).

The love of a woman leads Davis into his addiction, but it is at the urgings of various men, musicians and otherwise, that he ultimately tries to kick his habit. Most of his musician friends are as heavily into drugs as Davis is. But Gil Evans is able to reach Davis in a way that others have not, and he serves as means of checks and balances when Davis's life teetered out of control: "I realized that a person is lucky if he's got one soldier or Gil Evans in his life, someone close enough to you to pull your coattail when something's going wrong. Because who knows what I would have done or become if I hadn't had someone like Gil to remind me? Deep down inside, I have always been like that when I kicked my habit" (184).

Similarly, Davis's love for boxing and his admiration for Sugar Ray Robinson also inspire him to try to stay clean. Boxing is as much a boy's club as jazz, and Davis sees many similarities between the two forms in that "you've got to first learn how to be cool and let whatever happens— both in music and boxing—happen." (182).

Some of the most notorious passages from Davis's biography are his treatises on his relationships with women and why he often prefers white women to blacks. Davis's attitude toward black women seems to reflect a fear or powerlessness in relation to them. He resents their need to "be in control, them old-timey ones or those ones who are deep into their careers." Such women cannot allow an artist the personal space and freedom he apparently needs to be creative. In many senses, Davis echoes the same sentiment that Mingus does when he speaks of musicians as pimps. He tries to make the case that an artist, whether black or white, needs a woman who can "respect when he has to be creative. White women have been around artists a long time and understand the importance of what art does in society. So black women got a lot of catching up to do in that area" (402).

Artist or not, Davis falls prey to the common stereotype of black men who fear domination from black women. Seeking an escape from his own ambivalence with his blackness, Davis shares Mingus's fascination with the social significance of "whiteness." In his numerous encounters with the police and other authority figures, Davis often blames these incidents on the presumption that he is a "black nigger with a fine ass white woman." He seldom accedes that these clashes could be purely due to his own arrogance and defiance, which he admits to throughout the text.

The broad appeal of Davis as a legendary figure surpasses the considerable musical contributions he made to the jazz world. Rather, the core of this appeal arises from his unique and unequaled challenges to black masculinity, which could be viewed as empowering to a relatively insightful few but contrived and convoluted to the rest. According to Greg Tate, "The power of a Miles Davis was that he always seemed to be waving back from the other side of Black culture's transcendable horizon, from the post-liberated side of Black potentiality. That other shore was not emblematic of emancipation. What was over there was freedom from fear of a Black romantic imagination."[38]

The contradictions and brilliant innovations of jazz represent perhaps the most full-scale unleashing of the black romantic imagination the country has ever witnessed. Mingus's and Davis's biographies record their valiant attempts to revise black masculinity from their own experiences, needs, and abilities. Given the limited confines in which black creative expression has had to operate throughout the centuries, it is of little wonder that African Americans have so fiercely scrambled to keep their momentous contributions to American culture within their grasps. As a people, we value "the real" and test the authenticity of all things that attempt to approximate or typify the "black experience." But the images of black masculinity that circulate within these cultural arenas symbolize a stock prerequisite of the trade and allow for few radical deviations from the norm that fans come to anticipate and demand. These constructs remain consistent and are woven into the very fabric of the culture—they amount to the very name of the game. Thus, it is difficult to imagine a white woman as a jazz musician. And although the enigma of Dennis Rodman may incite a ripple of speculation and attention in the NBA, this will do little to change the association of a certain construction of black masculinity with basketball.

The odious *Titan arum* grows a remarkable four to six inches every day. Being the largest flower in the world, the *Titan* is a predictable draw. However, people are not as interested in the flower's girth as they are in its pugnacious smell, which has resulted in the plant's moniker—the corpse flower. Similarly, we can also call into question the appeal of the NBA, a pricey New York jazz club, or even hip hop aimed at a heterogenous mass market. Certainly, some skill is on display in the name of competition or creative expression. However, while the contributions of blacks to the world of athletics and music may be widely celebrated, we must start to think more carefully and deliberately about the price we pay for such accolades. I have to wonder what imaginative associations people make when they stand in the shadows of the *Titan arum,* which reeks of death.

Human beings cannot help but operate according to their expectations and precedents. While we logically understand that black folks are human beings and ought to be treated equally as such, it takes generations for many of us to internalize that thought and act upon it. Thus, in some facet of the mind, the *Titan's* audience probably cannot identify this rancid enormity as a flower, something sweet and delicate that can be handled and arranged in a vase or pinned to a lapel. Dwarfed by its stature and enveloped by its smell, people standing before the *Titan arum* may feel they are in the presence of a god, or possibly a monster.

NOTES

1. Frank Conroy, "Stop Nitpicking a Genius," *New York Times Magazine,* June 25, 1995, 28, 54; Tricia Rose, *Black Noise: Rap Music and Black Culture in Contemporary America* (Middletown, Conn.: Wesleyan University Press, 1994), 24.

2. Greg Tate, "Preface to a One-Hundred-and-Eighty-Volume Patricide Note: Yet Another Few Thousand Words on the Death of Miles Davis and the Problem of the Black Male Genius," in *Black Popular Culture,* a Project by Michele Wallace, ed. Gina Dent (Seattle: Bay Press, 1992), 243.

3. Pearle Cleage, *Deals with the Devil and Other Reasons to Riot* (New York: (Ballantine, 1993).

4. Stuart Hall, "What Is This 'Black' in Black Popular Culture," in *Stuart Hall, Critical Dialogues in Cultural Studies,* ed. David Morley and Kuan-Hsing Chen (New York: Routledge, 1996), 467.

5. Phil Rubio, "Crossover Dreams," *Race Traitor,* ed. Noel Ignatiev and John Garvey (New York: Routledge, 1996), 151.

6. Grover Sales, *Jazz: America's Classical Music* (New York: Da Capo Press, 1992), 35; Gene Lees, *Cats of Any Color: Jazz in Black and White* (New York: Oxford University Press, 1995).

7. Walter Benn Michaels, "The No-Drop Rule," in *Identities,* ed. Kwame Anthony Appiah and Henry Louis Gates Jr. (Chicago: University of Chicago Press, 1995), 411.

8. LeRoi Jones, *Blues People* (New York: Morrow Quill, 1963), 153.

9. Rubio, "Crossover Dreams," 153.

10. Robyn Wiegmann, *American Anatomies: Theorizing Race and Gender* (Durham, N.C.: Duke University Press, 1995), 85.

11. Andrew Ross, "Hip and the Long Front of Color," in *No Respect: Intellectuals and Popular Culture* (New York: Routledge, 1989), 85.

12. bell hooks, *Black Looks: Race and Representation* (Boston: South End Press, 1992), 34.

13. Eldridge Cleaver, *Soul on Ice* (NY: McGrew Hill, 1968).

14. Curt Sachs, *Rhythm and Tempo: A Study in Music History* (New York: Columbia University Press, 1959), 38.

15. Tony Scherman, "What Is Jazz? An Interview with Wynton Marsalis," *American Heritage,* October 1995. See also Frank Kofsky, *Black Nationalism and the Revolution in Music* (New York: Pathfinder Press; 1970), 123–39.

16. Jones, *Blues People,* 153.

17. Michele Wallace, *Black Macho and the Myth of the Superwoman* (New York: Dial Press, 1978), 39.

18. Gene Santoro, *Dancing in Your Head: Jazz, Blues, and Beyond* (New York: Oxford University Press, 1994).

19. Henry A. Giroux, *Fugitive Cultures: Race, Violence, and Youth* (New York: Routledge, 1996), 32.

20. Tate, "Preface," 245.

21. Herman Gray, "Black Masculinity and Visual Culture," *Callaloo* 18, no. 2 (1995): 401–5.

22. Burton Peretti, *The Creation of Jazz: Music, Race and Culture in North America* (Urbana: University of Illinois Press, 1992) 35–36.

23. Neil Leonard, *Jazz Myth and Religion* (New York: Oxford University Press, 1987), 24.

24. Robert Farris Thompson, *Flash of the Spirit* (New York: Random House; 1983), 104.

25. Leonard *Jazz Myth and Religion*, 61.

26. Ibid., 59.

27. Ibid.

28. Stephen Longstreet, *Sportin' House: New Orleans and the Jazz Story* (Los Angeles: Sherbourne Press, 1965), 195.

29. Kathy Ogren, *The Jazz Revolution: Twenties America and the Meaning of Jazz* (New York: Oxford University Press, 1989), 3.

30. Peretti, *The Creation of Jazz*, 35–36.

31. Charles Mingus, *Beneath the Underdog* (New York: Penguin Books, 1980), 55. Hereafter cited in the text by page number.

32. Calvin C. Hernton, *Sex and Racism in America* (New York: Grove Press, 1965), 24.

33. "Subsoil of Black Music," *Library Journal* 96 (August 1971): 2512.

34. Geoffrey Wolf, "Man with a Bass," *Newsweek,* May 17, 1971, 110.

35. *The Irigaray Reader,* ed. Margaret Whitford, (Cambridge: Blackwell Publishers, 1991), 58.

36. Miles Davis with Quincy Troupe, *Miles* (New York: Simon and Schuster, 1989), 7. Hereafter cited in the text by page number.

37. Leonard, *Jazz Myth and Religion*, 109.

38. Tate, "Preface," 245.

15

Stoned Soul Picnic

Alvin Ailey and the Struggle to Define
Official Black Culture

Thomas DeFrantz

STONE PONY: *Stand with a proud, wide foot stance. Hold your hands in fists at your waist, elbows to the back. Without moving your feet, turn your trunk to one side and push your weight forward. Swing your fists forward on the One. Snap your fingers as they release back on the Two. Let your back bone slip. Push forward again on the Three. Release the swing, snap, and slip on the Four, while simultaneously shifting your torso to face the other side. Repeat the four-count phrase with as much soul as you got.*

■ ■ ■

Choreographer Alvin Ailey often used contemporary social dance steps in his ballets, and the dance we used to call the stone pony (he called it the "hesitation" in his choreographic notes) provided the opening movement image for his ballet *Quintet*. First shown August 28, 1968, at the Edinburgh Festival in Scotland, *Quintet* gained prominence as the sole new offering from Ailey in his company's first Broadway season, January 1969. Before we try to unpack the soul step from its setting on the Broadway stage, where it was performed by five glamour-puss divas in blonde wigs and high heels, let's back up to consider Ailey's ascendancy as the postwar and civil rights eras' leading exponent of modern dance in the African American grain.

Born January 5, 1931, the only child of working-class parents who separated when he was an infant, Ailey suffered a difficult, transient childhood, moving with his mother from town to town and relative to relative. Strictly segregated life in Depression-era Texas offered a hostile environment for African Americans and nurtured a fear and mistrust of whites, Ailey later recalled; this background also created a fierce pride in black social institutions, including the church and the jook joints that figure prominently in his later work. In 1942 Ailey moved with his mother to Los Angeles, where his interest in concert dance was sparked by high-school excursions to the ballet and Katherine Dunham's 1945 "Tropical Revue" (DeFrantz 1995).

Ailey's soul vibrated in response to Dunham's theater, and he later credited the Dunham company as a guiding inspiration for his own. Dunham created dance scenarios resonant with social practice she observed as a cultural anthropologist in the Caribbean Islands. Although she achieved her greatest performing success within the commercial arenas of Broadway and Hollywood, she also wrote and lectured widely and developed a dance technique built upon aesthetic features of African movement retentions visible in the Americas. Ailey eventually established the Dunham Technique as a standard form taught at his school. For his own training, however, Ailey turned to dance only when a high-school classmate introduced him to Lester Horton's flamboyantly theatrical studio in 1949.

When Ailey began making dances in the 1950s, his classroom dance training had been acquired exclusively from the Lester Horton Dance Theatre School in West Hollywood, California. Modern dance was still in its first American generation, and Horton and his colleagues taught an idiosyncratic and experimental technique assembled from movement ideas representing a range of cultures: East and West Indian, African, American, Japanese, Native American, and Mexican. Horton taught his dancers to value emotional expressivity over strict dance technique, a strategy that diverted attention from the historical pedigree of specific dances and toward the overall sensory effect dance could have on its audience.

Horton, a white man from Indianapolis, Indiana, also enticed Ailey with his utopian vision of a multicultural dance melting pot. Horton's dancers included African Americans James Truitte, Don Martin, and Carmen de Lavallade; white dancers Bella Lewitzky and Joyce Trisler; and Japanese dancer Misaye Kawasumi. In later years, the Chinese American critic Frank Eng was Horton's lover. Even as he indulged personal and highly imprecise readings of non-Western dance forms, Horton offered his company the possibility of seeing beyond easy constructions of race. Ailey gravitated to this vision of personal and sexual liberation. In following Horton, Ailey conceived theatrical dance as the formalized display of movement narrative tempered by lighting, costuming, and the unique emotional presence—soul, if you will—of the dancer.

Ailey moved to New York in 1954 to appear with partner Carmen de Lavallade in the crudely stereotyped Broadway musical *House of Flowers*. Adapted from a Truman Capote short story, the show's exoticized libretto offered black dancers a host of familiar naive-primitive roles, framed by a tale of rival bordellos and mercenary intrigue. Largely popular with audiences because of its host of "wild, grotesque, animalistic" dance numbers created by George Balanchine and Herbert Ross, *House of Flowers* introduced Ailey to the New York dance scene as part of the titillating assortment of black bodies enacting racial stereotypes for mostly white audiences (Atkinson 1954, 7).

Ailey found the New York dance community to be remarkably fluid and available, especially to handsome young men willing to "play black" in a limited range of ethnic roles. He danced in several Broadway musicals and fulfilled his aspirations to be known as a professional dancer, but found he wanted to continue the creative work he had begun at the Horton school. While dancing in the Broadway musical *Jamaica,* Ailey gathered a group of dancers to fill an afternoon concert slot at the 92nd Street YM-YWHA on March 30, 1958, the premiere performance of the Alvin Ailey American Dance Theater.

Ailey's personal magnetism, combined with the artistic panache of his colleagues, brought terrific reviews and overwhelming audience response. Twenty-eight African American dancers and a number of musicians participated in the debut concert Ailey shared with choreographer Ernest Parham, with headlining guest artist Talley Beatty performing the role of Icarus in Parham's *Trajectories*. The unprecedented scale and ambition of the program arranged by Ailey and Parham suggested a strategic expropriation of the Kaufmann Concert Hall to confirm, in a single performance, the undeniable range of facility attainable by the black body in concert dance.

This thumbnail biography provides a map to understanding who Ailey was when he began making dances in 1958. His personal circumstances are all the more important when we realize that Ailey ultimately created a body of dance works that shaped African American participation in modern dance during the thirty-year period before his death in 1989. His company operations also defined a paradigmatic performance style that became the standard of dance in the African American grain from the early 1960s until the present. Working in a variety of dance styles and movement vocabularies, Ailey indelibly wrote soul onto the concert dance menu.

Ailey's Dances

Ailey's work began in the 1950s, an era of cultural assimilation, and his earliest dances embrace a range of thematic and movement vocabularies. He hoped to attract integrated audiences willing to question prevalent racial stereotypes surrounding black dancers in modern dance. Among these early works, *Mourning Morning* (1954) drew on characters and situations from plays by Tennessee Williams, while *Knoxville: Summer of 1915* (1961) built upon James Agee's libretto and Samuel Barber's music. The intimation that black bodies could inhabit white literature on public stages disturbed dominant stereotypical assumptions, but most audiences received these dances poorly. Ailey's largest success built upon lingering minstrel-era personae that tied black bodies to work songs, spirituals, the blues, and jazz. For example, the "barrelhouse" setting of Ailey's 1958 masterpiece *Blues Suite* played directly into traditional stereotyping of the black body as at once morally corrupt and titillating. As in *House of Flowers*, the women in *Blues Suite* portrayed hookers, and the men, their eager clients.

Ailey's choreography combined movements from several disciplines, echoing a layered approach to art-making distinctive to African diaspora culture. *Blues Suite* contains sections of early twentieth-century social dance, Horton dance technique, Jack Cole–inspired jazz dance, and ballet partnering. But audiences responded most immediately to Ailey's characters and their familiar milieu. Southern blacks recognized the truthful depiction of archetypal, down-home personalities, while white audiences appreciated the familiar spectacle of black bodies clowning and cavorting over money and sex (DeFrantz 1996).

This tension between familiar black archetypes and the transcendent dance invention routinely achieved by Ailey and his collaborators set a new standard for concert dance in the African American grain. Ailey allowed his dancers to bring themselves into their stage work—a profound shift from the blatantly stereotyped behavior solicited from Negro artists before the post-war era. Ailey and his contemporaries revised the minstrel stereotypes, investing them with personal truths drawn from their own experiences. Aided by the nationalistic reassessments of the civil rights era, Ailey fostered an important pedagogical shift that encouraged the enactment of core black performance strategies in concert dance. These strategies include subversion, secrecy, rupture, participation, dynamic interaction, and, above all, the pleasure of rhythmic musicality.

Ailey created his company with three goals in mind: to employ the scores of excellent black dancers in New York who had no performing homes; to create a repertory company that could perform both modern dance classics and new works by Ailey and other young choreographers; and to give artistic voice to African American experience in terms of concert dance. His largest success came in this last goal, as early performances of *Blues Suite* and *Revelations* (1960) established the Alvin Ailey American Dance Theater as the foremost dance interpreter of African American experience. While a concert tradition of dancing to sacred black music stretched back to the 1920s, when modern dancers Helen Tamiris, Hemsley Winfield, and Edna Guy all made pieces called "Negro Spirituals," *Revelations* eclipsed these earlier attempts and quickly became the company's signature ballet.

But Ailey always wanted "to take it to the wall," as he often said. He integrated his company within its first five years, adding Asian and white dancers into the multitoned African American mix. Though the company always featured its African American artists, through integration Ailey sought to subvert the critical eye that cannot see beyond race. "Some people like to put black people in a box. For example, when we first went to Europe [in 1964], many said: oh look at those black people do this and that. It was as though only black people could move in certain ways, and black people were limited to certain movements. I want people to see us as people. Further I think that having people of all colors and all cultures somewhat universalizes the material. It takes it out of the color bag, out of the race bag; it makes it easier to see simply as art" (Ailey 1989, 9).

Adding dancers unfamiliar with core structures of black social dance meant distilling those structures into abstract movements. In his choreography, Ailey attempted to locate an essence of black social dance style that complemented the various techniques his dancers studied. The resulting juxtaposition of styles—social dance followed by classical ballet, Horton-technique movements in the middle of Graham phasing, and so on—formed the crux of a hybrid aesthetic labeled "black dance."

But how did Ailey come to stand for "black dance"? And how did his interracial company maintain a status as the "official" bearer of black modern dance in the 1960s? The answer to these questions lies in the strategies of cultural intervention Ailey enacted to bring dance to the widest public possible. The Ailey company toured like mad. In its earliest years, the company spent much time on the road, bringing dance to people who had never heard of concert performance. This expanding audience of African Americans provided the wellspring of support essential to the Ailey enterprise. As Ailey noted, "We're giving the public the sense that dance in particular and the arts in general are important parts of their soul, especially to us black people. Our poetry, our music, and our dance have been able to sustain and fill spirit"(Ailey 1989, 9).

The Ailey company established its vast international reputation through a series of tours begun in 1962. A highly publicized and successful four-month engagement in Southeast Asia and Australia sponsored by the International Exchange Program under the Kennedy Administration established a pattern of performance in foreign countries continued by a trip to Rio de Janeiro (1963); a European tour including London, Hamburg, and Paris (1964); an engagement at the World Festival of Negro Arts in Dakar, Senegal (1966); a second, sixteen-week European tour including the Holland Festival in Amsterdam (1967); a visit to Israel (August 1967); a U.S. State Department–sponsored nine-nation tour of Africa (1967); and performance at the Edinburgh Festival (1968). To understand how large Ailey's international presence loomed throughout the 1960s, consider the May 1968 *Dance Magazine* layout that featured Ailey's face blown up across a map of Africa. Of course, there was no map with Ailey's image towering over Europe after his tours there.

Cast by the U.S. government as the cultural arbiter of Negro experience in dance, Ailey strengthened his choreographic language to revise lingering minstrel imagery. One of Ailey's favorite themes during this period was to expose the brutal ambivalence of the black body on public stages. *Quintet,* for example, describes the tension between the public performance of glamour, as in a Motown girl group, and the private despair and loneliness held by offstage life.

Quintet

Ailey set *Quintet* to six soul-inspired songs from Laura Nyro's album *Eli and the Thirteenth Confession*. Finished quickly during the company's one-week stay in Scotland (Goodwin 1968, 23; Latham 1973, 621), the dance remained in the company's repertoire for two years. A favorite among general audiences, and especially the college audiences the Ailey company taught in lecture-demonstration residencies, *Quintet* features five red-lamé-clad glamour dollies, armed with smart red pumps, over-done makeup, and Hollywood-style blonde wigs.

The curtain rises to reveal five women posed identically in a tableau of defiant Motown glamour. The women slowly lower their arms and begin doing the stone pony while lipsynching "Stoned Soul Picnic." Ailey doubles the minstrel imagery: blonde black women dance to white blues singing. The dance continues with flagrant juxtapositions of bold, streetcorner-style movements to small, glamorous struts and shimmies. The women perform a catalogue of contemporary social dances and connecting material, arranged by Ailey to follow the contours of Nyro's music closely. As the recorded singers rise to a climactic high pitch, the dancers execute expansive turns across the stage, their arms circling overhead and down again in a brittle staccato rhythm that echoes the rock drumbeat. Mysteriously, dancers drop out of formation one at a time to move in anguish to some inaudible, private score. The number ends with the women once again posed luxuriously across the stage, knees bent deeply with arms raised overhead, approximating an allure of feminized celebrity.

Quintet continues through five more sections, roughly one solo for each woman, in which the wigs, dresses, and shoes come off and the performers reveal a private anguish hidden behind their show-business drag. Recorded applause serves as a bridge between dances, satirically underscoring an oversized popularity of Ailey's mythic girl-group. When the dancers finally return, all dolled up, to repeat the opening stone pony dance movements, the thrill of glamour is gone. The women come back steely, angry, defiant, and forever fragmented.

In the dance's third selection, "Poverty Train," the soloist removes her dress to reveal a nondescript grey slip, (Goodwin 1968, 25). She angrily throws the high-heeled shoes binding her feet offstage; she drops her gown and, exasperated, kicks it away. The ensuing dance gently mirrors Nyro's shifting musical moods: slow-motion contractions and

15.1. "Quintet," members of the Alvin Ailey American Dance Theater. Photograph © Jack Mitchell.

rises to balance during out-of-tempo interludes; sweeping polyrhythmic swaggers to the hesitations of six/eight drumming in bluesy verses; repeated short phrases of two-count duration to a prominent rhythm-section lick. Toward the end of the solo the dancer falls to the floor, rolls toward the audience, and rises to hide her face in her curled right arm while pushing away with her outstretched left hand. The image of constraint is followed by a slow-motion rise to a one-legged balance, her arms and neck stretched beseechingly upwards. The dance ends when she collapses to the floor and pounds her fist, feebly, as Nyro moans the root of the problem: "Money." Taped applause sounds. Surprised, the woman suddenly notices her audience, gathers her gown from the floor, and exits, dazed, distracted, and wary.

223

In *Quintet*, Ailey reverses the framing device of *Blues Suite*, impli-
cating his audience in the false construction of celebrity. Where *Blues
Suite* suggested how social despair could be transformed into ebullient
social dance, the later work aligns public performance with private
sorrow. But by showcasing an idealized femininity, *Quintet* also exploits
glamour and the male gaze. The dance allows its women to be viewed
as fantasy objects: naive and hysterical "offstage," unresolved and passive "onstage." The binary construction is at once obvious and reduc-
tive.

Quintet became the first in a line of ballets exploring the intense
private anguish lurking behind a public façade of glamorous celebrity.
Among later works, *Flowers* (1971) chronicled the fame and tragic death
of singer Janis Joplin; *The Mooche* (1974) explored the persistence of
entertainers Florence Mills, Marie Bryant, Mahalia Jackson, and Bessie
Smith; and *For Bird with Love* (1984) built upon events in the life of
saxophonist Charlie Parker. The theme obviously spoke to Ailey's situation as a primary exponent of African American modes of concert
dance: feted by occasional government sponsorship, critical accolades,
and popular notoriety, Ailey faced constant financial hardship, inadequate business management, and a lingering private loneliness. Like
the other ballets created to this theme, *Quintet* offered no easy answers
to the convergence of private and public personae; its circular construction suggested instead an intractable association of celebrity and isolation.

Reflecting a Spectrum of Experience

Ailey's celebrity as the leading exponent of black concert dance advanced
throughout the 1960s and 1970s. He continuously spoke out for increased opportunities for African Americans in concert dance, and he
geared his company policies specifically to the canonization of an African American concert dance experience. In January 1969, just eight
months before Arthur Mitchell and Karl Shook founded Dance Theatre
of Harlem, Ailey wrote of founding the "Black American Ballet," a large
company of dancers, singers, and musicians exclusively devoted to the
cultural heritage of black America. He made plans for a three-act ballet
based on the life of Malcolm X; a danced tribute to Langston Hughes;
and a Duke Ellington festival, finally realized at the nation's bicentennial

in 1976. He wrote, "My greatest wish is for the Black American dancer to enter, through the front door, the mainstream of American dance" (Ailey 1969).

For Ailey, entering the concert dance mainstream through the front door meant bringing the healing power of black soul onto the concert stage. He understood social dance to be the site of pleasure and body knowledge, a "high" form of expression for many African Americans. In his dances, he situated soul proudly alongside classical ballet and modern dance forms, engendering a hybrid aesthetic with deep ties to African American cultural practices.

Ailey's legacy of soul hybridity now reaches firmly into neo-classical ballet, in the dances of Ulysses Dove, William Forsythe, and Twyla Tharp; and the postmodern dance styles of Donald Byrd, Garth Fagan, Bill T. Jones, and Jawole Willa Jo Zollar. Following Ailey, each of these choreographers has transformed black social dance into concert performance, connecting soul to a widening international mainstream of cultural production.

Ailey understood that soul pleasure is located in ties to the historical, the political, the subversively humorous, and the familiar. Black pleasure is in all of these, and seldom so gracefully realized as in dance.

BIBLIOGRAPHY

Ailey, Alvin. 1968. "African Odyssey; Two Months, Twelve Dancers, Nine Countries," *Dance Magazine,* May, 50.

———. 1969. Program Notes, Alvin Ailey American Dance Theater, Brooklyn Academy of Music.

———. 1989. "Alvin Ailey." In *Black Visions '89,* Tweed Gallery Exhibition Catalog, 8–9.

Ailey, Alvin, with A. Peter Bailey. 1995. *Revelations: The Autobiography of Alvin Ailey.* New York: Birch Lane Press.

Atkinson, Brooks. 1954. "Theatre: Truman Capote's Musical." *New York Times,* December 31, 1954, 11.

Barnes, Clive. 1969. "Ailey and Troupe in Triumph; Start Run on Broadway after a Decade Away." *New York Times,* January 28, 1969.

DeFrantz, Thomas. 1995. "Alvin Ailey." In *Encyclopedia of African American Culture and History.* New York: Oxford University Press.

———. 1996. "Simmering Passivity: The Black Male Body in Concert Dance." In *Moving Words,* ed. Gay Morris. New York: Routledge.

Goldner, Nancy. 1969. "Alvin Ailey's American Dance Theatre, Billy Rose Theatre, N.Y., Jan. 27–Feb. 1." *Dance News* March, 10.

Goodman, Saul. 1958. "Brief Biographies: Alvin Ailey." *Dance Magazine,* December, 70–71.

Goodwin, Noel. 1968. "Black Octave: Eight New Works from Alvin Ailey's American Dance Theater at the Edinburgh Festival, August 1968." *Dance and Dancers,* October, 23–30.

Latham, Jacqueline Quinn. 1973. "A Biographical Study of the Lives and Contributions of Two Selected Contemporary Black Male Dance Artists—Arthur Mitchell and Alvin Ailey." Ph.D. dissertation, Texas Women's University.

Marks, Marcia. 1969. "The Alvin Ailey American Dance Theater, Billy Rose Theatre, January 27–February 1, 1969." *Dance Magazine* March, 92.

McDonagh, Don. 1976. "Alvin Ailey." In *The Complete Guide to Modern Dance.* Garden City, N.Y.: Doubleday, 125–132.

Stoop, Norma McLain. 1971. "Of Time and Alvin Ailey: A Commodity the Head of the Alvin Ailey American Dance Theater Almost Always Lacks." *Dance Magazine,* December, 28–32.

Washington, Ernest L., ed. 1990. "Alvin Ailey: The Man and His Contributions." *Talking Drums! The Journal of Black Dance* 1, no. 4 (May).

16

The Legend of Soul

Long Live Curtis Mayfield!

Michael A. Gonzales

Sometimes, when I'm sitting in my boy's ride listening to the radio or flipping stations in my own book-cluttered office, I remind myself of one of those cranky old bastards lounging in some ghetto barbershop, inhaling on filterless Camels and screaming their aged opinions as though they were carved in Moses's tablets.[1] "They don't make soul music like they used to," I'm tempted to yell, over the latest sample-heavy Puffy/ Bad Boy remix blaring from the bleak landscape known as urban radio. Yet, unlike Nelson George suggested in his groundbreaking text *The Death of Rhythm and Blues,* I do not feel as though the music that was the soundtrack of my youth (until I became a traitor to race and began jamming to Led Zeppelin instead of Teddy Pendergrass) has been gunned down in some sleazy hotel parking lot like Sam Cooke, blood flowing into the gutters of urban radio. Rather, I think the music is in the process of aural morphing. Still, in my mind it's a shame when I check out videos on MTV and discover that so-called alternative groups like Nirvana, Soundgarden, Smashing Pumpkins, and Stone Temple Pilots have more of a funk-laced soulful Kool-Aid than black artists (Xscape, SWV, H-Town, or Silk) bopping dance electric style on B.E.T. "Who stole the soul?" is no longer the question, because it seems like the postmod brothers and sisters in the band merely gave it away.

Although much can be blamed on the lack of music education departments in city schools due to budget cuts, the limited number of spaces for young musicians to perfect their budding skills, and the lack of imagination on the part of record company A & R persons, still I wonder if the kids producing these lackluster sounds have ever bothered to study any records prior to the birth of New Jack Swing movement founded by Teddy Riley.

When I listen to a young artist like D'Angelo, whose *Brown Sugar* disc was one of the best albums of 1996, I can hear that this son of a preacherman has absorbed more than the flavor of his heroes Marvin Gaye, Curtis Mayfield, Isaac Hayes, Stevie Wonder, and Prince. Chilling in his downsouth bedroom as a teenager, D'Angelo studied these soul dudes like they were a science project in an attempt to figure out what to do next. Like a young painter staring in amazement at the canvases of Picasso or a novice writer reading the urban gospels according to James Baldwin or Iceberg Slim, D'Angelo fully understood that it was necessary for him to study the masters of soul if he wanted to create true soul music for a new generation.

But rewinding blaxploitation to da future, summer of 1972: one year after the shattered glass, shotgun blast of a bad mutha—"shut ya mouth"—known as John Shaft (wah-wah boppin' down forty-deuce to Isaac Hayes's soulful score) and six years before the pimp swagger of *The Mack* came creeping across da wrong side of those Oaktown tracks, the Afro-sheened/platform-heeled citizens of Black Metropolis were silently waiting to inhale some brand new funk.

In the village of Harlem, where my nine-year-old self dwelled, Sugar Hill was alive with the ghettocentric sounds of Curtis Mayfield's *Superfly* soundtrack 8-track bumping on da ave. Leaning from the sooty fifth-floor window in my daddy's apartment, my youthful eyes observed the neighborhood pimps (peacock-feathered hats, loud suits screaming) shining their boss Cadillacs—"hog" for its size and the amount of fuel it used—as Mayfield's "Freddie's Dead" came wailing from ebony car speakers. My innocent eyes scoped zombie-nodding King Heroin roaring down the block as Frankie ("Hollywood") Crocker's smooth, FM-radio voice introduced the brutal beats of "Pusherman" onto da chocolate city airwaves.

Opening on a humid summer afternoon at the Lowes' Victoria, a Harlem moviehouse a few feet from the neon-bright Apollo lights, the first showing of *Superfly* attracted the attention of the neighborhood Willie Dynamites with their stables in tow and hoodrat niggas dealing blow. Sitting in the darkened theater, baby-oiled hands clapped loudly as "Little Child Running Wild" erupted from the Victoria's audio system and a raven's-eye view of gritty Seventh Avenue was projected onto the aged screen.

Directed by Gordon Parks, Jr., whose father had helped define the genre of flaired pants flamboyance with the movie *Shaft*, *Superfly* introduced Young blood Priest (slick-haired, light-skinned actor Ron O'Neal), a Harlem cocaine dealer on a mission to get outta the drug game and flee to Europe with his sweet chocolate mama hanging onto his crushed-velvet sleeves. Yet, as actor Keenan Ivory Wayans would later say in his 1988 satire of the genre *I'm Gonna Git You Sucka*, "What's a hero without a soundtrack?" While Priest snorts blow from a small spoon that dangles from his neck, makes sweet love to his woman in the lingering bathtub scene, and hangs in the grand-styled club with the other midnight players "in the life," Curtis Mayfield's soundtrack becomes the inner voice of the character, giving him a depth beyond cocaine dreams. Darius James, whose book *That's Blaxploitation! Roots of the Baad-Asssss 'Tude* documents this fly film movement, notes that, "*Superfly* would not have become the classic that it is without the music. Gordon Parks, Jr., was a pretty third-rate director, yet Curtis Mayfield's music had a post–civil rights consciousness that really pinpointed what the reality of the characters in that so-called criminal subculture really believed." [2]

Much has changed in the twenty-eight years since the release of *Superfly*. Most important is the fact that Curtis Mayfield, whose innovative works influenced black rockers Prince, Lenny Kravitz, and former Living Colour guitarist Vernon Reid, as well as countless rappers, will never be able to play the guitar again. When I interviewed Curtis at his Atlanta home in 1996, he said, in hushed tones, "The guitar meant so much more than I could ever really express. Me and my axe, we slept together. I'd wake up out of the night and write songs. The guitar, while I never gave him or her a name, was like my other self. It would dictate to me as much as I would dictate to it. The guitar was like my twin."

In the summer of 1990 Curtis Mayfield was scheduled to perform two free concerts in the New York area. The first was part of the Central Park Summer Stage showcases, which proved to be a major event. "It was like a love fest," remembers bassist Jared Nickerson, whose group J.J. Jumpers opened for Curtis. "It was the largest turnout Central Park had ever had, with over eight thousand people. What surprised my group was what a regular cat Curtis proved to be. My guitar player had broken his strap before the show and was in shock when Curtis lent him his own. Sometimes artists who are legends can be a little seclusive, but Curtis was very normal."

The second appearance was in the East Flatbush section of Brooklyn, two months later. "I had spoken with him a few hours before the show," recalls his son Todd Mayfield, who runs the Curtom record label and studios. "I asked him what the weather was like and reminded him that if it happened to rain that evening he would still be paid." Pausing, as if still haunted by the reassuring words of his father, Todd says, "He said that the sky was overcast, but he didn't think it would rain."

Yet, in one of those nightmarish scenarios that would have a lesser mortal questioning the existence of God, tragedy happened the moment Curtis stepped onstage in Brooklyn's Wingate Park. Although it hadn't begun to rain, a freak windstorm knocked down a lighting tower, which fell on Curtis. Although he has been operated on numerous times and has undergone intensive therapy, the guitar strummin' brother man will remain paralyzed for the rest of his life. "The courage that I have is something that started with me years ago," he says. "Lots of people say, 'Well, you're still here, it must be for a reason,' but it's my children, my contribution [to music] and just the longevity I've had that gives me a lot of strength. It'll never be the same, but that's not what you expect."

Earlier on this sunny, cool afternoon Todd picks me up from my tacky hotel, which is directly across the street from one of the city's many strip joints—Nickii's V.I.P. From my window I could see honey-colored weave queens and Spandex mamas trooping through the door. Riding down the highway, we pass countless fast-food restaurants with neon hamburgers glowing toward the heavens and small, one-family houses off to the side of the road. Christmas is in two weeks and a few of the homes are covered in multicolored lights. Others have holiday wreaths on the door. I'm always amazed at how commercial Atlanta has become in the last ten years. Still country, just more commercial.

We stop at a red light, Todd's radio on a low buzz. A man wearing a red plaid shirt and black baseball cap stands on the side of the road selling towering Christmas trees. "What do you remember most about Curtis when you were growing up?" I ask. He laughs and says, "One thing about my father was that he loved to cook. Seafood, steaks, whatever. He was always trying to make you fat."

Shortly, passing through a neighborhood not far from Clarke College, I notice blocks of boarded-up two-story apartment houses. "Those used to be the projects," says Todd, "but the state has relocated all the families and they're going to make this property into an Olympic Village." Young black children run in the playground across the street from the decay.

"What was it like for you when you first heard about your dad's accident?" I ask.

Driving onto the smooth, narrow road that leads to Curtis's spacious but modest home in the suburbs, we are surround on both sides by trees whose leaves are just turning brown. Fall seems to come late around these parts. "It was very hard to seeing my father like that," he says. "He was in the hospital in New York for three weeks, then he was flown down here. Sometimes he doesn't push himself as much as he could, but that's understandable. It can be difficult when you gotta learn everything over again."

Before Atlanta became the black musical mecca that it is today, with LaFace Records and So So Def selling millions of discs, Curtis Mayfield decided that Hotlanta—as the Peach State natives affectionately call it— would become his adopted home. (When I asked him later why he moved here, Curtis's reasons proved rather simple: "At least living down here I would be able to find a place to park and I could escape the coldness of Chicago.")

Curtis Mayfield's music is still being played on classic soul stations. It can be heard on two Nike commericals, and new-jack soulster D'Angelo covers the vintage songs "Give Me Your Love" and "The Makings of You" in his live shows. The release of the fifty-one-track box set *People Get Ready! The Curtis Mayfield Story* should have the soul children screaming for joy. Accompanied by exhaustive liner notes by David Nathan, the three-disc set covers Mayfield's career from his early days with the Impressions to his masterful solo projects. This collection should introduce the quiet rage of Mayfield's soulful manifestos to a new generation of cyberfunketters. "When the old folks are debating with the young folks on what was and what is, I just hope that during those moments that someone will pull out a Curtis Mayfield record," Mayfield says, voice as soft as a kitten.

When we first arrive, Todd informs me that his father is on a business call. "Just have a seat in the living room," he says. "He'll be ready for you in a minute." Sitting on the couch in the cluttered living room, next to a polished wooden grandfather clock, is the imposing wheelchair that Curtis used when he accepted his Soul Train Award a few months past. As my eyes roam the room, taking in the three Ernie

Barnes prints (ironically, the print entitled *The Sugar Shack* was also reproduced on the cover of Marvin Gaye's *I Want You* album) hanging on the beige walls, a friendly chow mutt named Kid strolls in, wagging his fluffy tail. As his cold nose sniffs at my faded jeans, polished wing-tip shoes, and black denim jacket, I pet him, careful not to topple the numerous miniature Asian statues on the coffee-table. When Kid becomes bored with me, he walks away and pushes open the door to the study. From my seat I can see the floor-to-ceiling bookcase, and I can hear the soft purr of Curtis's voice.

When Todd first escorts me into Curtis's room, I am struck by how small he looks lying in the hospital bed. Although there are a few pillows to support his frail frame, the bed reminds me of a small prison. "Sit on this side," he motions with his head, indicating that he wants me on the right. During the interview, I am facing both the gray wool blanket that covers his body and the windows. While the sunshine almost blinds me at moments, at others the brilliant rays seem to form a halo over his head.

The first time I ever saw Curtis was that scene in *Superfly* when Priest goes to a restaurant called Scutter's—and there's Curtis onstage, looking like a geek, but with the voice of an angel swimming in an orchestral waterfall. With a scraggly beard, nerdy glasses, a gold silk shirt cuffed at the sleeves, and his Fender guitar hanging down, Curtis sings the spooky electric track "Pusherman." As he said early in our conversation, "The character came to life with me reading the script— Priest being the pusherman. It always sounded funny to me that his name would be Priest." Pausing to catch his breath, he waits a moment before finishing. "And reading what happened to Freddie allowed me to go into depth and make an example of him. While you may not know a lot of pimps and pushermen, you do meet quite a lot of Freddies about the world."

The generation of youth that spent their strobe-light nights dancing to the grooves of Mayfield's own records perhaps didn't know that they were grinding to his songwriting/production skills on Aretha Franklin's soundtrack to *Sparkle,* Gladys Knight and the Pips' noir swooning on the *Claudine* soundtrack, or da gospel wail of the Staple Singers on the *Let's Do It Again* title track. "Sometimes it's more important for a creative person to be able to do for others," he says. "It gives you chance to prove that you're not a fluke as an artist doing your own thing." What composer John Barry was to James Bond films, Curtis Mayfield was to the 1970s black film movement. Curtis, who grew up in the brutal Cabrini-Green housing projects, recalls, "What hooked me to scoring *Claudine* was it was a movie about welfare, young people growing up without a father. I had experienced all of that, recognizing it in my own life more so than *Superfly*. I knew welfare pretty good as a child." Screenwriter Richard Wesley, who penned both *A Piece of the Action* and *Let's Do It Again*, recalls being pleased when director Sidney Poitier informed him that Mayfield was doing the soundtrack for the latter. "It was two or three years after *Superfly* and we hoped that the song would help sell the movie. But when I finally heard the song I didn't think that the lyrics had anything to do with the plot." Still, the record was number one on the Billboard Rhythm and Blues chart for two weeks in November 1975.

Before he went solo in 1970, Curtis was the guiding musical force behind what music critics have dubbed the Chicago Sound. After dropping out of high school in his freshman year, Curtis recorded his first hit single, "For Your Precious Love," with his group the Impressions. Soon after lead singer Jerry Butler left the group (Curtis continued to write his material), the Impressions were dropped by their first label, Vee Jay Records. Within two years the Impressions would be recording classic tracks like the beautiful "People Get Ready" and the motivating "We're a Winner" (a track that came to him one night in a dream and a slogan that would later become his personal motto) for ABC-Paramount. Although his soothing falsetto did not seem to pose a threat, his lyrics were laced with vast thoughts and ideas that went beyond the usual lipstick-covered love songs of other R&B artists. Political before it was chic, the music that Curtis composed was proudly conscious of its blackness. "Whatever you're feeling, whatever your moods, whatever you were trying, whatever you had observed, whatever hurts, whatever made you laugh — all of those things were songs for me." Although the Impressions had often toured the chitlin circuit with Motown acts like the Temptation's and Smoky Robinson and the Miracles, Curtis remembers, "When the Impressions came onstage we didn't have any fancy dance steps and that's not what the audience expected. They knew that with the Impressions all they had to do was listen."

Another aspect that separated Curtis Mayfield from other performers of the time was his keen sense of business, which he proved by holding onto his own publishing (practically unheard of during the 1970s) and beginning the Curtom label (with his then-partner Eddie

Thomas). "I had heard horror stories of songs being sold for twenty-five dollars. Publishers were hitting the lottery off of people's songs. What was considered 'black money' was a Cadillac and $2,500 in fives, tens, and twenties. Everybody has to pay dues, but it doesn't mean you have to be broke."

When he stops talking, Todd asks, "Would you like a drink of water?" Curtis says yes. Todd walks over to the bedside and holds a plastic cup to his father's smooth lips. Curtis sips slowly, then continues. "I had so many long fights with record companies," he laughs. "They couldn't understand it. 'He wants his publishing,' they would say to each other. Like it wasn't mine to have."

Although Curtis has written songs for Major Lance and Gene Chandler, the talented but troubled Donny Hathaway remains one of his favorite artists. "I didn't discover Donny," he grins. "He found me. He had this singing group when he was attending Howard University and he had come to see me perform at a local theater. I've forgotten the name of his group at the time, but Donny later flattered me by asking my permission to call themselves the Mayfield Singers." After dropping out of college, Donny came to Chi-Town to work for Curtom Records with John Pate as an arranger. "Donny was a exceptional piano player as well as an intellectual."

Signed to Atlantic Records in 1970, Hathaway released the surpreme album *Everything Is Everything,* which includes the classic track "The Ghetto" (later remade by Too Short). While working on his second duets album with former classmate Roberta Flack in 1979, Hathaway ended his life by jumping from the fifteenth-floor window of New York City's Essex House Hotel. After the incident, Curtis reached out to Roberta and asked her to sing the theme for the *Piece of the Action* soundtrack, but the pairing didn't work out. She was later replaced by Mavis Staples.

Like Babyface in the 1990s, Curtis Mayfield's songs sounded good with most singers, but when there was a soul sister cooking on the mic it was often a special experience. And, as Aretha Franklin's beautiful, churchy vocals on the *Sparkle* soundtrack prove, sometimes a woman has the power. In the October 1977 issue of *Soul* magazine, Aretha told a writer: "It took us about five days to record the album, because Curtis Mayfield likes to work pretty fast. He pretty much let me have a free hand, but there were a few differences. Our only real disagreement was over one note—he wanted me to sing one way, but I had another way in mind. So we recorded both versions, and what you hear on the album is his concept. He was the producer, so I let him produce."

Curtis remembers these sessions as though they were yesterday. "I had everything prepared in such a manner that when Aretha came in I had my arrangements and all she had to do was sing the songs. And lucky for me they were good songs. We got into little disagreements, but who am I to tell Aretha how to sing. Her voice speaks for itself."

As I stand up to leave, I ask Curtis if he is looking forward to singing again. "Well, yes and no. It's not like it used to be years ago, but for some reason people want to see me do it again." Smiling, his eyes bright and his voice clear, he says, "And I'm going to take the challenge."

NOTES

1. An earlier version of this chapter appeared under the title "Mighty, Mighty" in *Vibe* 4, no. 3 (April 1996): 80–82.

2. Darius James, *That's Blaxploitation! Roots of the Baad-Asssss 'Tude* (New York: St. Martin's Griffin, 1995).

17

The Stigmatization of "Blaxploitation"

RICHARD SIMON

Popular culture has always been where black people theorize blackness in America. It has always constituted the sphere where black people produce narratives of pleasure, oppression, resistance, survival, and heroic performances.

—Manthia Diawara

In May of 1996, after some antsy weeks of waiting, I got to see the movie *Original Gangstas,* starring Fred Williamson, Jim Brown, and Pam Grier, with assists from Richard Roundtree and Ron O'Neal—stars respectively of the black action film classics *Black Caesar, Slaughter, Coffy, Shaft,* and *Superfly*—the *éminences brunes* of blaxploitation.[1] From the first precredit notes of the soundtrack, the movie delivers a densely packed parcel for the viewer to unpack at top speed. At the level of basic narrative, it is almost a textbook example of the genre: cool civilian comes back to town, finds once-tolerable illegality run rampant and cops helpless to stop it or in collusion with it, and—with the help of almost equally cool independent contractors—routs evil and restores order. But what struck me more than the common generic features were the layers of referencing within and outside the movie, thickening and "complexifying"[2] the experience of it for me and, I suspect, for much of the rest of the audience.

A few obvious examples from *Original Gangstas* of how we can read blaxploitation as revalorized through the homage paid to it by other maligned cultural productions. The title comes from the label given both to the stalwarts of the street-gang world which the movie's narrative turns on,[3] as well as to the first generations of rappers by artists who came to prominence a few years later (the temporalities of the music being such that if you were inclined to periodization you could mark several "generations" between, say, Grandmaster Flash and Furious Five's "The Message" in 1982 and, say, Ice-T's 1991 "Home of the Body Bag," not coincidentally off the album *O.G. Original Gangster*). Hip hop artists have acknowledged the influence of blaxploitation movies and their soundtracks (look at Snoop Doggy Dogg's "Doggy Dogg World" video, with its featured Pam Grier cameo, or Ice-T's coproduction of *Pimps, Players & Private Eyes,* a 1991 compilation of songs from the soundtracks of the best- and lesser-known black action films).[4] The soundtrack turns around and gives props to the prop-givers, again and again joining contemporary artists with singers and groups whose glory days overlapped those of blaxploitation. (Makes you wonder why nobody ever thought of pairing the Chi-Lites and the Geto Boys before.) More than a few of the younger artists had laid tracks for the scores of such films as *Straight Outta Brooklyn, Menace II Society, South Central,* and *Boyz N the Hood,* regularly classified under the genre "ghetto film" and called the direct descendants of blaxploitation. (At least one wag thought a better title than *Original Gangstas* would be *Grandpaz N the Hood*.)[5] The central irony of the plot has the middle-aged protagonists warring to the death with the Rebels, a gang they founded back in the day, ostensibly as a sort of home-grown equivalent of the Guardian Angels; the fathers have visited their sins upon the sons, and for that the sons must die. These echoes and ironies are clear even at the axis of reception: reactions in recent years to what gets labeled "rap" in general and "gangsta rap" in particular recapitulate in uncanny ways the critical reception—aesthetic, political, and psychological—of black action films two decades ago.

This chapter has its own roots in another essay where I intended "simply" to analyze the handful of black action films with female protagonists in terms of their engagement with the hard-boiled detective genre.[6] Looking at a wide range of contemporary responses and later surveys and discussions, I saw that the films were almost universally derogated in their heyday (which I expected), but that even the histories written (and rewritten) in the intervening years maintained one or more of the dismissive critiques of that time, distinguished from them largely by the replacement of urgency with the smugness of vindication by

history, or at least the market.[7] The films commonly called "blaxploitation" constitute an anathematized literature in the history of film, not
merely tainted by association in the way, say, the works of Bruckner and
Wagner are for their posthumous Nazi connection, but reviled for their
actual substance, much the way pornography has until recently generally
been abjured as worthy of contemplation for any purpose other than
juridical sanction or moral condemnation. This almost categorical stigmatization of the subgenre[8] convinced me that I had to scrutinize its
premises before I could talk about the films themselves in any responsible
way. In what follows, I first examine these critiques and the arguments
and assumptions on which they rest. I then draw on Stuart Hall's notion
of a diaspora aesthetic to outline what I think might be more useful
tools for engaging not just blaxploitation, but other popular cultural
production maligned by voices of cultural authority *within* marginalized
audiences.[9]

The Political Critique

The critiques of blaxploitation films can be read as turning on the three
axes of complaint mentioned above: the political, the psychological, and
the aesthetic—with some overlap inevitable, but usually focusing on
one. The political critique generally concerns itself with stereotypical
representations and the failure of audiences to recognize their complicity
in perpetuating those images, a failure fully understandable in light of
the internalized self-hatred of oppressed peoples.[10] It points out the
spurious racial awareness of films in which the white villains are portrayed as either gangsters or viciously dishonest cops (as in *Shaft, Superfly, Coffy, and Foxy Brown*), rather than showing the more subtle but
no less evil common racism people are likely to encounter in landlords,
teachers, business owners, government employees, colleagues, and loved
ones. Many of the critiques hold that people are as ill-served by unrealis-
tically powerful representations of black people *(Slaughter, Cleopatra
Jones, Three the Hard Way)* as they were by the shuffling, eye-popping
characters of earlier films.[11] Some critics prop up the straw man of the
black action film and dramatically shoot it down, attempting to reveal
at level after level how it not only lacks a revolutionary consciousness
but promulgates a false one, functioning as a facile catharsis machine
that gives impressionable young black men the illusion that they have,

for example, been a party to trashing the local drug syndicate when what they've done is squander their precious revolutionary energies cheering for ersatz agitprop.[12] And all of them castigate blacks who work on these films for aiding and abetting the enemy: "Those blacks who contribute to the making of these films, no matter how they rationalize it, are guilty of nothing less than treason." [13]

The Psychological Critique

This line of argument also focuses on the dangers of fantasy, but with an eye to how it damages the individual, not the race. Historian William Van Deburg, sounding the only negative note in an otherwise scrupulously sympathetic account of the Black Power Movement, sees in the black action films of the period depictions of an unfortunate phenomenon he calls Super Black:

Individuals [who] had trouble moving beyond the "blacker than thou" stage of their personal odyssey . . . [,] victims of arrested psychological development . . . [who] exhibited certain elements of the Black Power style, but little of its substance . . . [and] displayed many unfavorable character traits. Instead of materially assisting in the decolonization of black minds and the renewal of the black spirit, they provided little more than fantasy release. Stopping short of addressing broader issues, Super Blacks sensationalized and celebrated individual acts of revenge against whites as if, by themselves, these isolated confrontations could bring about group empowerment.[14]

Roy Innes called "the present Black movie phenomenon . . . in its ultimate destruction of the minds of Black youth, . . . potentially far more dangerous than 'step-n-fetch-it' and his lot." [15]

Psychiatrist Alvin Poussaint, known to readers of sitcom credits as advisor to *The Cosby Show,* offers the most detailed analysis.[16] He dismisses arguments that the films might have positive psychological effects on their audiences because they show that black people can beat the system, win against whites, and that "the white man is neither omnipotent nor invisible." Instead, Poussaint cites several studies that claim to show a direct correlation between viewing representations of aggressive behavior and such behavior itself. His argument breaks down to four points: Black teens (he consistently conflates "youth" and "male") use fantasy to deal with or escape from the challenges and terrors of life in the inner city,[17] they need positive role models to channel their fantasizing constructively;[18] these *can* be found in film, but are washed away in the torrent of blaxploitation pictures whose protagonists teach their target audience that the shortest distance between two points is a great crime,[19] as a result, "many black youths have leadership capabilities that are being misdirected and wasted, in part because of the new films."[20]

In face of the claims that blaxploitation pictures exert a pernicious social influence on their audiences, it is worth noting the essential social conservatism of the movies themselves. Nearly every assault on them speaks of the glorification of the criminal and the criminal's way of living, no small testimony that these writers feel free to totalize on the basis of a fraction of the whole. Outside of *Sweet Sweetback's Baadasssss Song, Superfly, The Mack, Black Caesar,* and *Panic up in Harlem,* it is almost impossible to find a widely released black action film with a professional criminal for its protagonist. Far more common is the law enforcement professional or good citizen *in loco legis* whose rule-breaking is plainly presented as end-justified means—long the standard motif for detective and action dramas of any hue: the restoration of order through the suppression of the anti-social, by any means necessary. Virtually all black action films have among their characters pimps, pushers, corrupt public servants, and professional gangsters; but these characters are almost invariably cast in negative light, in a spectrum ranging from buffoonish to heinous.

The weakest link in the reasoning behind the political and psychological critiques is the narrow conceptualization of the role of fantasy and the "bad influence." To deny the appeal of the illicit, not least to the young, whose conceptions of the world are still supple enough to rankle easily at notions of the Law, is effectively to criminalize not only forbidden behavior but the impulse to it. The normative imperative cannot conceive a positive value in fantasy, especially fantasy of breaking rules and inverting norms. I suspect that anyone who has had the good fortune in her youth to break the law and get away with it even momentarily knows the thrill of discovering that the rules that cast so long a shadow can—however briefly, whatever the consequences—be thrown to the wind. For ninety glorious minutes the young woman or man watching the action film can be the Reyne or Roy de la Basoche and experience, however vicariously, the liberatory rush of seeing an oppressive "natural order" utterly disordered. The spectatorial positioning of this filmgoer in relation to the action is less likely to diminish the power of the experience than to heighten it, since the baffling quotidian details and choking frustrations of extra-diegetical life are generally swept away in the crust in the crush of narrative events.[21]

The Aesthetic Critique

The aesthetic critique also finds fault in the fantasy element of black action films, not for the political and therapeutic reasons outlined above, but on the grounds that the extremes of the genre make it bad art, art in bad faith. Although many of the reviews make this claim, they tend to do so by way of pronouncements without elaboration.[22] Authenticity— that most modernist of concepts, problematized well before Heidegger's recent eclipse[23]—is regularly invoked, questioning whether the films truly embody, for example, "the action, color, tempo, mood, and music . . . called 'the black style.' "[24] These arguments either hold up dramas such as *Sounder* (1972) and *Nothing But a Man* (1965) as representative of "more serious and *truthful* black films" for contrast,[25] or originary films like *Shaft* and *Superfly* as the real thing, with all those that followed dismissed as mere epigones.[26]

Thomas Cripps's *Black Film as Genre* (1978), which devotes its first chapter to definitions of black film, black genre film, subgenres, and "blaxploitation" film, is less polemical.[27] Although his definition of black film is expansive enough to include, "though rarely, film produced by white filmmakers whose work attracted the attention, if not always the unconditional praise, of black moviegoers and critics,"[28] in an elaborately polarized scheme Cripps maps out a series of specious distinctions between "genre film" and "exploitation film":

Genre film can easily become exploitation film, through which tastes are teased but no deeper needs are met. While genre film tends to treat things as they are and avoids the trap of advocating them, exploitation film sensationalizes them. Genre film merely speaks from a segregated point of view; exploitation film prefers it. Black genre film ritualizes the myth of winning; exploitation film, as its worst, merely celebrates and dramatizes revenge as though it were a form of winning.[29]

On the one hand, these binary oppositions set up standards unlikely to be met by any one film; on the other hand, they create negative criteria so damning that any "exploitation film" might be shown not to be "*that* bad" and have claimed in its defense numerous points where it rests comfortably within Cripps's definition of genre film. This Manichaean catalog is all the more suspicious in a book that claims, in the auctorial plural, "like the French semiological critics who borrow from the science of structural linguistics, we shall seek to define black genre film through social and anthropological rather than aesthetic factors," [30] and also claims to know what people's "deeper needs" are and who does and does not meet them. [31]

Despite Cripps's claim to be setting aesthetic considerations aside, his list valorizes moderation over excess pair by pair, intimating in laden language that the former beats the latter in every match: "treats" over "sensationalizes," "celebrates" over "trumps," "chooses" over "bleats," and so on. Cripps's tropes, like Van Deburg's and Poussaint's, cloak subjective distaste under the mantle of a neutralizing discourse of dispassionate concern for "the good." [32] If the black genre film and the blaxploitation film can stand as metonyms for the *aesthetique du cool* and the funk tradition, respectively, what Cripps is rejecting in Column B ("merely," "redundantly," "only") becomes much clearer: funk is not cool; it has no class.

The Critiques Critiqued

The dynamic of a cultural production marginalized within a population itself already marginalized can be seen in various kinds of class policing. When Spike Lee, in an April 1994 appearance on *Arsenio,* said of gangsta rap that "it's got no class," he spoke the truth of his own perception (the music lacks or even opposes the values he subscribes to, those that embody or advance the "classy"), but he also showed that he could not or would not engage the music: he gazed down upon it from on high and found it wanting.

The expert's conceit of standing *above* popular culture, of "getting it" better than the lumpen masses, of privileged insight given only to the elect, itself functions as an instrument in social stratification, in its own way "perpetuating the flawed model of art as a pipeline for delivering meaning, rather than as a social field for constructing, negotiating, and contesting it." [33] If an uncertainty principle à la Heisenberg obtains in any act of measurement, no matter how metaphorical, then no critique of popular culture that positions itself as above the consumers of the cultural production under scrutiny—that does not try to take its own measure, or pretends such a measure cannot be taken—is likely to offer a sufficiently complexified interpretation of the consumer, the production consumed, or the processes of production and consumption.

To note that the political and psychological critiques both signify a hoary brand of paternalism is not to deny the value of positive role models for anybody, let alone people who generally see the groups of which they are members reflected in mass media badly if at all. These critiques say, in effect, that "they" (a particular group of people whose oppression is structurally organic to a larger society) are incapable of distinguishing between entertainment and a societally acceptable reality. This "they" is incapable of resisting an impulse to act out the implausible or pathological behaviors it sees on the screen, or of reasoned moral choice overall. "We" (the cultural dominant, or the enlightened vanguard of the oppressed) by stern contrast, are best able to judge for the benighted "they" what it needs, and what it must not see.[34] From this stance, none of the critiques discussed is able to address the sheer enormity of the popularity of these films in their heyday, let alone what that popularity might mean.[35] They never address the issue of the pleasure the audiences plainly got from these films, proof that "it is easy to forget that culture exerts the influence it does because it provides us with pleasure."[36]

In scorning these films as too nakedly commercial ("exploitative") to be considered as art, the aesthetic critique ignores the subgenre's context as a commodity in a consumer culture. More to the point, the films were produced on extremely tight budgets and notoriously tight production schedules for audiences whose leisure reading was more likely to be comic books than the Great Books. That these viewers would have been better served by an equal quantity of noble narratives on the order of *Sounder, Brian's Song,* and *The Autobiography of Miss Jane Pittman*—that they would have *consumed* these products even if they had been available—is unlikely.[37]

As with many cinematic trends, the makers of black action films strove to understand and respond to the whims and dictates of the market, proliferating with the wild surge of demand, mutating in response to or anticipation of greater specificity of consumer tastes, redefining (in some cases, into the kung fu subgenre), waning and dying as demand tapered off into oblivion. To call them exploitative presumes a deficiency in judgment on the part of their African-American viewers that is rarely imputed to white viewers of action and fantasy movies; to quote James Earl Jones, "If they're going to put the damper on John Shaft, let them put it on John Wayne too, and they'll find out that there are a lot of people who need those fantasies." [38] It also presupposes as norms certain aesthetics, models of behavior and psychological development, and paradigms of political awareness and action, all born and raised in western Europe.

To dismantle these discourses of aesthetic, therapeutic, or political value doesn't constitute an argument that the movies *are* art (good or bad), or spiritually uplifting or politically motivating, or in some quantifiable way beneficial to the identity formation of the young black people who made up the bulk of their audience. The critiques that take blaxploitation to task for *not* being these things build their cases on very small plots of very shaky ground. They almost never address *how* the movies actually functioned in their time, except in the most begrudging and perfunctory ways, and then with the invariable conclusion that the benighted were buying into their own oppression. They do not ask what the appeal of black action films was, how they related to (contested, apotheosized) the genres in which they positioned themselves, how the mercurial dynamics of their market shaped them, or how they spoke to one another.

I have not tried to prove the bankruptcy of these discourse for the interpretation of black cultural production, but rather to problematize them. For an alternative, I am inclined toward what Stuart Hall calls "the dialogic strategies and hybrid forms essential to the diaspora aesthetic." [39] It seems to me that a diaspora aesthetic can be inclusive enough to welcome consideration of cultural forms that do not on their faces uplift the race, that speak in terms simultaneously more outrageous and more subtle. Maybe one or some of its schemas can account for the production *and* reception of such otherwise disavowed forms as black action films and gangsta rap in a way not predicated on hierarchies of taste, accumulations of cultural capital, or degradation/deficit models of behavior. And if not a diaspora aesthetic, then another; or not. As the ongoing histories and interrelationships of black action films and gangsta rap show, it is in the processes of production and reception of popular culture that marginalized groups—especially the doubly marginalized—continually theorize themselves.

NOTES

1. An earlier version of this chapter was presented at the conference "Race, Rights and Regions" at the Center for Critical Analysis of Contemporary Culture at Rutgers University, New Brunswick, N.J. on December 2, 1994. The current version incorporates portions of another paper, "Superbadd(e), or, The Case of the Hard-Boiled Soul Sister," presented at the conference "Soul: Black Power, Politics, and Pleasure," at New York University, April 10, 1995. Thanks to Andrew Ross and Richard Green at NYU; likewise and then some to Scott Brewer at Harvard and Glenn Sandberg at Rutgers, both soul brothers of the first order.

2. A word and notion I picked up from Tricia Rose; you probably won't find it in her *Black Noise: Rap Music and Black Culture in Contemporary America* (1994), but it is implicit throughout.

3. See Scott (1993).

4. See also Rose (1994, 55): " 'Blaxploitation' films such as Melvin Van Peebles's *Sweet Sweetback's Baadasssss Song* . . . are also especially important in rap."

5. Gabrenya (1996).

6. See note 1 above.

7. Darius James's priceless *That's Blaxploitation: Roots of the Baadasssss 'Tude* (1995) had not yet come out when I first looked.

8. Here I follow Cripps's (1978) use of the term, which I discuss below.

9. E.g., the various brands of stigmatization of drag among gay men, pornography among lesbians, and gangsta rap among African-Americans.

10. This position is typified by Wesley (1973), Mattox (1973), and Washington and Berlowitz (1975).

11. "The black film, as a genre of cinematic art, is degenerate, debased, and an insult to the integrity of audiences of black people, who, starved for the sight of *anything* black on the silver screen, flock to see these manifestations of celluloid prostitution. . . . These films, for the most part, portray blacks outwitting the white man at every turn, or else beating him to death. Quite naturally, an oppressed people will relate in a positive manner to such pictures. But these films have created a 'legal' white whipping boy—the gangster. The white gangster or the hopelessly crooked white cops are the only white villains blacks are allowed to deal with. Mere low men on the totem pole. Never mind the corrupt federal officials who fail to safeguard black people attempting to vote in the South. Never mind the 'jive' meat and produce inspectors who continuously allow substandard foods to find their way into the supermarkets and grocery stores of black communities. Don't deal with the Strom Thurmonds, James McClellans, *et al.*, who are daily engaged in activities designed to stifle the lives of the black, Chicano, Puerto Rican, Native American, and poor. No. Let these

'niggers' see their heroes deal with the most obvious villains only." Wesley (1973, 65).

12. "The films present any semblance of revolutionary struggle in terms of adventurism, tactics of 'revolutionary suicide,' one dimensional machismo, and violence. They obfuscate black-white unity and questions of class struggle by posing all conflicts on exclusively racial lines. The street hustler and the more 'respectable' social climber alike represent the most petty bourgeois individualism. Blacks involved in organized political struggle are denigrated as buffoons." Washington and Berlowitz (1975, 23–24).

An open letter from The Black Artists Alliance to Jesse Jackson, in *Variety*, August 18, 1972, states: "We will no longer tolerate the visual images of Black people that are paraded across the screen as little more than reincarnations of racist stereotypes which demean our women and make ludicrous caricatures of our men. The image of black people in the various forms of media has changed, but the John Shafts and their women of today are no closer to black reality than the Mantan Morelands and Beulahs of years gone by." Cited in Mattox (1973, 190–95).

13. Tony Brown, then dean of the School of Communications at Howard University, quoted in Michener (1972, 239).

14. Van Deburg (1992, 287–88).

15. Quoted in Leab (1975, 258).

16. Poussaint (1974, 22, 26–27, 30–31, 98).

17. Ibid., 27, 30. This take on fantasy can be found throughout the political and psychological denunciations of the black action films, though nowhere as systematically as in Poussaint. It would be interesting to know these studies used for controls, and if Poussaint really means to suggest that "normal" teens by contrast spend their adolescences learning practical skills like spreadsheet analysis, in intellectually nourishing enterprises like reading Homer (preferably in the original), or in spiritually uplifting endeavors on the order of bringing the Word to the heathens.

18. Ibid., 98. The argument that "realistic" portrayals do poorly at the box office because most black films do not show the black family at all utterly ignores the likelihood that extraordinary behavior is far more likely to attract attention than the ordinary. In this light, see, for example, Wollheim (1993, x): "It seems to me natural to think that art is more deeply rooted in human nature than morality, and I am surprised that philosophers make little of the fact that, though good art is more likeable than bad art, virtuous people do not enjoy this same advantage over those to whom we are drawn primarily for their charm, or their gaiety, or their sweetness of nature, or their outrageousness."

19. To some black youths, drug pushing and the related violent life-style are the shortest and quickest means out of poverty" (Poussaint 1974, 30) As far as I know, they were then and still are. To contend otherwise is to dismiss reality.

20. Ibid.

21. An interesting discussion of these and related ideas can be found in Wollheim (1993, 112–31).

22. Wesley (1973, 65) is once again examplary: "Questions of art, relevancy, *truth* have little to do with what they are all about in any real sense."

23. See, for example, Grass (1963), where everyday language and understanding are debased by the discourse of transcendence.

24. Wesley (1973, 69).

25. Ibid., 70.

26. "From 1970 to 1976, black-themed movies were a Hollywood staple. In retrospect, the range and tone of the films were wider than the term 'blaxploitation' suggests. Yet there is no question films bastardizing *Sweet Sweetback's Baadasssss Song* into a repeatable formula set the tone." George (1988).

27. Cripps (1978, 3–12)

28. Ibid., 4.

29. Ibid., 11.

30. Ibid., 9.

31. "Black genre film celebrates the *aesthetique du cool,* the outward detachment, composed choreographic strides, and self-possessed, enigmatic mask over inner urgency that have been admired in both Africa and Afro-America. In contrast, so-called 'blaxploitation' film trumps *aesthetique du cool* into mere sneering and bravado. The black genre film chooses hyperbole as a mode of celebrating the combination of triumph over adversity, fellow feeling, and moral superiority of the oppressed, known most recently as 'soul'; 'blaxploitation' film only bleats in shrill imitation. The anatomy of black life in black genre film is an instrument of communication *to* the group *by* the group . . .; 'blaxploitation' film redundantly depicts only what has been done *to* blacks, not *by* them." (Ibid., 12.)

32. As for what *my* tropes do, I don't claim to be agenda-pure, or "merely analyzing"; even if something we might call an objective stance to cultural production were somehow desirable, I have seen no evidence to suggest that it is possible.

33. Walser (1992, 39).

34. The high-toned classics of this breed are Kael (1972), which sighs ruefully at the "they" that has traded the Martin Luther King dream for the "consumer-media society" lie (p. 262); and Poussaint (1974). The flip side of this is the reduction and condescension that often inform receptions claiming to recuperate previously stigmatized cultural productions as kitsch, such as the cable television network Nickelodeon's *Nick at Nite.* This Lettermanic ethos of self-congratulation against the stunning dopiness of the denizens of the past is a counter to the kinds of appropriation that have been fundamental to hip hop.

35. In 1972, when the annual industry output was to be about two hundred

films, fully one-quarter of those planned for the year had primarily black casts (J Murray 1972, 249).

36. Walser (1992, 55; italics mine).

37. This is not the place for a detailed economic or audience-response case study, but the history of the black action film from 1971 to 1976 provides a remarkable picture of the industry genius for market research and product development. Even allowing for the lag between production and distribution— much shorter here than for "A" pictures—and without ignoring the fact that the majority of these movies were financed by white-owned production companies and many of them were written or directed by white men, a model to chart the origins and evolution of the form over its five-year lifespan would be fascinating. It would probably not be difficult to graph, for example, the stripping away of elements some consumers might have found extraneous, and the expansion of those known to give pleasure. The pleasures of narrative are harder to commodify than sex or violence, but almost without question those movies in which the plot—however fanciful in its details—is most tightly constructed, and the characters not only most consistent but in some ways generative of plot, were the most commercially successful. The exception is *Friday Foster*, which had the highest production values and the most conventionally competent technical work, but the disadvantage of release a year after the action boom had crested.

38. Quoted Michener (1972).

39. Hall (1992, 29).

WORKS CITED

Bogle, Donald. 1973. Rev. ed., 1989. *Toms, Coons, Mulattoes, Mammies, and Bucks: An Interpretive History of Blacks in American Films*. New York: Continuum.

Cripps, Thomas. 1978. *Black Film as Genre*. Bloomington: Indiana University Press.

Gabrenya, Frank. 1996. " 'Original Gangstas' Separates Men from the Boyz," At http://www.dispatch.com/news/movies/gangst.html, May 1996.

George, Nelson. 1988. *The Death of Rhythm and Blues*. New York: Plume.

Grass, Günter. 1963. *Hundejahre*. Darmstadt: Hermann Luchterhand Verlag.

Hall, Stuart. 1992. "What Is This 'Black' in Black Popular Culture?" In Gina Dent, ed., *Black Popular Culture*. Seattle: Bay Press.

James, Darius. 1995. *That's Blaxploitation! Roots of the Baadasssss 'Tude*. New York: St. Martin's Griffin.

Kael, Pauline. 1972. "Notes on Black Movies," Reprinted in Patterson (1975; 258–68).

Leab, Daniel J. 1975. *From Sambo to Superspade: the Black Experience in Motion Pictures.* Boston: Houghton Mifflin.

Mattox, Michael. 1973. "The Day Black Movie Stars Got Militant," Reprinted in Patterson (1975, 190–95).

Michener, Charles. 1972. "Black Movies." Reprinted in Patterson (1975, 235–46).

Murray, James P. 1972. "The Subject Is Money." Reprinted in Patterson (1975, 274–57).

Parish. James Robert, and George H. Hill. 1989. *Black Action Films: Plots, Critiques, Casts and Credits for 235 Theatrical and Made-for-Television Releases.* Jefferson, N.C. McFarland.

Patterson, Lindsay, ed. 1975. *Black Films and Film-Makers: A Comprehensive Anthology from Stereotype to Superhero.* New York: Dodd, Mead.

Poussaint, Alvin. 1974. "Blaxploitation Movies: Cheap Thrills That Degrade Blacks." *Psychology Today,* February, 22, 26–27, 30–31, 98.

Rose, Tricia. 1994. *Black Noise: Rap Music and Black Culture in Contemporary America.* Hanover, N.H.: Wesleyan University Press/University Press of New England.

Scott, Monster Kody [Sanyika Shakur]. 1993. *Monster: The Autobiography of an L.A. Gang Member.* New York: Atlantic Monthly Press.

"A Symposium on Popular Culture and Political Correctness." 1993. *Social Text* 36 (fall): 2–7.

Van Deburg, William L. 1992. *New Day in Babylon: The Black Power Movement and American Culture, 1965–1975.* Chicago: University of Chicago Press.

Walser, Robert. 1992 *Running with the Devil: Gender, Power and Madness in Heavy Metal.* Middletown, Conn.: Wesleyan University Press.

Washington, Michael, and Marvin J. Berlowitz. 1975. "Swat Superfly: Blaxploitation Films and High School Youth." *Jump Cut,* October–December, 23–24.

Wesley, Richard. 1973. "Which Way the Black Film," Reprinted in Patterson (1975, 65–72).

Wollheim, Richard. 1993. *The Mind and Its Depths.* Cambridge, Mass.: Harvard University Press.

Question of a "Soulful Style"

Interview with Paul Gilroy

RICHARD C. GREEN AND MONIQUE GUILLORY

This interview with Paul Gilroy took place in the spring of 1996 in New York City. In recent years, scholars and writers have begun to investigate the international dimensions of soul as it emanates from the Caribbean, Great Britain, and other urban metropoles. Gilroy's work has been crucial to our (and others') critical (re)considerations of soul because it calls for a rigorous investigation of the impact that the exchange of ideas and commodities across various national borders has had on these global communities. Similarly, he calls upon us to interrogate both the differences and commonalities among black diasporic communities in light of differing relationships to such issues as nationality, race, and class. Taking up Gilroy's pun from The Black Atlantic, *one might propose that any project that attempts to excavate and explore the "roots" of soul requires mapping the "routes" it has traversed through places such as England, the Caribbean, and Africa.*

■ ■ ■

PAUL GILROY: First of all, it seems to me that soul is the mark of a particular cultural axiology. It is first and foremost a sign of value. What's important to me about the political language of soul and the language of cultural value in which the trope of soul circulates is that it is a sign that the axiology of the market does not work. It is a sign that we are dealing with a realm of cultural production, cultural utility, cultural dissemination where the calculus of worth cannot apply or applies rather problematically. So for me, the value of soul and the idea of soul is that they mark that realm which resists the reach of economic rationality and the commodifying process. Soul is a mark of how that precious, wonderful, expressive culture stands outside of commodification, how those cultural processes and the history in which they stand have resisted being reduced to the status of a thing that can be sold.

RICHARD C. GREEN: How would you relate this, then, to the Afro-picks, the actual material manifestations of soul, for example during the seventies, the actual soul products which were marketed between segments of *Soul Train*. How would you view those in terms of this expressive culture which lies beyond commodification?

GILROY: Well, we didn't have *Soul Train,* and we didn't have an instant vernacular economy that sought to meet the needs and demands for those small desires. We didn't have anything like that. Obviously we did have our own version of intimacy with African-American cultural forms. We had a version of the desire for soul as solidarity, but we didn't have that kind of economic cannibalization of it. For us, soul certainly wasn't spatialized through any sort of immediate or simple notion of community as territory. I think that the yearning for soul, for its social moment, floated around and stimulated the idea of community as territory, which was beginning to break down under the pressure of economic changes even in that period. Soul in that sense belongs to your American apartheid, and we didn't have anything quite like that in our urban worlds. We didn't have a black visual culture of soul that was separate from the visual culture of the Black Power period. They were continuous for us and soul wasn't something that had been colonized by corporate concerns. Of course, we wanted to buy combs to blow out our hair with, but that was to do with wanting to have an Afro. Getting an Afro comb was necessary for having an Afro, and that was a kind of liberatory moment.

GREEN: Did you have an Afro?

GILROY: Of course. But for me soul was not simply of a piece with that desire for a distinctive unassimilable style, because soul for me was always culturally marked. The relationship between soul and Black Power was uneasy. Though I didn't appreciate it at the time, it was an early version of the fateful tension between politics and culture, a symptom of the problems involved in founding a cultural politics that remains political. Perhaps there were material objects—perhaps even Afro-combs—and other things which mediated that tension.

My point is that soul wasn't the word which we applied to that political process. Soul wasn't a word which we used to examine the politics of that moment. The question of a "soulful style" was something that we sort of took for granted—that wasn't the problem. But soul meant the music and the music stands for black sublimity, it stands for that moment when the unfolding of the musical event presents that sublimity. It also stands for the dramatic, oppositional moment where the processes of fragmentation and commodification begin [to], if not exactly break down, then at least lose some of their totalizing power.

MONIQUE GUILLORY: When you were growing up, you say you did not have something like *Soul Train*. But what would you identify as one of the first things you recognized as soulful, and how would you describe that experience?

GILROY: I can remember following the Voices of East Harlem around when they came to England in 1970. They had Doug Rauch on bass, who was seriously funky, had a huge 'fro and some extremely cool snakeskin boots. I remember going to see Curtis Mayfield when he came to play in London—it must have been in 1971 or 72—and feeling myself inducted into this ultraserious, sepulchral kind of celebration of soul. That same pain, that same pleasure—it took me by surprise and changed the quality of pleasure the music yielded to me. I must be careful not to project backwards, but I do think that it was really only at that point that I realized how close that particular public world of the vernacular was to a religious experience. Before that moment when he sang "People Get Ready," "Stone Junkies," and "We the People Who Are Darker Than Blue," I hadn't appreciated that. My encounter with Christianity had ended as a child when I discovered the parable of the talents. I knew my Bible because I had been to a religious school and so on, but the moment I discovered that parable, I left Christianity behind and I've always felt that the cornerstone of my modernity is a very strictly enforced sense of the secular. Soul for me, now, is about marking those intensities of feeling that were readily assimilated into a religious language and experience, a spiritual exploration, but it allows us to value them as a secular and sometimes profane phenomenon. I think that's the power of the concept. That's why I didn't give up the idea, and that's why actually I'm sad that the idea is being lost.

GREEN: You say lost, but do you think it's being transformed into something else? Some people were suggesting that perhaps hip hop or perhaps other musical forms have some of the same elements of soul. Could we see these as some sort of continuation?

GILROY: No. I see it more as a break with the past, as a rupture. People don't use the word much these days. Right now back home, most of what used to be called soul is referred to as swing if it's up-tempo and slow jams if it's not. The word *soul* also has to be seen in a particular representational economy. One of the other key terms that works with and against it in that setting is the term *funk*. For me, soul and funk have a sort of co-evolution, and I see them existing in a kind of contingent equilibrium in much of what I value in the best expressive culture of the seventies. Think, for example, of those albums that Aretha recorded for Atlantic in the early to mid-seventies: *Let Me in Your Life* and *Hey Now Hey the Other Side of the Sky*. Think of *Donny Hathaway Live*. These were recordings that set new standards in the evaluation of what counted as a soulful performance. The thing about soul which distinguished it from funk was its relationship to the idea of embodiment and its very particular attachments to notions of bodily performance, where the voice is the dominant aesthetic issue, not the rhythm.

GUILLORY: You talk about mourning this loss of soul almost with a similar sentiment as you discuss the loss of discourses around freedom, particularly in "After the Love Is Gone." These two concepts seem almost interchangeable.

GILROY: Yes, I do think it's connected, in our period, which is a quarter of a century later . . . now everything is everything. I do see what I would call a changed relationship to the embodied self in much of black popular culture. We are well past the point where a particular set of conceptualizations derived from religious language in the relationship between the flesh and the spirit, the body and the soul (which gets secularized in an uneven way) were blasted apart. Those old pieties have been replaced by an acquisitive but emphatically post-Protestant notion of individuality and by a changed sense of the value of life and living which suggest that carnal vitality is the most intensely felt experience of being in the world that you can find. I think that extraordinary shift redefines the horizons of freedom—it shows how the orbits of freedom have shrunk. They shrank initially to the dimensions of the family, then to the space around the body, and then moved from the surface of the skin—the moment of epidermalization—into the interior of the body, into the imagined interior of the embodied black self. I'm always wary about this argument because I feel it has a kind of generational specificity to it, and I would not want to turn around and be seen to be saying, well, this particular quality has completely disappeared from the musical culture. It may still be there, but I know that I can't hear it. Of course, most of the funk has gone too. That was killed by the technology and the de-skilling process instituted by digital technologies. I think that soul is only soul in relation to funk and without funk it loses something of its value. As funk is squeezed out of the frame by some of the technological factors at work and some of the de-skilling issues involved in musical production right now, these political changes are paralleled by new kinds of limitations and shrinkage of the creative horizons of musicians and performers.

That precious quality of soulfulness is becoming harder to find in the secular world of global black pop. The guy from Jodeci models himself on Bobby Womack but you'd never confuse the two of them. I thought his version of "If You Think You're Lonely Now" (on the *Jason's Lyric Soundtrack*) was an embarrassment. Look at the ways that Mary J. Blige and company simulate soulfulness by means of video. The great Chaka Khan was the last one to work that particular seam of creativity with any conviction. Nothing authentic about her, too; she was raised as a Catholic, so let's not cheapen her art by making it something easy that she didn't have to work for. I can enjoy Brandy's records, like "Best Friend," but not because they're soulful. I suppose if you move into the church you can still find that quality of tone, phrasing, and expressiveness, that way of pulling the sounds out of the body. I found myself moving towards church music in pursuit of a certain quality of performance that I find there. I regard that as something of a defeat although I take the same pleasure in it. You know what I mean? It's a defeat because it used to be so much easier to find. D.J. Rogers doesn't make records anymore! I remember the first time that Vanessa Bell Armstrong came to London to sing. I was very privileged to be able to hear her that night, but it saddened me too because I wasn't getting those same sorts of pleasures from listening to people who were op-erating in the secular equivalent of that sacred style. I went to see Anita Baker around the same time and only got the shivers up my back once.

That was in a small venue too! I didn't expect her to be so shallow. At home we use the word "deep" to specify that quality of soulfulness.

GREEN: Speaking of coming to England, a lot of your work focuses on the crossings back and forth through the black Atlantic. What I'm thinking about is how this notion of soul migrates to other countries.

GILROY: Yes. Have you ever seen the film *Soul to Soul?* With the Voices of East Harlem and everybody in Ghana? It was a big movie in the early 1970s and it represents precisely that reconciliation of African-American cultural production with Africa. There's an album from that tour, which commemorates the package of African-American rhythm and blues and soul performers going to Africa and that reconciliation with the motherland. They're all interviewed in the movie and it's very moving to them that they find a different constituency. They respond to a hunger for what they do in Africa which is both the same and different from the one that is familiar. Of course, that exceptional creative capacity travels and resonates very strongly in differently places. I think we have to be very cautious about interpreting those moments of connection. We know what that language articulates because we know about the intensity of pleasure that we discover. But I think sometimes that language of an essential particularity, which we use to explain those moments of affiliation and linkage, represents a kind of shortcut to the more obviously political work involved in explaining how solidarity happens and how culture, technology, and language mediate that solidarity. I think if we could be just a little harder on ourselves before we start celebrating, we might have something more worthwhile—a more politically coherent understanding of what those fragile solidarities add up to. Maybe then the party can start, and I don't mean the vanguard party.

GREEN: So I'm wondering about the African-American cultural community in terms of our global colonizing effect. What happens when the black American sphere becomes the primary site and market for articulations of black diasporic cultures. Also, I'm wondering about the shift in U.S. centrality depending on global economic and political changes.

GILROY: But there isn't a shift of centrality. Black American culture *is* the dominant global resource for all of that activity. We can unpack it and see where it contains inscriptions, conversations and dialogues across the Americas and beyond, but it is American—the core of that black global culture as a world culture is American. Now there are all sorts of interesting reasons for that, but I don't think that we can doubt it. The difference is that being from England, our relationship to the Caribbean and to Africa is a more present one. And we have had to deal with all the arguments about the consequences of American imperialism for the development of black cultures in the Caribbean and in Africa. My mother's family comes from Guyana and they come from the woods, from a distant and remote part of Guyana, far from the capital. They had to deal with the fact that an American air base turned up there. My mother's brother gets taken over, under the wing of African-American military men on that base, and they teach him to be a mechanic, which then gives him a new life. He was endowed with new skills under a kind of fraternal relationship conducted through particular racial categories, which do and don't really translate into what's going on in Guyana. The same sort of story might be constructed in Trinidad and other places as well. It represents a very ambivalent becoming. I'm sure that there are all sorts of other stories like that. The American military was also a source of his culture. Louis Jordan and the "new calypso be-bop" came down the same wire. When you think back to my own period of growing up in the seventies and so on, when I wanted to listen to soul on the radio, what station did I tune to? I tuned to the American Forces Broadcasting Network transmitting to black soldiers in Germany. That's where we heard that part of our music. It wasn't the only place, but it was one of only two or three places on the radio where it was possible to hear that culture at all. For us it had an authentic stamp.

GREEN: What do you think about the resurgence of interest in soul right now? What we're seeing in America right now, there is a renewed interest in things like blaxploitation films, styles and music from the seventies, Spike Lee's film *Crooklyn*. How do you see this nostalgia for this historic moment?

GILROY: I think it expresses a yearning for a scale of sociality, which is denied everywhere. It speaks to the desire for an authentic, face-to-face version of democratic interdependence and mutuality. In this case it is not, of course, gender specific. That's one of the other things that matters about soul. If you look at what was going on at the Million Man March, it's gender coded. But here, under the sign of soul there's a cosy world of mutuality—a way of becoming brothers and sisters that is both secular and open to all, at least in theory. So I suppose it would have something to do with that. The interest in soul registers dissatisfaction that what's left of black public culture has been impoverished, debased by the absence of that mutuality. Nothing more than nostalgia for the social.

GUILLORY: So would you say that soul is something that is open to all—that anyone can possess soul, be soulful? Or is it racially marked?

GILROY: That's the idea, that's what the concept says. It says: "This is our racialized uniqueness." The problem about the music and the problem about loving the music is this: That is not the story that the music tells you. It is only on the most superficial level, but if you dig into the history of the music you find that is an untenable position. To make the music tell that story, you must do violence to the music. A good example for me actually would be this: People talk a lot of bullshit about Sly and the Family Stone. I guess I wanted to be Sly for a spell in my teens. I suppose my teenage life as a guitar player at a certain point in the 1970s was musically and imaginatively triangulated by the figures of Sly, Miles, and Hendrix. I can remember going to a festival in 1970 and seeing them all in the space of a twenty-four-hour period on the same stage. The message that came to me from all of that was that that quality of soulfullness was something that wasn't the specific property of blacks. This is an old argument. From Du Bois and Alain Locke on down, it has to do with the extent to which the music is recognized as an American phenomenon. This recognition compromises and complicates a sense of how it might be thought of as a black phenomenon. Now it certainly is the case that I recognized and still accept a kind of priority which is attached to the African-American component in that creativity. But I don't think that it's possible to argue that the music can be that exclusively, prescriptively. It just can't—it doesn't work. I remember that day, watching John McLaughlin, Dave Holland—the English bass player—and Joe Zawinul playing with Miles and thinking, well, what do you know! Then when Jimi came on he was with Billy Cox and Mitch Mitchell. The Hendrix issue is a much more complicated one, of course, because nobody liked Mitch Mitchell's drumming anyway except Jimi. The point is this. He heard something in that Anglo simulation of Elvin Jones that was important. And I'm not sure that I could hear it even now. The constitution of Family Stone might be used to reinforce the same point. "Don't Call Me Nigger Whitey, Don't Call Me Whitey Nigger"—isn't that paradigmatic at some point? What were Pat Rizzio and Jerry Martini doing in that band? It expresses an entanglement, a kind of political and cultural complexity that is localized, of course, in the Bay Area—at least that's how it looked to me as an outsider. I found all of that exciting, liberating, and empowering. The music showed me that race was limiting and offered concrete utopian resources in the struggle against racisms. The presence and participation of white players was no obstacle to soul. In a sense, it may even have enhanced it by making "race" irrelevant and symbolizing the possibility of white agency against white supremacy. Those "outsiders" venerated the tradition of black music before that was fashionable. Their collaboration signified something profound. Let's not forget that Sly, Miles, and Jimi were all rejected by African Americans to some degree. It's a different story now, but how long did it take people to catch up with them?

GREEN: I was thinking about *Young Soul Rebels* and that particular moment of cultural contact/conflict that is depicted on the dance floor and the airwaves. I found it to be an interesting exposition on the notion of soul from a different perspective, from a black British perspective. What did you think of that particular film and the way it portrayed a young black British vantage of soul?

GILROY: Well, we didn't have a communicative infrastructure that we could simply plug into. That meant that when we made that infrastructure it had an even greater distance from the corporate world because it was content to be an underground phenomenon and to stay there in the darkness. Actually, I'm sure that everyone would say that this is me being such a crusty conservative, but I've never believed, looking at the development of black culture, that anything gets better by going overground blinking in the daylight. It doesn't; it's always destroyed. Everything gets destroyed by that process of being exposed on that massive scale. I'm very happy that people are able to make money off of their art and culture and happy that they want to cultivate new audiences and constituencies for their work and I wouldn't want to inhibit any of that, but I also know that all but the rarest people are destroyed by that variety of exposure, and all but the most precious and unusual minds are exhausted. There are maybe a half a dozen exceptions to that rule. Nothing gets better by being served up like that. I think in a sense *Young Soul Rebels* speaks to a number of contingencies about the consolidation of counterculture as an underground form which doesn't aspire to be anything other than that. It may not articulate that directly, but then the recovery and simulation of that moment was something from which people could draw solace in the present. That was an important intervention. The music was the site of that argument—and let's remember that the film is not a narrowly realist one. The music is all mixed up timewise to underline the utopian possibilities.

If I think back to my own encounters with the music in the seventies, rather than as it's celebrated in the film, the story was very different. We might go see the MC5 or Freddie King one week, and the next week we would go and see Maggott Brain–era Funkadelic and they would be stoned out of their heads, playing this dull, very "white" music for hours and hours which was, for all intents and purposes, the most rebarbative form of rock. The lines were not so clearly and simply drawn. I guess that being in Europe, they felt all the freer to act out and so that's what they did. In the face of all that, I would want to distinguish soul much more carefully as a distinctively African-American phenomenon defined initially by its proximity to the sacred. It transcodes that religious quality of expression, which then gets secularized and politicized. Even this isn't the whole of that story—there are a number of other parallel processes going on. Funk isn't the first of those, just the one which was most important to me.

GUILLORY: Can you talk a bit about this notion of soul being linked to some sense of suffering, and also the expression of pain as in slavery and returns to the freedom question?

GILROY: I don't know how to talk about this stuff if you want to get serious about it. I don't know what to say because for me, the word *soul* was a useful way of talking about precisely those communicative qualities that exceed the power of language to recapture. That's true when we sing and play and it's true when we try to talk about it. You can be technical and say, well we're talking about melisma and all the old examples come out, like James screaming "Please" or Jackie Wilson filling the word love with fifty-two different syllables and notes and yes folks, that's the referent. But I think it's also the site of a kind of ambivalence about the memory of slavery and the desirability and the obligation to forget things which are difficult. Soul suggests that this suffering is without redemption. I don't understand for a moment the kind of complicated psychosexual mechanisms which result in being transported into those democratic, antiphonal performances, and I'm sure that lots of people think that those precious aesthetic and social

259

moments aren't there at all, that we all imagine it. And yet, we know that we don't imagine it. It is our open secret. I suppose that this is the place where I get accused of being a complacent essentialist or something like that. I don't want to sound facile. What does the song say? "When it hits you, you feel no pain." And if that notion wasn't so repeatedly cited it wouldn't speak to a very simple but fundamental truth about what it means to occupy our particular modernity. I don't think there's any sort of sense in which the music or the soulful quality of the music we're talking about is a redemption of our history of suffering—it isn't. It's not redemption but a sign of the impossibility of that redemption. That's why it recurs, and that's why I wonder now, what other forms of redemption are around? If my suspicions about those changes in the collective palate are well-founded, if I'm right about the dwindling of that secularized Protestantism and the anachronistic notions of freedom that governed it, then what other surrogate forms of compensation are being worked up into a counterculture today? Maybe it's just easier to fantasize about being a superhuman black man like Grant Hill. I think I've got some ideas about this change of perspective, but none of the answers I have make me feel any better. They all have to do with embracing a kind of vitalism and embracing a kind of regression that the signature of soul doesn't permit or sanctions only in certain carefully defined sets of circumstances. I remember working in this child day-care center, this is back in 1972, the year I was leaving high school. There was this other black girl—I will say girl because that's what we were, we were boys and girls at that time—and she had an Afro, a very big one, beautiful. And she was talking about the quality, the intensity of feeling she felt when she was embracing her boyfriend and their Afros rubbed against each other—and I always remembered that and won- dered what became of her.

GUILLORY: But what about our tendency to mythologize soul icons and perhaps the "soul" period with a sense of tragedy and with a deep sense of loss?

GILROY: Well, I don't know if it's tragedy, but it is loss, yes. Again there are some other problematic features to it. I think there is this sense in which we invest our artists with the obligation to represent it to us. That is a poisoned chalice for them. When I look back on that period, the notion that someone like Aretha was the "queen" of it, there is a whole set of arguments about the particular kind of hierarchy that's being sought there, the particular kind of authority that is invested in those exemplary figures—and in her case, there are things you can't say about her while the tape is running. But many of us recognize in her the sources of that pain. For me soul has marked some of those boundaries. And there are many other people who probably are able to listen to Billie Holiday records without encountering that quality of address and they probably mark it elsewhere in their lives. I suppose that in terms of soul, the obvious equivalent in terms of vocal performance with the same sort of intensity and feeling is someone like Donny Hathaway. And look how his life ended. I know people who can't bear to listen to Donny Hathaway records who in fact can listen to Aretha. It's uncanny how his daughter sounds like him, though.

GREEN: Turning back to Aretha for a moment. Your essay in *Small Acts* on record album covers was an interesting way to address the question of exportation and importation. Previously you mentioned the lack of images, but at the same time you analyze these nontraditional, what we generally consider insignificant, sleeves of the albums. And what about the disappearance of these large cultural artifacts and their replacement by smaller CD covers? There are these questions about how these images circulate and where they appear that your essay begins to address. Your work in general shows us how we need to look elsewhere, to "read" between the lines. . . .

GILROY: Absolutely. I mean, looking at the significance of sportswear ads today as sources of black particularity and black visual culture is a depressing activity. The album sleeves offered the opportunity to put some text in there, to kind of cultivate the meeting point of text and image. Image may have been dominant, but it did not erase the text. It could lead people towards literacy, which was sort of inherent in the earlier forms. I regret the loss of that. I am worried about rates of illiteracy. It's harder to read CDs or to use them in that way because the scale upon which the object has been constructed is so different.

GREEN: Did you also put them on your wall?

GILROY: No. My records were much too precious to be used as wallpaper. I'd probably do that now. I knew people who did that, but to me they were holy relics of a sort. I don't look after them as well as I should; if you look at the photographs from *Small Acts,* they're all very crumpled around the edges, and that wasn't just a means of getting around the copyright issues. When I went to see Curtis Mayfield that night or any night of five hundred nights, similar nights, that have passed since then, the atmosphere retains that kind of sepulchral mood. That holy burden of expectation bound to those profane delights.

It's beginning to change now, but when I first came here, fourteen or fifteen years ago, I would talk with African-American "intellectuals"— most of whom were academics actually, not intellectuals—and they would take all this stuff entirely and bizarrely for granted. I'm pleased that now people have woken up to what they should have been apprecia- tive of in a different way much, much earlier than this. I think that this has got to do with questions of class. Maybe privileged people remain dependent on poor people for their soul, or their access to soul comes via the cultures those people erect against their sufferings, which the elite do not share. I wasn't going to put it quite as straightforwardly as that, but maybe there's a kind of estrangement from the vernacular which the elite experience as a complex form of ambivalence. They don't want to associate themselves with anything disreputable; on the other hand, they need it. This is the source of important kinds of emergent consciousness about self, conscience, solidarity, the outer limits of community and obligation, the hypertension between the place of origin and the place of sojourn, and so on.

GREEN: We often talk about the parasitic relationship of American society on top of black expressive forms, and rarely do we address particularly a certain group of black people who are also parasitic— maybe parasitic is too strong a word.

GILROY: But yes, we call it parasitism because we're talking about a very interesting form of symbiosis actually. A complex interdependence— certain things we remember and certain things we don't remember. And there's also a strong sense of the differentiation of sameness that makes that symbiotic relationship possible.

GUILLORY: Could you talk about this a bit more in terms of black academics and where they stand today in terms of a resurgence of interest in black popular culture, the underclass, and this estrangement that black academics do have from the community and which they are charged with.

GILROY: A lot of the black professoriat expend their energy pretending they're not estranged from that culture. Soul was a good alibi for the black middle class because they had their Roberta Flack records and albums on the Kudu label—and they were good, good and safe. Now that option has gone and the poor have reemerged as the custodians of authenticity. The quality of the black professor's engagement with the forms of black popular culture suffers from their obligation to pretend that they may be more into it than they really are. Of course, I don't think that it's only black academics who suffer from this—this is also the banalization of cultural studies and the tragedy of the upwardly mobile—but I do think that it's intensely visible in recent writing about black cultures. There are all sorts of debates about what exactly should stand for the repository of black authenticity in the cultural domain today—Sports? Comedy? Cassette tapes of speeches by Dr. Khalid Muhammad? I can remember something that Michele Wallace once wrote. It was a harsh rebuke against me because I went on about music all the time. I'll plead guilty to that charge. What we should really be talking about, she said, is black visual culture—really, it was the visual realm that quickened the pulse of the black community! Now, I have never tried to say that nothing else counted. I just tried to say that for me, where I am, and actually for most of my life, wherever I have been, the music has been the primary medium for composing community and channeling culture, and there are many interesting traditions of reflection on why that should be. I think that wonderful fact has endowed our culture in the world, your culture in the world, with an amazing strength and suppleness. It has acquired an amazing capacity to travel, and it has reproduced its important moral, ethical, and political insights wherever its seeds have found sustenance. It has a wide range of influences, and without the sublime power of that antirepresentational element in musical culture, I don't think that it could have happened. I feel greatly privileged to have any kind of access to that culture. I think sometimes how much poorer the life of this planet would be without it.

GUILLORY: In an exchange between dream hampton and Baraka at our conference on soul, Baraka seemed to claim that hip hop could by no means be considered a continuation of soul and that it is the complete commodification of soul—somehow no political or community intervention was involved—while dream hampton tried to defend her generation, that for her this is the soul. Can you recognize that when young people now go to hip hop concerts, they do experience this kind of euphoria.

GILROY: Well, I really don't know if I know that answer to that, because I don't think that going to the hip hop concert is the primary moment for consuming hip hop culture. Of course they find euphoria there, because that's as close as they can get. But the concert hall is the last place to make an assessment of hip hop. I would suggest that the screen is where that might take place. These hip hop users are screenies. They connect with it through video, not audio. Where do they listen to the music? Certainly not socially and collectively in real time, but in a privatized mode. Cars, not dancehalls, are the primary context for listening to that stuff; perhaps they might be where that primal moment of consuming takes place. It's barely even the radio nowadays, and so I'm against assimilating hip hop to that particular older mode of soul centered on the stage and its dramaturgy. When we think about hip hop, we should remember how long it has been going on. Sixteen years or so? How many records can you honestly say have that quality, that unforgiving, intense quality that arrests you every time. There are a few—there aren't very many. "Eric B is President" and how many more solid classics, tunes you need to revisit periodically to measure your own growth as much as to enjoy their internal qualities? Maybe fifty, maybe a hundred, but not many more.

GUILLORY: But there are definitely some people who would disagree. Who do find those qualities in the music.

GILROY: Well, I'm sure they're right. They're probably right and I'm wrong, actually. I defer to them if they can find those threads. But that claim raises another problem: Who is in a position to evaluate that type of thing? Anyone who tells you they is lying. They can't possibly be. The sheer volume of the product pumped out by the industry defeats that operation. The fact that there are just too many records out there defeats any kind of certainty. It defeats that kind of categorization. I just don't think the music can be known in its totality. Whereas that was possible in the previous period.

GREEN: The question is, Is it useful to make a distinction between having soul and soul as a particular moment historically, politically, a moment in the dance, so to speak? I think that's an interesting thing about hip hop, and also specifically the idea of the being there, being present. And you've mentioned a couple of times having gone to see these shows.

GILROY: Yes, being present, face to face and in real time. The forms in which people become present to one another and the technological mediation of that presence is the decisive issue. Those are very big issues and I want to supplement them with some arguments about what hip hop does with performance values. In hip hop, we often talk about the poverty of the live shows, the particular quality of drama, what it means to have them just messing about with the DATs, simulating a performance. Here I don't want to get hung up on a set of arguments about authenticity. I'm not saying that there are any guarantees in the older mode, but I'm thinking there might be a way of talking about the regression of performance. What has happened in the provision of musical education in this country during the same time? How is music being taught in schools and passed down in churches and other community institutions these days? Cast your mind back twenty years. We were not then trying as creative users of the culture or as producers of the culture to replicate the quality of the music that we had heard in the 1950s. We were not in a retro mode. We enjoyed Louis, Wynonie, and Cleanhead, but we didn't want to be them or play their music—we wanted to be modern. When you think about that, particularly given the acceleration of technology in the past few years, I'm not sure I would go the route dream hampton did. I know I wouldn't go with Amiri Baraka, but I'm not sure I would go with dream either.

Part Four

BLACK CONVERSATION

19

"Ain't We Still Got Soul?"

Roundtable Discussion with Greg Tate, Portia Maultsby, Thulani Davis, Clyde Taylor, and Ishmael Reed

GREG TATE: Supposedly, it's not an easy thing to meet your maker—not unless you're a writer, that is. Our profession provides the once-in-a-lifetime opportunity of inventing your parents, of creating a lineage and ancestry out of words others have set down on a page. The Soul Conference wasn't the first time I found myself in the company of Amiri Baraka and Thulani Davis, but it was an occasion to pay homage to three writers I'd claim for birth canals any day. If not Baraka's tales *System of Dante's Hell* and *Black Music*, I'd have never run up on prose as mind-jolting as Marvel comics. If not Ishmael Reed, I'd never have thought a novel could be as mock-heroic as a Marvel comic. If not for Thulani Davis's insistence that I send some clips to the *Voice*, I would have never thought you could get paid for writing Marvel comics–style Black music criticism.

Listening to their definitions of soul threw my own into sharp relief. I was made to realize what a difference a day, or at least a decade, can make in the fast-shifting world of Black popular culture. As a child who came of age in the late seventies, by the time my generation reached its teens soul was something to be revered and parodied. Hence, our soul men were George Clinton and Prince rather than James Brown and Wilson Pickett. In retrospect, even the late Marvin Gaye has a self-parodying element to it—that sense of a man drowning in his own sexual excesses, not unlike Elvis in his decline. The upshot of this is, as I listened to the firm Baraka, Reed, and Davis reconnect the term *soul* with its Yoruba, hoodoo, and Black nationalist roots, I mulled how my own thirty-something generation and the hip hop generation's definitions of soul were more a function of reference than essence. In other words, soul wasn't nothing but a word to us—a way of describing how folk felt about the condition their condition was in back in the day.

What's funny in all this is how a word once so loaded down with the weighty task of upholding Black authenticity can become frozen and fossilized once Black authenticity moves on. These days, the odious phrase "Keep it real" labors under the burden soul once did, distinguishing the truly Black from those merely passing for blues people. "Keeping it real" is generally used when one wants to let the world know how much you're sacrificing for the cause of true, sho-nuff Blackness. This can lead to excessive measures, like citing one's illiteracy or criminal record as evidence of how real you've been keeping it.

The upshot of all this is, of course, that the more fragile and fractured the Black community becomes, that is, as Black identity grows ever more complex, the more desperately the desire to name, proclaim, and defame an essential Blackness will rear its you-gly head. The only definition of soul that ever moved me was the one Bobby Byrd offered to anyone within earshot: "I know you got soul cause if you didn't, you wouldn't be in here." If that ain't loving us, baby, all I got to say is grits ain't groceries and the Mona Lisa was a man.

PORTIA MAULTSBY: Soul, as a concept, originated in African-American communities during the late 1960s. It evolved from the ideology of Black Power, which promoted Black nationalism. Therefore, soul has both sociopolitical and cultural functions and meanings. From a sociopolitical perspective, it advocated self-awareness, Black empowerment, and a Black identity. From a cultural perspective, it identified expressions symbolic of a Black style or a Black way of doing things, as well as a range of traditions unique to African Americans. Within this context, soul identified cultural symbols (clutched fist, African-derived fashions, ornaments, hairstyles, etc.), Black behavior (greeting one another with a unique handshake, walking with a glide in the stride, and other forms of physical expression), a unique cuisine (chitlins, ham hocks, black-eyed peas, okra, etc.), Black cultural institutions (soul radio), and creative expressions (dance, visual art, and music).

Soul music evolved in response to the call for Black nationalism. Its performers served as messengers and cultural icons for the Black Power Movement. Their lyric themes advocated Black unity, Black empowerment, and a Black identity; their musical style captured the spirit and intensity of the movement; and their African and African-derived fashions, hairstyles, and other visual images reinforced an African heritage. The songs "This Is My Country" by the Impressions and "Say It Loud: I'm Black and I'm Proud" by James Brown epitomize the concept of soul in music. I incorporate the concept of soul in my work by examining the aesthetic ideals unique to Black music styles within the context of an African continuum. I also explore issues related to resistance and the representation of a Black identity in music. The latter considers social, political, and cultural contexts for music evolution.

Since the 1960s, many changes have occurred in African-American communities, which, in turn, have produced new attitudes and interpretations about the concept of soul. During the 1960s and early 1970s, for example, the critical mass of African Americans from various regions and generations united for a common purpose—Black empowerment. Soul music, which resonated this philosophy, emerged as the ONLY new popular music genre. However, since the mid-1970s, many new forms of contemporary expression have evolved and coexisted. For example, funk, disco, rap, and go-go, along with personalized styles akin to soul and mainstream popular music, were created during the 1970s and early 1980s and became popular among various segments in African-American communities. This diversity in musical expression corresponds to social upheavals in African-American communities, which resulted from new aspirations, ideals, and cultural values acquired during the post–Civil Rights and Black Power eras. Therefore, new popular musical styles mirror these changes—changes that resulted in ideological differences among African Americans along generational and social class lines. The movement of the middle-class to the suburbs widened the gap between this group and those that remained in inner-city communities.

Even though the soul concept undergirds most post-1960s musical styles, its representation varies as determined by new social situations and new forms of expression. For example, George Clinton's P-Funk style fused humor and themes of party with social commentary, while many funk groups such as the Bar-Kays, Cameo, Gap Band, and Zapp emphasized party-oriented lyrics. Stevie Wonder, on the other hand, advocated a social agenda, and Teddy Pendergrass commented on personal relationships. Despite differences in lyric content and musical styles, these and other African-American performers preserved the essence of soul in its original or modified form. Their music also brought a soulful relief to the frustrations experienced by American communities in their struggle for post–Civil Rights racial equality and Black empowerment.

In the mid-1970s, Black popular music began to change. Corporate America entered the Black music market to increase its profit margin by expanding its consumer base across cultural and national boundaries. The commodification of Black popular music for mass consumption forced many artists to modify their style. By the early 1980s, new functions and meanings had been assigned to the music, and nationalist connotations of soul had faded from the productions of most record companies.

In inner-city communities, rap artists revitalized the original soul concept by promoting a Black nationalist consciousness. Beginning in the late 1980s, Afrocentric rappers such as Public Enemy and later KRS-ONE, Poor Righteous Teachers, Paris, A Tribe Called Quest, X-Clan, Sister Souljah, and Prince Akeem expounded on the tenets of Black Power as solutions to the social problems that plagued inner-city communities. The musical tracks, which sampled soul and funk recordings, echoed the spirit and intensity that had faded from the musical landscape. Other rap artists, such as Rappin' Is Fundamental, shied away from political commentary but put the soul back into Black popular music by adapting the sounds of Sam Cooke, Curtis Mayfield, B. B. King, Muddy Waters, Wilson Pickett, and Otis Redding. Mainstream America and many African Americans dismissed rap music, which they interpreted to promote separatism, but inner-city youth embraced this music and its message. Eventually, Afrocentric rappers provided inspiration for many college-age students and members of the Black middle class whose dreams for racial equality faded.

The concept of soul has always been preserved in Black churches, whose rituals are informed by Black cultural values and ideals. Black churches historically have been integral to the struggle for racial equality and many adopted a nationalist agenda. Regardless of political orientation, however, many of these churches have been central to the dissemination of soul to the larger African-American community. Sunday morning radio and television broadcast of Black religious services transmits not only the sermons of Black preachers but Black culture as well.

Outside the church, gospel music and other cultural features have always been part and parcel of everyday life. The structures of Black institutions and organizations, for example, are derived from the Black church. Black church culture also influences the play of children, whose activities often mimic the style of Black preachers, musicians, Sister Ann or Deacon Ware, who have sat in the same seat for forty years physically and verbally responding to the preacher. Thus, the soul of the Black church has always provided a cultural vitality that defines life in African-American communities. In conclusion, soul is a concept that has many meanings and applications. It embraces a philosophy, behavior, symbols, cultural products, and, in general, a cultural style—a style informed by African values and traditions and a style unique to peoples of the African diaspora who subscribe to the concept of a Black identity.

CLYDE TAYLOR: This soul concept is a passage, a medium through which we can access what has happened to Black people over the last two or three decades. Because when we're talking about soul, we're talking about survival—our very existence and the stuff we're made of.

I found soul to be the feeling in the room at the conference yesterday when we were at the University Center; it was soulful because we were there. I think it was brought there by the people, and I began to think that that is where soul is. This doesn't specify what soul is but demonstrates where it is—wherever there is a gathering of Black people who are bent on being together, soul emerges from that kind of context. I feel that it is in this room as well, but I think the Greek columns are sort of holding it back. But then again, the circular design could be an African vision, to offset that Greek tradition. I think that soul, then, is the identifying spirit that emerges among Black people when they come together.

It's kind of a cosmic aura. Portia Maultsby has given us useful images for it. But I also feel that the most concentrated nexus for soul is one that might locate in African religions. I appreciate what Portia said about African-American religions, but I think African religions are a further source behind that. And then again, soul comes from something even beyond that, something called the evolution of humanity in various languages but flowing into African religious references. It can be seen there as most concentrated and can perhaps be speculatively looked at in literature, particularly Ishmael Reed's very important novel, *Mumbo Jumbo*.

I am fascinated by how soul has undergone various transformations. It was very burgeoning there in the sixties, as Portia said, so that it brought all the music together, and it was very rooted in that politicizing

273

action. It could be present in so many different contexts—of course it could be there in a church service, but it was then sort of secularized. Through this political movement and also the cultural movement of the sixties, it reached the apex of its history. It is somewhat analogous; we're searching for soul, but where has it gone? Is it still here? Would we ever recognize it if we saw it again? I think these remarks may be a premature obituary for soul. We need to think of this decline and wonder what that loss is about so that soul (or a lack of it) becomes a type of barometer for historical losses: losses in the momentum for making social change.

And so movements were crushed, leaders were killed or invalidated, talent was bought off. I think that . . . the commodification of soul is a very important aspect of this transformation and the extensions of narrative that we are speculating about. Soul has also been internally abused; I think we were silly with it. I am afraid that if we get the right pied piper to give us a soulful tune, he could lead us to any kind of disaster, bopping all the way with him to concentration camps, predators, or whatever. Soul has got to be seen in all these great kinds of services. So it was modified, it was sensationalized, it was overexposed, it was cheapened, it was exoticized, it was sent out to the world too quickly, and it lost some of its commentation with social justice. I think that was the final indication that the case was epidemic. At a certain point, soul got so weak, it almost evaporated under the critique of essentialism, which is another one of the things that happened to it with recent years. Soul became marginalized under the discourse of gender, and although those debates were in no way inessential or inappropriate, the possibility of a unified perception of Black people became something that was almost considered to be subversive. But soul is almost always, and this is my point, a by-product of something else, and the something else can be very different in different contexts—and so we have to examine it closely and often to see what it is doing.

It is most noble particularly when the cause for which it emerges is one of justice and righteousness. But it can also be a mask for corruption, for mendacity, for cryptofascism, as well as a carnivalesque diversion. So when I think about soul, I have an ambition—a weird ambition, I think—about questions of Black consciousness. I think that one could make a map or a grid of all the issues that might have a relationship to Black consciousness so that when you engage a person or a concept, you could go to that grid and there might be a key word or an adjective, or even a quotation from Fanon, that would give you better insight into how this subject pertains to Black consciousness. So when I get to the question of soul, the key word that comes to mind is Brazil. I think of some of the trips I made to Brazil, when I saw the most enormous and lucid manifestations of soul you can see on the planet. In Brazil, you can make the whole planet rock with soul. It's Africa connected to the Americas through African religion; the Orishas are deeply worshiped there. The most powerful influence of African culture in a non-African country is in Brazil, where African religious values dominate the cultural scene to the extent that on New Year's night, two million people will walk to the shore of Rio, to the ocean shore, with candles awaiting Imanje coming in. It's a powerful manifestation, its carnival everywhere. But, of course, there is another side to this which can not be glossed over. The poorest people are in Brazil; they are the ones who have maintained the traditions. The people who get beat down, whose kids have been shot by police, whose leaders are now being murdered, eliminated. The people at the very bottom of Brazil's social structure are some of the most soulful folks in the world. Soul is not enough; it must be taken with everything else going along with it. I want to refer to the three questions I always ask when I think about the value of something to Black people. I go to the Ayi Kwei Armah question: "Why are we so blessed?" Why are we so blessed when compared to our fellow human beings who are not living so well? But I think it's also a question of why are we so blessed to have this manifestation of soul around us. Secondly, I go to the Les McCann question: "Compared to what?" And, finally, I go to the Sonia Sanchez question, "Uh-huh. But how do it feel?"

THULANI DAVIS: In the world I grew up in, which was the segregated upper South, soul was the world we lived in. Two years ago, I was recording in the Sea Islands near South Carolina, and these people were telling me about the time when Black people first started to vote there. They explained that on two of these islands the majority of the population was Black, and White politicians started learning that they needed the Black vote. They were told that they should go to the Black churches and campaign there. So they did and they were told that when they visited these churches, they would be expected to offer a prayer. These White politicians would come to these Black churches and they would take out a little piece of paper with a prayer on it and start to read. At that point, they lost the congregation, and although the people were very polite and heard them out, no one in the room considered voting for these people. And the politicians never had a clue. But that was soul, and that anecdote also illustrates who we thought had soul and who we thought did not have soul. Being able to offer a prayer from the heart was an indication of soul. I think many more of us offer our prayers from paper now, so I think that there may be an obituary to write on soul, although it may be a premature one. But some of us do still come from that place where I'm trying to come from—a place of offering that prayer from the heart, a prayer that no one has to write down the words.

Another part of soul which is related to that for me is the idea of taking a solo—having something to say within the context of the room where you find yourself. Papa Joe Jones said he had known nothing about slavery; he had played the blues and he had lived free. But when they asked him was the count colored, he had said, "Very. Because I have stood up with people who could play with nothing but the rhythm." And I think that that's the kind of soul that I'm talking about—that every person has a solo to take but you have to find it in the rhythm, draw it from the knowledge that you grew up with, express it in the language of that knowledge, and find the words to make that solo count.

Some years later I was teaching at a Quaker School in Washington, and I was the only Black teacher there and probably the only child of the sixties there as well. I was widely regarded in the school because the second week I was there some of my students discovered I had seen Jimi Hendrix live in my lifetime. The day after I told one of my English classes this, they were discussing Cream, and they thought I had never heard of this group. I said, "Now wait a minute, you were born after those people. That was music of my era." So then, when I told them I had actually seen Jimi Hendrix, who had died before they were born, a line formed outside my classroom of kids who were looking through the glass window to see the teacher who had seen Jimi Hendrix. Now every year at this school—and this, by the way, is the school Chelsea Clinton goes to—there is a theme day and the whole school participates by adopting the attire of whatever theme they think up. My second year there it was "sixties day," and when I came to school that day, the children were running up and down the halls with flowers in their hair, and cross-dressing, and they had a mock rock concert outside. Now, given my newly established expertise on the era, all day the students kept coming up to me and saying, "Is this what it was really like, Ms. Davis, is this what it was really like?" So it is a little disjunctive for me to answer the question, "Ain't we still got soul?" I really am trying to be in the nineties all the time. I feel a little passé, like a retired person, but I am trying to be in the nineties. But when I do think about soul, I am thinking critically about things that were part and parcel of those times, things that we took issue with, and I think it's okay for us to defend that. But I think at the same time, there is an element of loss to be looked at. A memorable example of this is when I went to this grocery store near Union Square one day, and I went to the cashier, who was a young Black woman, with a whole batch of kale and collards. And she looked at me and said, "What are these?" and I thought she meant which was kale and which were collards. But she registered even more confusion, held them up and emphatically asked again, "No. What *are* these?" Of course, I thought to myself, "We are in big trouble."

I think soul for me is made up of a lot of things. I always understood it to be part and parcel of resistance and endurance. I think improvisation, taking a solo, is a big part of what we learned growing up in soul—that it is something that has to be transmitted. Sharing was a big part of it—and sharing, today, is in deep trouble. Barry White is the only one offering to do something for us, and I think he only wants to do it for women, so are we still sharing? And then song was an enormous part of it—and, of course, greens. The greens are really a serious symbol of that part of us who are interested in health and interested in survival and endurance—a part of our survival we cannot afford to take for granted.

Soul also has written within it some degree of ambivalence towards the culture that represented oppression. I wouldn't have thought so thirty years ago—I thought everything was Black and White—but I think soul has an uncomfortable response to the notion of the beautiful, for instance. I don't think that once James Brown sang that song "Black Is Beautiful," that the ambivalence went away. I think we move in a certain direction, but I think if you look around today, that question is still uncomfortable for many of us. A friend of mine, who is my age, grew up in Washington, which had a de facto segregated school system in the sixties. In her elementary school, the classroom was arranged by color. Now mind you, this is a Black classroom in a desegregated environment with all Black children. The light-skinned children sat in the front and the dark children sat in the back and they went back by degree. Our standard of beauty is so cultured to some extent. Who sat at the front of that classroom? Has that standard of beauty, which we kept pushing Black towards the middle of that room and the back of that room, has that standard of beauty now put them in the front? It seems to me with the aid of technology and chemicals that it's back with a vengeance. There are lots of people who spend a lot of time inventing chemicals to alter Black looks.

Soul has historically had a male leadership stance; it needed to be addressed and has been addressed. But soul is ambivalent about the strength of women. Soul martyred women and it put women on a pedestal. We had race struggles over whether women could lead. Soul, as Clyde said, became an exotic product that was divorced from social change, and we're seeing that again. The market is forcing us to have more visibility and presence in certain social fields; there is actually a feeding frenzy for things that we are making. But this trend is also causing us, in a way, to respond to just making products. When I was growing up, what I understood to be soul was politics and pleasure. Resistance, endurance, laughter, sharing, improvisation, song—those things seem to me to play a decreasing role in pleasure as it circulates in the mainstream now, and this is perhaps best demonstrated in books which emphasize our apparent pathologies.

I want to talk a little bit about artists because it seems so tragic that literature, film, and music tend to be moving away from soul. This, I believe, is something we need to be vigilant about and insist that soul should try to resist this. Salman Rushdie said that because the writer only needs a pen and paper and not even a room, literature is the freest form of the arts. He said the more money a piece of work costs, the easier it is for someone else to control it. Film, the most expensive of art forms, is also the least subversive. I think we need to look at our literature in terms of that. Because we do not control the publishing, there is a lot of work being published which undermines us. What is being printed more and more every year is the pathology of Black people. In oppressive societies, writers have used metaphor, symbolism, and coded language to keep getting the truth across. Here I'm speaking not only about writers from forty years ago, but twenty years ago in Argentina, Uruguay, or wherever they had a police state. Many writers went into exile but continued to use a language which was understood by people. My question is, Do we still have that common language with which to resist? We in America have always given, willingly or unwillingly, our language to the mainstream. As long as we have cohesive communities, we produce more language. When we were talking about Charlie Parker and bebop, when we were talking about rap, we have continually been able, as long as our community stayed together, to continue evolving the language which was at first our language and a language of resistance. The artist must be searching for a language of resistance—particularly now, when we are at a time when language itself is a popular product. As I express this, I hear Stuart Hall speak at a film conference last year and I will end by quoting him. He asked a question about differences and stressed that what we need to look at is our shared commonness—what is distinctive, not about our color, but how we have been installed in a history of modernity. We should look for the continuity in our relationships to difference. This means looking at soul and resistance over a larger landscape. If we are talking about diaspora, it means we have talk about the culture we have entered and transformed. We have to inhabit it, contest it, inhabit it and displace it. That has been going on in both directions across the borders we live on. We have inhabited this culture and contested it. In many ways we have displaced the culture that has resisted us at ground level. The power of the culture was our soul. Do we still create a culture of resistance? Aren't we also being displaced, at least as we knew ourselves once? Do we recognize ourselves in soul, in the mirror? Having transformed the culture in our own likeness, what do we do now? Do we resist what we ourselves have made? My answer is yes. We measure work by what is needed now, not what was needed before. It is the essence of our greatest music; we honor what we've made and resist it—Miles Davis did it, and even dear old Mom.

ISHMAEL REED: In the mid-eighties, I embarked on a study of my ancestry and found it to be more complex than I would have imagined, having been schooled in a system in which African Americans had to camouflage their bloodlines in order to make some people, nouveau whites—that is, European Americans who were considered "Black" maybe fifty years ago—comfortable. But now a younger generation is beginning to assert their biracialism, or their multiculturalism, in a way that my generation could never have imagined. For this, they're being criticized by an older generation who insist upon Blackness that has often been used as a cover for racism, indicating that the germ that Europeans brought to the hemisphere—the English in New England and the Spanish in the Southwest—has infected African Americans. Just listen to some of these people—even some of those who can figure out what Derrida and Foucault were driving at—carrying on when discussing, say, miscegenation, and you'd think that you had David Duke

standing before you. The Native Americans whom the Europeans encountered when they arrived had no concept of race. Columbus describes Native Americans of different colors, and the Pueblo Indians in
the Southwest believed that all people, no matter what color, were
children of the earth.

Our West African ancestors didn't arrive here racist either. Studying
their customs and language also demonstrate how different we are from
what they were. One out of four of those Africans came from Yoruba
land in West Africa. Two thousand years before Calvin they believed in
a work ethic and a free market system (that we find in the United States).
The British found them to be cryptic, also a trait that African Americans
share. My great-grandmother, who was born in slavery, always told her
children not to allow anyone to get into one's business. She operated a
business from 1917 to 1934. I'm sure that this cryptic style has generated
cultural forms among African Americans that outsiders find inaccessible.

Translating Yoruba literature, one finds that Western intellectual
trends were anticipated by the African oral tradition by thousands of
years, which ought to encourage us to translate more African orature
rather than becoming bogged down in the discussion about whether
Plato, the bulk of whose work is hampered by useless metaphysical
speculation, was Black. Our intellectuals, even when they oppose what
some call "Western intellectual values," seemed to be hexed by them.
The task of many of them seems to be that of missionizing African
Americans. One appeared on one of the right-wing monocultural centers, the PBS news hour, and said that he preferred the intellectual
environment of the French Enlightenment to that of Black studies, when
the Enlightenment thinkers engaged in a considerable amount of hum-
bug speculation and helped to foster the scientific racism that characterized the next century. They prepared the way for Adolph Hitler. Voltaire,
for example, believed that Black women mated with monkeys.

Yoruba also have some practical advice for their descendants.
Though Africans in the diaspora concentrate on ritual and the "saints"
of the Yoruba, the Yoruba, as I read them, instruct us that we should use
our minds. (In fact, in Yoruba literature such as *Igbo Olodumare,* which
I am currently translating, humans are capable of defeating "the saints,"
upon which those in this hemisphere place such emphasis.) Your head,
your *ori,* is the only god that you can rely upon. According to Bolaji
Idowu, author of *Olodumare,* the *ori,* the head, is a symbol of the *inu-
ori,* the inner head, and it is the inner head, not the soul, that rules,

controls, and guides the "life" and activities of the person. There is a heart (*okan*) in the Yoruba system, but no soul.

Soul is an English word that African Americans have borrowed to explain something that defies empirical investigation. The *American Heritage Dictionary of the English Language* quotes Claude Brown when defining soul: "An aggregate of elemental qualities that enables one to be at harmony with oneself and to convey to the others the honest and unadorned expression of the hard side of life: 'Soul is bein' true to yourself . . . is . . . that uninhibited self-expression that goes into practically every Negro endeavor.' " If this is what soul means, then it doesn't represent the multimillion-dollar marketing that goes into such products as *Soul Train,* where the environment is controlled, or the use of "I'm a Soul Man" as the theme song of Bob Dole—a presidential candidate who is anything but uninhibited.

And so when we say soul, I think that we mean style, and there is no doubt that African Americans have a style, a way of cooking, of dancing, that's so attractive that even those who are pathologically hostile to Blacks adopt this style. Take fascist rock-and-roll bands, for example. The late Lee Atwater, one of the creators of the notorious Willie Horton campaign, was a rock-and-roll performer who received a better review in the *New York Times* than Black musicians usually receive. This style, which they had no hand in creating, is making these performers billions of dollars. Soul has become little more than a marketing device.

But the folks who did create this style, we're not using our heads in an organized manner. The difficult task that the well-financed adversaries of African Americans have set up for them has gone unchallenged. Toni Morrison was correct in her Howard University speech when she likened the current political atmosphere to that of pre-Hitler Germany. But I don't think that we have to leave this continent to find a parallel to the current conditions. Native Americans had been subsisting in this hemisphere for thousands of years until the Europeans arrived and disrupted their economy, made them dependent, and ultimately destroyed millions of them. No matter how assimilated African Americans might become—after all, the Cherokee assimilated very well into American society—what finally happened to the Native Americans haunts the experience of African Americans in this country (millions of whom have a Native American heritage).

And so though soul, a style, is entertaining and provides pleasure

that helps African Americans get through the hell that they find themselves in, the ultimate liberation of African Americans will be due to
their using their heads, not their souls. Their *inu-ori.*

Our ancestors were right, and there is still more that we can learn
from them.

DREAM HAMPTON: I think I'm having a different problem and, no
disrespect, but I think that there's this intergenerational thing. I'm
twenty-four, grew up on hip hop, and considered hip hop to be soul. I
felt that the soul tradition is still maintained through hip hop and maybe
now we have transformed it into something new. But a lot of times,
when we talk about soul being dead, about reclaiming soul, it's as
though we must reinvent it, as if there's nothing there. Ishmael Reed was
referring to Biggie Smalls, and there's like a plethora of artists out there,
not just hip hop artists, but young intellectuals. Of course, not NYU and
other institutions that we're at war with while we're within them. I just
want to kind of address that, bring it to the forefront, because we're
talking about a generation that landed from nowhere, that invaded our
communities as opposed to being born and nurtured within them. We
still represent soul and have something invested in the survival of our
communities. It's as though we're trying to go beyond this generation to
save the next. Like we're a write-off and everyone else is moving on.

MAULTSBY: You allude to a point that I made. Soul is a concept that
defines a distinctly Black worldview and a way of being. Because Black
culture is not monolithic nor stagnant, each generation employs this
concept in ways that reflect its unique set of circumstances, which are
informed by cultural, social, and political environments. You mentioned
hip hop. I believe that Afrocentric rappers are largely responsible for
revitalizing the 1960s application of soul as an ideological and cultural
concept. In the process, they have raised generation X's consciousness
about a historical past and the ideals of Black nationalism. These rappers
have also made Black suburbanites and the larger society aware of the
social ills that plague inner-city communities. Therefore, I agree with
your comments.

HAMPTON: But I think even naming the Afrocentric rappers, it's been a
long time since an Afrocentric rap album came out—in the traditional
sense that you're talking about. The binary poles that have been constructed in hip hop around good and bad, around narratives and mes-

sages, are ones that I don't think existed twenty to thirty years ago. It's been this kind of moral construct. Biggie Smalls and Nas—you may not consider them to be Afrocentric, but I would argue that they still operate within a certain tradition of soul in our communities.

MAULTSBY: I agree with you. Soul is expressed in different ways within and across generations. Your comment indirectly alludes to the commodification issue discussed earlier. Once a Black cultural product has been commodified for mass consumption, it is assigned a different function and, thus, acquires a new meaning suited to the new context. However, and within African-American communities, its original meaning and sociocultural and political significance are preserved or adapted to meet the demands of a new situation.

QUESTION: Why are we tied to content and not style?

MAULTSBY: It's all the same content—that was my whole thing. Soul is a style—it's a style distinctive to African Americans characterized by improvisatory components. The call-response, community participatory components, defined by a worldview that's all a part of the concept of soul that is manifested in a style. There is a style of the seventies; there is George Clinton and the P-Funk. That was his soul. The rappers have their soul—in a different way. But also they maintain some of those fundamental aesthetic features—this is what links African Americans from two to four hundred years ago to the present day. We share a core of aesthetic qualities. We share a particular worldview that's been shaped by an oppressive existence that has not changed for four hundred years; now it may have taken on a different form so we're still creating out of that experience, drawing from our aesthetic qualities and expressive styles of an African past. So we're part of a continuum, of a legacy that is just redefined with a new set of circumstances, but it survives of the culture of the past.

20

From This Ivory Tower

Race as a Critical Paradigm in the Academy
(A Discussion in Two Acts)

Introduction

MONIQUE GUILLORY

In a book about soul, a roundtable discussion on race as a critical paradigm in the academy may appear a bit incongruous, a sacrilege even. Academics have fallen under heavy fire for sapping the fun out of everything. From movies and music to the blind security most people feel with their own identities—we nitpick and dissect everything of value into nothingness. And now, after submitting "soul" to our unforgiving knife, we have to throw something about "critical paradigms" into the mix.

But soul-searching is second nature to the fledgling Black academic who must constantly reevaluate and second-guess the personal, spiritual, and economic investment that graduate school demands. Many of us were drawn to the academy by the lofty intellectual tradition Blacks such as W. E. B. Du Bois, Zora Neale Hurston, and Angela Davis have honed there. In recent years, the country has reveled in a second Black Renaissance that tempts and tantalizes aspiring Black intellectuals with unprecedented power and visibility. When Toni Morrison won the Nobel Prize, when bell hooks bridged the academic divide on *Oprah*, and every time we read an op-ed piece in the *New York Times* by Henry Louis Gates Jr., we are charged with fire for the fight and earnestly believe, "I can do this."

Yet, determining whether you can get your Ph.D. usually is not the question facing black graduate students, but rather the more profound question of whether you should. Once inside the hallowed halls of the academy, one of the first lessons you learn as a Black graduate student is that institutions of higher learning have not opened the floodgates to Black studies, aesthetics, texts, theories, or students for that matter. The above examples are precious exceptions, but they are so ubiquitous and renowned that they start to appear to be the norm. Not until you are deeply embroiled in the system, on the verge of that nebulous space known as "the market," do you start to recognize how difficult it can be to navigate the political tides of academia and not soon find yourself stranded and soul-sick.

Thus, at the Soul Conference, we convened the following group of scholars and academics to offer us reassurance and inspiration. Our logic was that they had done what we were trying to do, so all we needed to do was sit down and have some honest heart-to-heart discussion about how to get through the experience of grad school with (1) a job, (2) as little pain as possible, and (3) as much soul as we could salvage. The academy is not the most hospitable place for soul—an abstract and essentialist construct imagined by an imagined community. It may have been different thirty years ago, but these days upon entering graduate school, you check your soul at the door and in exchange for it you receive a bushel of dialectics, universalisms, theories, critiques, texts, and discourses. And while your soul sits in some existential coatroom with your name on it, after five or six years of academic programming, you may not even know how to ask for it back.

I found the comments that follow to be enormously helpful in both practical and personal ways. It was surprising and a bit jarring to me, however, to realize that the women academics felt in no way as secure or finished with the professional battles in the academy as they appeared. I should not have been surprised by the stories of tenure wars, of having to contend with sexism and condescension no matter how high you scale the Ivory Tower. The women in this conversation stress the importance of anchoring yourself to a reliable support system early in the battle of your education. They caution against trying to find yourself or your mother in the often cold and indifferent clime of the academy. The tone of the men is notably different. They were able to offer a practical and pedagogical guideline through the graduate years. The men emphasized issues of specialization and concentration, how

285

and what to teach to market yourself for as broad a consumption base as possible.

I conclude with a scenario that serves as a common denominator for academics everywhere, regardless of stature or stability. Any academic could give you his or her version of how they survive these ever-impending tests of the will and wits, but here I offer my most recent trial as a preface to the comments and encouragements these scholars offered to conquer the banal and discouraging chores that pose a considerable threat to every intellectual's soul.

The Parable of the Books

In two days, I am moving from Brooklyn, New York, to Santa Barbara, California, to complete my dissertation in a more serene and struggling-student-friendly place. In light of the impending move and the incomplete manuscript, my life of late has been the predictable whirlwind of mental and physical activity that moving entails. From stocking up on ten-pound sacks of kitty litter (trying to make it easier for the sublet) to working feverishly on the book, it feels like everything that I have learned, accumulated, and worked for in the past four years conflates to some impossible detail I must tend to in these final East Coast days. But today, all the reasons why I feel the following roundtable discussion is pertinent to the question of soul crystalized for me in a rather grueling and taxing way.

The day began at 7 A.M. with me, pissed and frustrated, pouting behind a fort of twenty-eight boxes on the sidewalk in front of my apartment building. I was fortunate enough to find a sublet who was willing to watch my cats for the year I would be away. But while he could handle the cats, this fellow graduate student had a library of his own, of course. My cats could stay, but my books had to go. Which was perfectly fine by me. After too many times of frantically scrambling for hours to find a book I know I own, only to realize that it's collecting dust under someone's bed across town, I have become extremely protective of my books. I could picture the chaos upon my return if my books commingled for a year in the same small space. I'm sure some of them would couple up and I'd inevitably lose a few treasures.

To avoid that costly horror (I am absolutely positive that I have bought *Flyboy in the Buttermilk* at least three times), I squirreled away the vestiges of my academic career in twenty-eight specimens of the best book boxes you can rummage from the trash. Banana boxes are the best—they're durable, usually have a cover (very important for vertical stacks on hand trucks), and come with easy-grip slots on the sides. I once swore by milk crates for moving books, but you can never get them level (very important for vertical stacks on hand trucks) and if your library compounds every year, as mine did, storing milk crates in a tiny Manhattan coup quickly becomes a decorating nightmare. This selection of boxes was pretty impressive as it ought to be after all the experience I have had lugging my modest library across the country and through the boroughs of New York. Of my four years in New York alone, this was my sixth move.

Waiting for the ever-elusive truck, I fantasized about getting a job that would pay my moving expenses—an unlikely dream for an academic. I imagined myself directing the movers hither and thither, making them fresh lemonade as they indifferently schlepped my belongings along the trajectory of my rapidly rising career. I thought of Edward Said's essay on unpacking his library in the same way that he recalled Benjamin's experience with boxes of books. Somehow I felt convinced that they had not packed their own stuff in boxes pulled from the trash.

The reverie abruptly ceased when the man at the storage space showed me where my precious library would reside for the next year or so. Although the lease claimed I was getting a five-by-six-foot space, the cavity I peered into seemed no bigger than a shipping carton for a twenty-five-inch TV. But it would have to do, because although these folks can make you feel like you're committing yourself to a summer cottage when you get a storage space in New York, I simply refuse to pay anything that even feels like "rent" to have my belongings just sit there. By some miracle of geometry I figured I could manipulate the twenty-eight boxes into the bin, but it did concern me that the space was about five feet above my head.

I maneuvered the mobile staircase over to my cubical and tried to calculate how I would manage to stuff these ridiculously heavy boxes into this space without lifting them over my head or scaling the rickety scaffold twenty-eight perilous times. I certainly couldn't throw the boxes up there, nor could I stack them up on the stairs and then load them into the space because there wasn't enough room for that. I struggled to shrug off the self-pity that inevitably slinks up to me whenever I find myself in a circumstance in which it would be really nice to have a man around—someone big and strong who had read all the books the boxes contained and discussed them with me as he effortlessly toted them up the stairs two at time.

I soon stopped wasting time and accepted my fate—each box would have to be carried up the stairs. The tragedy of Sisyphus flashed before my eyes. I studied the pallet of boxes and, with x-ray vision, espied their voluminous and bulky contents—two volumes of the unabridged *Oxford English Dictionary* (complete with magnifying lens), complete box sets of Campbell's *Myths of the World* and Shakespeare's plays, unruly binders of assorted articles, and an asymmetrical deck of over-sized art books—just to name some of the more formidable heavy-weights.

As I struggled, wrenched, and wrestled the twenty-eight bundles of hell into their grave, I was ready to bid them a final farewell. Never would I want to see these books again—half of them I probably have never read and will likely live out the course of my life without the morsels of insight they may contain. I laughed at myself and the irony of the considerable material burden academia can be with such little material return. I tried to reason away the absurdity of the situation by thinking that my physical strength simply could not accommodate the physical manifestation of my considerable mental strength and fortitude. But I found little consolation in that thought and resigned myself to the crude reality that I was out of shape, mainly because I had been sitting on my butt for the past four years either reading a book, writing a paper, or talking about my lack of motivation to do either.

In spite of my limited conditioning and bitter mood, after only two and a half hours, a broken nail, and a few bruises and scrapes, I finally snapped the lock onto D-951 and nearly floated out of the maze of mini-storage. I signed and snatched up my reams of paperwork, listened to the automatons behind the bulletproof glass drone on about late fees and insurance, and felt so physically drained that I could bid adieu to every text and title I had hauled into that chasm. After considerable maneuvering and contortion, the exact configuration of those boxes remains emblazoned on my mind—the brilliant colors of *African Ark* pressed up against the door waiting to tumble out onto the first unsus-pecting soul to unlock that Pandora's box.

But I know I will go back for the lot of them in D-951 because I realize that I could no more abandon my books than a tortoise could vacate its shell. I accept that this education is simply never complete and that I will have more coursework, only this time it will be on the other side of the table. As I approach that facet of my academic tenure, I was encouraged to hear the stories of those academics I admire and trust. Through the experiences they relate here, and even more so in their own work and intellectual paths, they each demonstrate that a graduate education ultimately remains a highly personal and individualized event. There are requirements and expectations, obstacles and rewards, but the kind of life and the kind of career each person makes of those factors depends significantly upon what they bring to the table as well.

I, myself, will bring twenty-eight boxes of books.

Act One

MANTHIA DIAWARA

In the spring semester of the academic year 1994–95, I added Jean-Paul Sartre's *Black Orpheus* to the reading list of my course "Introduction to Pan-Africanism." Because I wanted to emphasize the Harlem Renaissance and the Negritude movement as cultural and political components of Pan-Africanism, it seemed to me that Sartre's long introduction to the art and philosophy of the Negritude movement, like Alain Locke's manifesto at the beginning of his book *The New Negro*, would help to set the stage for further discussions of the problematic issue of race and its relation to culture and universalism.

The class began with W. E. B. Du Bois's *The World and Africa,* which refutes the racist thesis, primarily associated with Eurocentric historians, that of all the continents, Africa had made no contribution to world history and civilization. Du Bois's main objectives in this celebratory book, as in his classic *Souls of Black Folk,* were threefold: to write the history and culture of the people of Africa and African descent; to enable African Americans to identify with Africa as a proud and dignified source of identity that could be placed on an equal footing with Europe, Asia, and North America; and to posit Africa's humanism and rich heritage as a compelling argument against racism and colonialism. Du Bois believed that freedom was whole and indivisible, that Black people in America would not be completely free until Africa was liberated and emancipated in modernity; his Pan-Africanism was born out of the consciousness of freedom as a common goal for Black and Brown people.

That first week, the class's reaction to *The World and Africa* was aggressive. One student from Africa challenged the very idea of Pan-Africanism, warning us that Africans were very different from Nigeria to Ethiopia, and that African Americans, like White Americans, were ignorant about Africa's complexity. Another accused Du Bois and other Pan-Africanists of the same colonial intentions as White people, and added that race should not be used to justify the paternalism and elitism of African Americans and West Indians in Africa. One woman also raised a question concerning the links between Pan-Africanism and sexism. But the majority tended to focus on Du Bois's attempt to raise consciousness about the worldwide exploitation of Black and Brown people by people of European descent, and on his quest for freedom.

I knew that the class was not going to be easy. I had to find some texts by women and Afrocentrists to add to the reading list. But, one might wonder, why *Black Orpheus,* a text by a dead French White male? Because the Du Boisian ideas of race unity are more interesting if they are studied together and repositioned by other racial theories in time and space, such as the nationalism of the Negritude movement, the Afrocentric movement, and Sartre's thesis of antiracist racism as the basis for combatting colonialism and paternalism. I wanted to know what would happen to the core idea of Pan-Africanism if it were taught as a history of often contradictory ideas instead of a chronology of events and historical figures. What were the common links, for instance, between Du Bois's statement that the problem of the twentieth century was the problem of the color line and the Diopian, or Afrocentric, theory of the cultural unity of the people of African descent; and by extension, what were the intertextual relations between Du Bois' Pan-Africanism and C. L. R. James's appropriation of the central themes of the French Revolution for Black liberation struggles and his repositioning of the Haitian uprising as the first paradigm of race unity between Black and Brown people in the modern world; or Sartre's call for an antiracist racism, in *Black Orpheus,* as a reason for unity among Black people against racism and colonialism? Sartre is important to me in this debate not only because of his role as an intellectual leader who was involved in several revolutionary movements in France in the 1940s and 1950s, including Negritude—I shall say more about this later—but also because of the similarities between his position on antiracist racism and the Diopian essentializing of race.

Black Orpheus was written as an introduction to the *Anthologie de la Nouvelle Poésie Nègre et Malgache de Langue Française* (1948), edited by Léopold Sédar Senghor. It is the most famous essay on the Negritude movement, serving on the one hand to define the concept for Western audiences, and on the other hand to encourage some of its poets and writers to embrace Marxism in their search for a universal road beyond skin color. For Sartre, Negritude is a separation and a negation in the existential sense; it valorizes a word that was until then an ugly and dirty word in the French language. A French dictionary, *Le Nouveau Petit Robert,* gives the word *Nègre,* from which Negritude is derived, the following meanings: a person of the Black race, a slave; to work like a *Nègre* is to work hard without earning the right to rest; to be a *Nègre* in the literary world is to be a ghostwriter for famous authors; to speak *petit Nègre* is to express oneself in a limited and bad French. In other words, a *Nègre* is a person without a soul and a mind; a dirty person; the opposite of a White person, of a human being. For Sartre, Negritude derives its authenticity from the unhinging of the word *Nègre* from these traditional connotations in the French language; from the destabilization of the meanings embedded in the roots of the concept; from its revelation that "there is a secret Blackness in white, a secret whiteness in Black, a vivid flickering of being and of nonbeing."

Sartre defines Negritude as an operative power of negation, an antiracist racism, which unites Black people in their combat to reclaim their humanity. He finds in the poetry of Aimé Césaire, Senghor, Léon Gontran Damas, and many others from the French West Indies and Francophone Africa, an authentic élan driven by a new meaning of Blackness; an existentialist affirmation liberated from fixed and atavistic connotations in the French imaginary; an obsessive energy sending the Black poets after their Negritude. Sartre is reminded of Orpheus's descent into Hell to rescue Eurydice. The Black poet, too, will leave no stone unturned, will reverse the meaning of every French word that has contributed to his subjugation, and rescue his Negritude with positive values. Sartre sees another analogy in the manner in which the Negritude poets defamiliarize the French language: to Prometheus stealing the fire, symbol of knowledge, from Zeus. This leads the French master to declare Negritude a *poésie engagée,* "the sole great revolutionary poetry" in French at that time.

At first, Sartre's celebration of Negritude's racial essentialism does not seem to allow room for criticism. Like the poets, he sings the African's closeness to nature; he speaks of the synthetic African versus the analytic European, the capacity of Black people to display emotion against the cold rationality of White people, and the African's blameless role in modern history's catalog of genocide, fascism, and racism. For Sartre, the White worker is incapable of producing good poetry because he has been contaminated by his objective and technical surroundings. The Black man, on the other hand, is subjective and therefore authentic; his poetry is evangelical; the Black man, as Sartre puts it, "remains the great male of the earth, the world's sperm." The Negritude that Sartre describes here resembles that of Cheikh Anta Diop and Senghor, who believe that Black people live in a symbiotic relation with nature, unlike white people who dominate and destroy their environment.

But Sartre is not content to define Negritude as only an antiracist racism uniting people around race consciousness to combat French colonialism, paternalism, and imperialism. He also sees Negritude as a becoming, a transcendence of Blackness into a future universalism. For Sartre, there are two ways of constructing racial concepts, one internal and the other external. Those who internalize their Negritude and make of it an irreducible difference are mobilized by the desire to constitute a unique history and to shield themselves from outside contamination. They are traditionalists. On the other hand, there is the vanguard that deploys Blackness as an antiracist racism, or uses racial consciousness as a social movement, because it "desires the abolition of all kinds of ethnic privileges; solidarity with the oppressed of every color." Here, Sartre anticipates the Blackness of C. L. R. James, who discovered that Black unity coincided with the quest for liberty, fraternity, and equality, the central themes of the French Revolution that Toussaint L'Ouverture appropriated for Haiti; of Césaire, who wrote *Discourse on Colonialism;* and of Frantz Fanon, who stated that "a nation which undertakes a liberation struggle rarely condones racism."

Sartre, too, sees the ideal of the French Revolution in Negritude:

The Black contribution to the evolution of Humanity is no longer savor, taste, rhythm, authenticity, a bouquet of primitive instincts; it is a dated enterprise, a long-suffering construction and also a future. Previously, the Black man claimed his place in the sun in the name of ethnic qualities; now, he establishes his right to life on his mission; and this mission, like the proletariat's, comes to him from his historical position: because he has suffered from capitalistic exploitation more than all the others, he has acquired a sense of revolt and a love of liberty more than all the others. And because he is the most oppressed, he necessarily pursues the liberation of all, when he works for his own deliverance.

Black Orpheus provoked the ideological divisions in my class to come to the surface. There were those who felt invigorated by Sartre's call for a common struggle for a universal humanism. They agreed with Sartre that Negritude was about class struggle, that racism and colonialism themselves were conditions of class antagonism. Others felt that this movement toward the universal was preventing the Black struggle from defining its own agenda for freedom and recognition; they felt that Sartre was diluting the meaning of Negritude.

I asked the class to think seriously about the passage quoted above, and to put into brackets, in a Husserlian sense, the words "it is a dated enterprise, a long-suffering construction and also a future." With these words, I felt that Sartre had historicized Negritude into a grand narrative and conferred upon it the same mission as Christianity or Marxism, two of the most important teleological social movements of modern history.

Negritude's utopia calls for a society without racism and class division. Sartre placed his hope on Negritude, which he believed would create the society that Europe failed to realize at the end of the Second World War. Richard Wright also believed that Europeans had abandoned the spirit of modernity by refusing to give up racism and xenophobia. What better people than Blacks, therefore, who have known racism and suffering, to charge with the mission of ending the evils of humanity and bringing the grand narrative to closure? Negritude contains the romantic ideas that the oppressed would not persecute their brothers and sisters because they knew how it felt to be oppressed; that the excluded would know the meaning of ostracism; and that those who suffered the pogroms would teach the world to love. Confident that decolonization was the most important revolution of the last half of the twentieth century, the Negritude poets would identify with suffering, as Christ did, in order to end all suffering.

I feel that this Sartrean view is worth pursuing in Pan-Africanism; it universalizes Black struggle by positing Africa and other continents involved in the fight against colonialism and racism as the future of the world. Negritude and other decolonizing movements, before being coopted by the Cold War and forced to align themselves with NATO or the Soviet Bloc, held the promise of the world renewal: Black and Brown people would have the right to shape their own destinies; and the White people would rid themselves of the guilt accumulated through centuries of racism and paternalism. Modernity would be finally fulfilling its true mission in the Habermasian sense: to go beyond the visible difference of skin color and save humanity from obscurantism and oppression.

Suddenly, this changes the goal of Negritude into something larger than the Black poets who invented it. Negritude will not be limited to Africa and turned inward into a narcissistic contemplation of the self, or fixed as a blinding determinism of skin color. Its poets will seize the leaven of life away from those who hate and exploit, in order to provide energy to those in need of freedom and emancipation. The mission of Negritude is now universal freedom, which encompasses not only the colonized subjects of Africa and the Caribbean, but also the exploited working classes of Europe, America, and Asia. Clearly, the struggle for Black rights in Negritude coincides with Sartre's Marxian analysis of the condition of the working class in France, and with the Civil Rights Movement in America. The role of the Black poet, like that of a demiurge, is to create a new man and new woman in a new world, and not to ghettoize the muse. In his pathbreaking book, *The Wretched of the Earth;* Fanon, a young writer coming out of the Negritude movement, was the first to agree with Sartre and to declare the pitfalls of racial identification "the unconditional affirmation of African culture has succeeded the unconditional affirmation of European culture."

I wanted my students to know what this meant to some of us growing up in Africa in the 1950s and 1960s. The idea that Negritude is bigger even than Africa, that we were part of an international movement that held the promise of universal emancipation, that our destiny coincided with the universal freedom of workers and colonized people worldwide, gave us a bigger and more important identity than the ones available to us until then through kinship, ethnicity, and race. It felt good to be in tune not only with Sartre himself, but with such world-renowned revolutionaries as Karl Marx, Leon Trotsky, Albert Camus, André Malraux, Fidel Castro, Angela Davis, Mao Tse-Tung, Martin Luther King Jr., Nelson Mandela, and Frantz Fanon. The awareness of our new historical mission freed us from what we thought then were the archaic identities of our fathers and their religious entrapments; freed us from race and made us no longer afraid of the whiteness of French identity. To now be labeled the saviors of humanity, when just yesterday we were colonized and despised by the world, gave us a feeling of righteousness that bred contempt for capitalism, racialism of all origins, and tribalism. In fact, the universalism proposed by Sartre became for some of us a new way of being radically chic, of jumping into a new identity in order not to deal with race, which was not mentioned except during discussions of racism. It was not until the mid-sixties, when we became sufficiently immersed in Black American popular culture, that race reappeared as a significant element of culture.

Ironically, this awareness of common struggle, of the worldwide demand for human rights from White supremacists and capitalists, seems to take away Negritude's first claim to authenticity and singularity. As some students in the class pointed out, it may not be possible to take everyone in the direction that Sartre is taking Negritude. The desire to appear universal may cause Negritude to forget or ignore some of its constituent elements, and therefore to disintegrate. The students were concerned about Sartre setting the agenda for the Negritude poets, a White man telling them what to do and how to do it and therefore diluting the radical ideas in the movement.

It is true in this sense that Negritude is primarily a poetry by Black people about Black people. It is also true that every movement has its own internal coherence, which is kept alive by the specific way in which the movement sets its elements into motion and maintains a specific relation between them. This autonomy imparts to a movement like Negritude its singularity, enables it to shine among other movements, and even to be admired and imitated by them. One risks rendering invisible these constitutive parts by emphasizing too quickly the similarities between Negritude and the proletarian movements around the world.

But, I asked the class, is the movement toward the particular necessarily a move away from the universal? Or, to put it in another way, is the movement toward the universal a selling out of Black culture? My own answer is no in both cases. When the particular is successful, its central themes begin to illuminate other struggles and creative projects. And conversely, when the universal is truly universal, it takes away from the particular the need for resistance and ghettoization and brings freedom to the elements that used to constitute the particular. This is what Sartre sees in Negritude, a movement he thinks is capable of shedding a new light on the meanings of freedom, love, and universal beauty. The light coming from Africa and from Black poets, visible enough to influence liberation struggles elsewhere and release energies in other parts of the world against racism and exploitation, is what constitutes the universality of Negritude. It is important, therefore, to distinguish Negritude from its emanations. The universality of a thing is not the thing itself—it is what the thing reveals or teaches to others; it is external to the thing itself. Sartre emphasizes that which is external to Negritude: the Black poet's gift to the world; in other words, the lesson of freedom.

Some of my students said that Sartre's universalism was Eurocentric; his sources—Orpheus, Prometheus, the Bible, the proletariat—were all from a European scholastic tradition, not from Egyptian or ancient sub-Sahara African sources. It did not grant the Negritude poets time enough to digest what their Blackness meant to them and what they wanted to do with it. Yet Negritude, as part of decolonization, was important because, for the first time, it enabled Black people in France to assert themselves in the political, psychological, and artistic spheres. This would later lead to the independence of several African countries with Negritude writers among the heads of state. Negritude enabled Africans and West Indians, for the first time, to deploy Blackness as a positive concept of modernization: be proud of your ancestry, discover the beauty of Blackness, and let Negritude unite you against colonialism. It is because the Negritude poets turned inward to become conscious of their own historical situation that they discovered a truth bigger than themselves; it is because they sang their love song from within this specificity that it shone and inspired other liberation songs.

It was then time for me to make an argument exposing certain ethnocentric definitions of universalism. I explained to the class that I understood the need to celebrate Negritude on the ground of particularism. I myself might not have been their teacher today, had it not been for the nationalism of the Negritude poets. My generation was drawn to Negritude because of its promise to make us equal to White people, to lift us above the tribe and the clan, and to provide us with our own nations. Many of the children of my generation, overlooked by the colonial system, only went to school and learned to read and write because of Negritude and independence. It is in this sense that we say that Negritude invented us, taught us how to think in a particularly modern way, and put us inside history. It is easier to ask those who would have known modernity without Negritude to forget about it than to demand those of us who owe our modernity to Negritude to abandon it for the universal. As Sartre himself puts it, "The colored man—and he alone—can be asked to renounce the pride of his color." The universalist tendency carries with it, and against the separatist tendency, a threat of destruction of identity, a shift of priority, an aggressive attitude that leads the separatist to feel anxiety over being cast aside and neglected.

It is important to remember again that the universal is always a gift or a revelation to the world. The modes of actualization of this gift lead, under certain social conditions, to control, resistance, or disempowerment. First of all, the universal may take on particularist or racist features whenever people, in order to control it, choose a selective way of dissemination. Césaire was right in calling the colonial experience in Africa a controlled gift system, because it was willing only to selectively educate and to partially Christianize the native Africans and was never interested in letting people take full advantage of the universal potential of education and Christianity. But a gift must be total in order to have a positive cultural significance.

Today, people still give selectively, and there remains an essentialist tendency that links Whiteness to such universal practices as scientific inquiries and classical music. For example, the reluctance to give generously or let go of things leads some scholars to keep referring to the novel as a Western narrative form, as opposed to a form invented in Europe at a particular moment in history. Clearly, to write a novel today one does not have to be European or agree with a European way of life. A parsimonious gift system colors our vision of America itself, whose civilization is called "Western." But notwithstanding the presence of Americans of European descent and the development of certain ideas and practices that originated in Europe, the fact remains that the identities of Americans derived as much from a flight from Europe and its monarchist, Victorian, and religious cultures as from Africa and Asia; America is not culturally interchangeable with Europe, just as it cannot be with Africa and Asia.

Interestingly enough, the reference to America's Western identity is no more than the European Americans' desire to insert themselves permanently in the very image of Americanness and to maintain the power to reproduce themselves as the ideal and universal Americans. This type of essentialism remains a problem as people continue to lay claim to certain universal elements discovered by their ancestors at a particular time in history; obviously they are still suffering from a separation anxiety. The mishandling of the loss of a country of origin and the psychological split engendered by the flight from Europe to America leads to a denial of new American identities, to a permanent misrecognition of these new identities as purely Western, and consequently to racism and xenophobia.

The desire to control the universal element in Negritude, or to give selectively, haunts also some Black people in Africa and the diaspora. Here, though, social agents are faced with a different problem because, unlike the European Americans who possess the means of disseminating what is universal and of exercising control over its deployment, they have no mechanism of distributing their Negritude in the public sphere and therefore are unable to control its definition universally. Faced with the dearth of political, cultural, and scientific resources with which to position audiences for their category of the universal, Black people who cannot stimulate or impose reality through their representations rely either on Euromodernisms such as Marxism or Christianity to define their Negritude or retreat into narrow particularism and resistance. For example, Afrocentrists resort to the binary opposition schemata of Euromodernism, which freeze into an eternal antagonism Black and White, good and evil, sedentary and nomadic, sun people and ice people, as a mode of defining their Negritude. The proponents of ethnophilosophy in Africa, on the other hand, posit tribal religions, oral traditions, and drumology as the basis for identity formation and rationalization of their Negritude. Clearly, social agents can be pushed to retreat into the comfort zone of identity politics because of lack of access to the tools necessary for the distribution of universal ideas and objects, the wide commercial dissemination by others of what they perceive as their culture, or the continued absence of their images in what is perceived as universal. But such resistance movements risk deviating from the very modernity that revealed itself to them in the Negritude poets' struggle for liberation.

In contemporary debates on universalism, it is easy to see that people who refute the existence of race on biological and cultural grounds are among the same groups that deny the large majority of Blacks access to the political, economic, and cultural means that will enable them to move beyond the simple determinism of color. It is increasingly easier to point to the homophobia, sexism, and xenophobia in groups that espouse particularism, and harder for public intellectuals to try to provide such groups with access to the economic and political means that cause White males to become less xenophobic, homophobic, and sexist. Currently, White male control over the definition of what is universal, beautiful, and rational also excludes particularists from discursive spaces. Writer and critic Ishmael Reed is right to refer to English departments as White ethnic studies because, like black and Chicano studies departments, English departments refuse to democratize the aesthetic criteria that give other literatures access to their lists of great books. One cannot continue to defend the claim for the universality of art while resisting at the same time the universalization of access to the social and economic conditions that produce a taste for art.

On the last day of class, I brought up Sartre's *Black Orpheus* again and asked the students if they thought it had a place in a class on Pan-Africanism. The debate was as animated as the first day of class. Most students had not been swayed from their original positions, but they were more friendly this time. I was not surprised. As a teacher, I see my role as a facilitator; in other words, I wanted to provide students with enough arguments to defend whatever position they chose to occupy. There was one bright moment for me in all of this. One student confessed that she took the class because of the authentic sound of my African name. All the courses on Black people and Africa were taught by White professors. She did not trust them. She wanted to study with a real African and see what it was like. "And?" I asked impatiently. "Oh! Now I know that white people are not all the same, just as all Black people are not the same. With more Black professors like you around, I no longer feel mistrust of White professors and their knowledge of Africa; and I am glad that you made us read Sartre."

Act Two: Summaries of Roundtable Discussions by Houston A. Baker Jr., Phillip B. Harper, Trudier Harris, and Tricia Rose

HOUSTON A. BAKER JR.

Since the reflections that follow are meant to serve as both sheltering reflections and as a series of stories within stories, what better sign than imbrication to cover the whole. There are myriad poststructuralist uses of the term *imbrication,* but I want to use it in a rather literal sense. Imbrication, simply, means layering or overlapping, as with the tiles on a roof. Remove one tile and you have a serious leak, or an entirely different story. In what follows I briefly suggest the imbrication or roofing of a built environment called "Black Studies." There are so many layerings in the present conservative climate of the United States that perhaps the only way to proceed is by such large framings as the following.

Academically, Black Studies may be seen as an empiricist outgrowth of the "Negro History" movement. I mean this only in the sense that the word *study* marks a particular, public space of Negro schooling. Whether most of us knew his name or not, Carter G. Woodson was who we were experiencing in those meagerly resourced, but nevertheless committed, Negro History weeks of our youths. We saw the blackboard decor from last year come out again, and we recited the mantra of Negro contributions to America: from George Carver's peanuts to Ralph Bunche's Nobel Prize. Of course, W. E. B. Du Bois and many thousands gone, from John Russwurm and Wells Brown to Wilmot Blyden and Anna Julia Cooper, have made a conceptual claim upon us with respect to Black Studies. Aware of "race" as the great seismic divide of American life, these conceptualists offered sometimes panoramic—sometimes merely Pan-Africanist—schemata and prolegomena for rethinking, re-writing, and revisioning relations of "race" in the United States. If Woodson was an empiricist believer in the "contributions" and archives school, Du Bois and company, as conceptualists, were surrounded always by an aura of idealism (even in their sometimes darkest hours) that seemed to reflect a sense of convergent interests. Black and White together in America; the heady prospect of a better (shall we say "hybrid") life ahead. Much of this had to do, I think, with the public space of the schools, with access to and mastery of certain forms of scholarly address, and with certain strenuous wrestlings with at least two key queries. First, "What matter who speaks?" And, in tandem, "To whom and with whom does one speak?" While a sometimes (to be charitable) acerbic Woodson came increasingly to mark out a public space of K–12 as the discursive territory of his work, Du Bois and company seemed dramatically more divided in their articulations. From *The Brownies' Book* to *Black Reconstruction* is an astronomical leap.

I offer these brief remarks as an overly general way of characterizing some traditional Black Studies personnel and problems in the United States. What I have not said, of course, is that these questions of subject position, public sphere constructivism, and audience determination are as clear markers of "modernity" (in the sense powerfully suggested and illustrated by Manthia Diawara and an urbane Africana Studies at New York University today) as one is likely to find articulated in these United States.

Let me give a somewhat too densely metaphorical "just so" tale, by way of clarification. Several weeks ago, I had the honor of visiting Tuskegee University to deliver the first Ralph Ellison Memorial Lecture. On the afternoon of my visit, I discovered three things. First, that the whole of this historically Black university is designated as "historical," and as such it is meta- and macro-managed by the United States National Parks Service. "Smoky [as opposed to "Jack"] the Bear meets the New Negro," I thought to myself. Second, I went to the George Washington Carver Museum, where that inventive genius is constructed and preserved as a stunning example of the conversion to "aesthetic"—a recognition of Black subsistence confinement on somebody else's land. Third, under the fierce, clear (and possibly contemptuous) eyes of a portrait of Booker T. Washington, I lifted a telephone receiver, pushed a button and heard the recording that the great B.T.'s son made of the famous 1895 speech in Atlanta. It was epiphanic: the rolling periods, trilled *R*s, sonorous and entirely Standard English information and flow. I remember learning as a boy that you could always tell by someone's voice on the telephone if he or she was "Black." Well, on that receiver in that museum at Tuskegee there was no way—even with the inexactness and skips of early recording technology—to unequivocally identify those Washingtonian periods as "Black."

Now if Washington was, in tone and timbre, an empiricist, he achieved his results through a complete reconceptualization of what "Black" public speaking should sound like—how it should be "identified." The conjuncture (to borrow a word from the excellent vocabulary of Stuart Hall) that Washington effected between the conceptual and the empiricist is a marvel of Tuskegee.

But if it seems that I have emphasized the downside of Tuskegee confinement, it must be remembered that at the University of Pennsylvania, where I work, there are many many Black students who have never ventured into the W. E. B. Du Bois residence with the fixed intention of surveying the history of "Black" struggle permanently displayed on the walls of that building. Such students have no concept or empirical evidence of where they are. Jack the Bear has them happily in a hole of his devising. One also suspects there are many many Black students at fair Harvard who do not even recognize the habitational and locative imbrications of 77 Dunster Street. They are in a public hole, rather than articulate to the public as a whole. Which cohort of the young, Black, restless, and talented at the University of Michigan could recite the résumé of Harold Cruse and position him on an empirical or conceptualist continuum? Under which Kente cloth buntings do the young at Temple come to understand the deeply colonialist, fundamentalist, and religio-visionary "acres of diamonds" foundation on which their program subsists?

Question: Were those Washingtonian periods of the Atlanta speech merely Black sermonic oratory turned to public service account? I don't think so. There is something far more deeply interfused in those accents than simply greets the ear. Our Black Studies graduate aspirants—no matter where they are situated (HBU or HWI)—must begin to infer at least four points from the foregoing reflections.

1. Always make ideological maps of the broad disciplinary field you choose to pursue. Know how to distinguish the empiricists from the conceptualists and what is entailed by the program of each camp.
2. Remember the metonymic relationships to urban "modernity" of the sign "Blackness." The notions of subject, identity, progress, and technology are all dramatically revised or extended under the sign of urban and international "Blackness."
3. Make and keep an ideological map of your own home institution. Make sure it is not a "theme park" and you, its chief exhibit. Keep a good log, record, and journal. Hold onto hard copy. Do this on a daily basis.
4. All of the foregoing points hang in the balance on your ability to "read." But the notion of "reading" signifies for me a performative interpretiveness. It implies an active, comprehensive taking of texts and metatexts. Reading and critical memory elide in the emergence of what I call the Activist Intellectual.

Back in the day, in the 1960s, some of us began trying to construct, perceive, learn, and create strategies enabling us to heed the wisdom of a four-point plan for Black Studies advancement. We made mistakes, to be sure. But a number of us are still trying both to find interpretations and actively to perform them—outside of academic theme parks of confinement. We are looking for our own peculiar imbrications before we begin pointlessly to do nothing but shout: "The roof, the roof, the roof is on fire!" Black Studies has always been a remarkably resilient and infinitely adaptable public enterprise. Its successful future resides, precisely, in its graduates' abilities to grasp its imbrications.

PHILLIP B. HARPER

There are three points that are primary in the comments that I want to make. But I guess I would begin by talking a little bit about my own relatively recent graduate school experience, at least one aspect of it. As a graduate student, and even now to some extent, I very strenuously resisted being pegged as an African-Americanist. And I still do that to a large degree even though I talk almost exclusively about African-American culture in my work. But I want to make it very clear to people that I really see myself as someone whose field of is twentieth-century U.S. literature and culture. It just so happens that no matter where I look at U.S. culture, I see Black people. And that's why my work looks the way it looks. But it's also what makes me, quintessentially, a scholar and critic of twentieth-century U.S. literature and culture That is to say, given the racial politics that have so intensely informed U.S. culture, I don't see how you can get around dealing with Black folks and their history if you want to talk about U.S. culture at all in any of its guises. So I've very strenuously resisted being pigeonholed for those reasons. That was good for me because it meant that if I wanted to live up to my rhetoric about specializing specifically in twentieth-century literary cultural studies, then I really had to make it my business to establish as solid a foundation as I could in the tools of that calling. And I still think that that is a really important thing to do. It seems absolutely of paramount importance to me that I familiarize myself as extensively as possible with the tools undertaken by literary critics because that's what I am, and I didn't have any problems saying that's what I am. And if I'm going to be that, then I'm going to have to figure out how you do that. And if I want to figure out how do that, then I'm going to have to learn the tools of the trade. And I say this not as a way of speaking against interdisciplinarity, because I believe very strongly in interdisciplinarity. But interdisciplinarity implies discipline to some degree, and what you do with that discipline is open to question. But that is not to say you throw out discipline or disciplines necessarily. This strategy has served me comparatively well, and it's something that I do try to counsel current graduate students to take seriously, at least as an option.

I think there are a lot of different possibilities for how you can sell yourself in this business. But I do encourage people to at least try to consider learning a discipline thoroughly as an option—the strategy that I just outlined. That's related to the second point that I want to make, picking up on a subject that Houston spoke about—imbrication—and thinking about it in different terms. In my own work, I am less concerned with the delineation of African-American cultural traditions because that seems to me to be self-evident—there is such a thing—than I am in the exposition of how those traditions are thoroughly implicated in what we think of as U.S. culture. Now, this is related to what I said earlier about not wanting to be pegged as an African-Americanist for reasons that have to do with the baggage generally attached to that term. Being tagged as such sets limits, not necessarily on one's work but on one's ability to operate within the academy. This is a concern that really has to be taken seriously by people of various identifications, but certainly people in racial minorities. How you are positioned to operate in the context of the academy, if you decide that that's where you want to operate, is a crucial question for all of us to consider continuously. For my own part, it has been generally helpful to situate my intellectual work in such a way that what I'm dealing with are the imbrications of African-American culture within the context of the U.S.

Finally, and this a very general comment, but no less important for that fact, in thinking about the future of African-American studies in the academy, I recalled a conversation I had with Manthia which has stuck with me because it seemed to me so absolutely right. He said that what marks African-American studies now, what ideally should mark it now and in the future, is that it is characterized by an absolute lack of fear to talk about anything, to think about anything that seems to bear upon our project. I remember Manthia was talking specifically about questions of gender politics, sexuality, class divisions, so on and so forth— things I think we all talk about and think about, but have not necessarily always been easy to talk about and think about in a public forum. For us to reach a point in the field where we could undertake that kind of inquiry without betraying any fear whatsoever about it—because ideas can't hurt us—I think is a real mark of the maturity of the field. I would like to think that it is actually a point that we've reached by now. I sort of use that idea as my touchstone; to ask myself at every turn is the work that I'm doing at this moment measuring up to that standpoint. That has worked for me in the most recent past as a really helpful backdrop against which to pursue the work that I'm engaged in now.

TRUDIER HARRIS

I'm going to talk about the personal first, and then I'm going to turn to talk about you. Perhaps the most constructive thing I could say about my ventures into the predominantly White and hallowed halls of academia is that it teaches you resilience. Having grown up in an all-Black community in Tuscaloosa, Alabama, my arrival as a graduate student at the Ohio State University in 1969 was something of a shock. I had never been around so many White people before, and I had never had my intellect questioned in the way it was in that environment. From being assigned the first C I ever made in a literature course to being denied permission to audit a course, I experienced what it was like to be rejected by some of my professors. From an environment where I was always expected to be at the top of my class, always expected to succeed, I moved into one where some of my professors perceived my success to be a constant question mark. One course at Ohio State led me to do something I had never done before—stay up until 2 A.M. working on a paper. I did that to put the finishing touches on a paper on Arthur Hugh Clough's *The Ten Decalogues,* which you've probably never heard of, only to discover that if I had stayed up all night, every night, for two weeks, it would have made little difference to that professor. When he wrote comments such as, "Your classmates would not agree with you," it was clear that he would resort to whatever means necessary to assure that my confidence was shattered and that I would not make a respectable grade in that course.

And he almost succeeded. After my encounter with him and with another professor who was not appreciably different, I decided to leave Ohio State after my first year as a graduate student. Very early on the morning after I made that decision, I received telephone calls from two deans asking me to come by their offices to talk about the situation. I received notes from professors who thought I had done well and those from whom I had earned *As*—ones who had allowed ability to overshadow race. After many conferences and much persuasive maneuvering, I was convinced to remain in the program. And most of the time now, I remember the pleasant things about Ohio State rather than the trials those three insensitive professors put in my way. That resilience was repaid in 1994 when the chairman of General Motors of Ohio and I became the first recipients of the Distinguished Alumni Awards now given annually by the College of Humanities at Ohio State.

When I arrived at the College of William and Mary as an assistant professor in the fall of 1973—after eleven interviews at MLA and two job offers—I did not exactly feel invincible, but I did feel that I could handle the interracial situation a bit better. It was the wrong school to have made such a choice. Please understand, however, I was treated wonderfully well by most of the people at William and Mary. I received support to attend as many as seven conferences a year, and I learned how drink martinis and mai tais because there were two or three dinner parties or receptions to which I was invited and became the centerpiece every week. It used to puzzle me, however, as to why my many, many hosts and hostesses never paused to consider that maybe, just once, they should have invited another Black person to just one of those gatherings.

My colleagues, mostly male, came in a number of political and interactive guises, but two of them I remember vividly. Every year when we were evaluated for merit raises in the department, one other woman faculty member and I would receive the highest student evaluations for teaching and consequently received fairly decent merit raises. After one such evaluation, when these two guys served on the committee, they met me in the hallway afterwards and commented, "You had better stop getting those good teaching evaluations or we're going to break both of your legs." Of course this was said with broad smiles, but imagine the implications of that imagery. In exchange for solid teaching, I had to be crippled. They might just as well have said, "How dare you make us look inadequate, you little upstart, Black thing you. You're rocking the boat and it would be preferable if you fell back into line."

Somehow, I always flunked falling into line as they wanted. It's not in my nature, and it's not what my mother taught us as we grew up in Alabama in the 1950s and 1960s. And falling in line is not an attribute of resilience. So I used to leave William and Mary every two months or so. I would either attend a conference or go home to Alabama for what I called my "spiritual renewal" because my family and my community were the things that sustained me in that environment. Going home was essential because there were no "living mirrors" on the William and Mary campus. Of the 425 faculty members there were only two Black folks—me and a guy from Haiti. Imagine being 50 percent of the Black faculty on a university campus. And I was the lucky one. At least I was exclusively in the English department. They had him spread out over French, anthropology, and political science.

Attending conferences worked as inspirationally as going home. After each outing, I would revise the paper and submit it for publication somewhere. Being at William and Mary, therefore, made me realize that I had to write my way out of that environment. Not because people were necessarily inhospitable, but because of a lack of culture and a society of people like myself. I would drive down to Hampton Institute when I wanted to see Black people who were not taking the garbage out of my office or who were not pruning the beautiful lawns at William and Mary.

My memories of those early days are vivid because the newness of the transracial interaction at the professional level left me more impressionable at that period. After a few years, you begin to feel like Superwoman negotiating the academic waters, and you keep going because you see the pattern that is larger than the few idiots who try to stand in your way—the White guys who say, "You're a Black woman. You can go anywhere and get anything you want." Those who say, "That's it Trudier, you always go for the balls" anytime you have a disagreement with them. Those who think you should never be more successful than they—one of my colleagues at Chapel Hill I remember questioning me because I built a new house. "What do you want to move into that neighborhood for?" he asked me. Those who never let you forget your accomplishments and how they separate you from them. "Of course you can afford a new car, Trudy, you're a chaired professor," and so the beat goes on.

I have remained sane throughout the years because it would be criminal of me, after all the training and encouragement from my mother in the years after my father's death, to let White folks drive me crazy. Resilience. I keep on keeping on because I've made a choice. I like what I do. I love teaching, and I like working with graduate students, especially those who are motivated to move through programs in a timely fashion. I've had my share of academic madness, some of it racially motivated, some of it utterly sexist. I've been tenured twice, and the second time was not as pleasant as the first. I've fought tenure cases for other people because they were being discriminated against on the basis of their scholarship or their sexual preferences. I've gone toe-to-toe with department chairs on a number of issues ranging from teaching, to appointments, to salary and equity. If I were to write the story of my life in academia, however, I would probably focus less on the battles than on the ideas that have come as a result of teaching, interacting with the students, or just sitting around thinking. I still like what I do, but I like the climate in which I do it today far less than I did a few years ago.

Now about you. When I became a folklorist in 1973 along with being a scholar in African-American literature, there were approximately eleven African-American folklorists in the United States. The scholarship being done in African-American folklore was being done by European-American scholars and even Hispanic scholars. I am concerned about the development of future scholars, so when we talk about what is happening in terms of Black studies, I see my generation as a very special generation. When you look twenty years ahead of me to people who are in their mid to late sixties now, you can't find many African-American women scholars. When I look behind me, twenty-some years, to people getting out in literature, I don't see that many African-American women either. So the question I ask is, where are the African-American scholars? Where is the energy to produce? More and more, I run into a lot of people who are in the profession with me who are very lethargic; people who do not finish projects, who lack the ability to produce, who receive grants and do not do what they say they are going to do while they have the grants, who get contracts from publishers and do not deliver the manuscripts. This is especially the case with Black women scholars, those currently out there, and I hope you will somehow change that. Who will have the authority, in other words, in the study of African-American life and culture five years from now, ten years from now? I train many more European-American scholars than I train African-American scholars to do what I do. I am concerned about graduate students who delay their exams because they're afraid of getting out and discovering what the real world is about. I am concerned about graduate students who never finish their dissertations or take five, six, seven years to do so. Publishing opportunities are much more extensive today than they ever have been, so I'm concerned about how we inspire young African-American scholars to get out there and do the work. One major problem, as I see it, is that people have a fear of writing and you have to write in order to be a scholar. I had a young student come into my office the other day, a sophomore in undergraduate school, who said that he loved to write, and I asked him if he knew what a rarity he was because so few African Americans who come into my office actually express a love for writing. So that is something that is absolutely necessary for us to do, what we need to do, and I hope we can talk about that more during the discussion period.

TRICIA ROSE

Much like the chicken-or-the-egg question, it is hard to know which comes first for academics and intellectuals: a form of alienation from society, or a commitment to a life of the mind. Either way, the problem of how to continually reflect critically and broadly about the world in which you live and still remain in touch with the ground, to be able to connect with and gather support from the faulty, broken, and ill-conceived institutions that define us, is an underlying preoccupation for many of us. This is not to say that such preoccupations are conscious, or directly expressed in our teaching or scholarship. But for many who want to share the insights that funded, sustained rumination encourages with the rest of society, this problem seems to surface and resurface in a variety of ways. Academic debates over the use of various disciplinary "jargons," the relationship between theory and practice, the importance of the policy implications of our work, the high-culture/low-culture skirmishes over meaning and value are, at this moment, repositories of this sort of anxiety.

For members of those racial, gender, and ethnic groups who have fought long and hard for a chance to participate in the institutions of higher learning that hone and refine the skills of critical cultural reflection, this matter—or dilemma, as it has been frequently called—is even more charged. What will you, community and family members have asked—Black, woman, Latina, Jew—do with this golden opportunity? How will you insure that this luxury is not squandered, make sure that a lifetime of social reflection and cultural analysis is not reduced to years of socially irrelevant navel-gazing?

For this generation of Black scholars, intellectuals, and professors, socially irrelevant scholarship has been increasingly equated with race treason. The pressure to "contribute" to the lives of everyday people through one's scholarship or teaching has seemingly increased in the post–Civil Rights era; the sacrifice and bloodshed to improve Black participation and opportunity has amplified the notion that increased opportunity for the individual should translate into collective Black gain.

Fifty years ago, simply being a Black intellectual was a sign of collective gain; now, the standards are much higher. This, coupled with the continued crises facing the vast majority of African Americans, can produce immense pressure and conflict in a cerebrally oriented Black person—especially one who attends or teaches at a predominantly White institution.

Some seem to respond to this tension by self-imposed exile. Others become political activists/intellectuals. Others understand their contribution to the field of African-American studies to "represent" their community commitment. Still others understand their desire/decision *not* to research Black subject matter as helping Blacks by expanding Black opportunity. Regardless, few can truly escape this problematic, no matter their location or political persuasion.

This tension, or crisis of belonging, increases as one's commitment to academic life and institutions grows more entrenched. As Black intellectuals move along in their careers, the impact of this aspect of one's professional/public identity becomes greater, not only because of the cloistered, isolated nature of writing and research, but also because academic research tends to direct its attention primarily (if not solely) to others who share this pursuit.

The irony is, I think, that awareness of the full weight of the impact of becoming a Black intellectual isn't revealed in theory or analysis, but in practice. By this I mean that the longer and more seriously one takes up this role/identity, the more complexly and intensely one can feel this form of alienation. So, it seems to me, the most appropriate time to consider and ponder this question—graduate school—is not a very productive moment to be able to fully comprehend the weight of this dilemma, nonetheless resolve it. Not only is graduate school a time of intense work and ability-related anxiety, but the desire to succeed institutionally (remain funded, get funding, etc.) can direct students' attention away from philosophical examination of one's chosen vocation and toward disciplinary mastery. Furthermore, the limited number of Black peers and professors (some of whom are not interested in grappling with this issue openly or do not perceive this as central to academic apprenticeship) does not create a profitable setting for serious and extended examination of this sometimes painful and unanswerable problematic.

Consequently, I think, Black graduate students are in an especially vulnerable position, and because of this they can be more intensely invested in whatever model of Black scholar best matches their style, interests, and strategy for responding to this unspoken dilemma. Sometimes the most accessible and visible Black scholar in one's department or field, regardless of a student's affinity to the professor's chosen negotiation of this tension, or the fact that one's department does not have any Black faculty, can subtly shape one's expectations about becoming a Black intellectual. So, too, can the number of Black students in one's department, program, or classes. Being the only Black student in my incoming class of fourteen American Civilization Ph.D. students at Brown (the only Black woman and one of a total of four Black students over the preceding five years) with no Black faculty (the only one in the program was on leave) by all means had a variegated impact on my intellectual development during that first year and in the years to follow. No doubt, a large coterie of such peers and teachers might produce similarly complex and contradictory effects.

Graduate school is a liminal space and time that can encourage some sorts of interrogations, while masking others. Struggling to master one's chosen area can obscure a potentially important need (especially as related to the dilemma posed at the outset) to continue interrogating what this vocation offers and why a specific field and institution is attractive. The factors that go into making these decisions are multiple and complex, not all of them purely intellectual or logistical. Working toward a clearer sense of *why* can help illuminate the impact of various situational influences, and anticipate the sometimes debilitating queries about one's social value as a Black thinker.

Academic home institutions are only one source of intellectual and emotional support, and relying solely on them, especially when one's intellectual choices are not looked upon favorably by nearby mentors or peers, can profoundly impact self-confidence and self-worth. While it may appear that only other poor current or former graduate student souls can understand student struggles and fears, such thinking can augment one's isolation and heighten the negative impact of professorial and classroom critique. Although many departments are supportive and congenial, they are not families, nor should professors be perceived as parent-like figures. Being a good teacher or scholar says nothing about one's ability to nurture, and the frequent ego-related power dynamics of the faculty-student relationship are not to be underestimated. This is not to say that significant and valuable bonds cannot be established; it is to say that as with any relationships developed under structurally unequal circumstances, the less powerful have special concerns.

Academic cultures, like broader American society, tend to operate along highly racialized lines. Black students are sometimes shuffled off to Black professors, even when their intellectual interests are not as well served there as they might be with other faculty members. Even more importantly, though, discomfort and legitimate fear can discourage Black students from seeking intellectual support or knowledge from unobvious sources. Given that my interest in Black cultural theory was not the direct interest of any of the faculty related to American Studies during my years in graduate school, I was forced, by necessity, to look more broadly for intellectual mentorship that I might have otherwise overlooked. I was, therefore, attentive to the value of some professors whose work, race, gender, or politics were not, shall I say, closely linked to mine. This was sometimes frustrating, but it has helped me to see that what you're looking for may not always come in expected places and that all of what you need never comes from one source.

The dilemmas associated with becoming a Black intellectual are at once collective and idiosyncratic. Representing oneself is a full-time job; representing a race is an impossible task that nonetheless remains a potent subtext for Black scholarship and critical commentary. Honest self-reflection about the possible ways in which academia and its relationship to the legacy of African-American collective struggle can impact one's sense of place is critical to one's chances of remaining at least partially sane under seemingly irreconcilable circumstances.

CONTRIBUTORS

HOUSTON A. BAKER JR. is the director of the Center for the Study of Black Literature at the University of Pennsylvania. He is the author of several books devoted to black literature and culture, including *Black Studies, Rap, and the Academy* (1993), *Workings of the Spirit: The Poetics of Afro-American Women's Writing* (1991) *Modernism and the Harlem Renaissance* (1987), and *Blues, Ideology, and Afro-American Literature: A Vernacular Theory* (1984).

ANGELA Y. DAVIS has been teaching, writing, and lecturing about African-American and women's social theories for the last twenty years, during which time she has also been active in a number of organizations concerned with issues of social justice. She presently teaches in the history of consciousness program at the University of California, Santa Cruz.

THULANI DAVIS is an accomplished writer in film, theater, fiction, and poetry. She has written for *American Film,* the *New York Times,* the *Washington Post,* the *Village Voice,* and other magazines and journals. She is the author of the libretto for the widely acclaimed opera *X: The Life and Times of Malcolm X* and of an adaptation of Bertolt Brecht's *The Caucasian Chalk Circle* and other plays. She has published two books of poetry and her first novel, *1959,* was nominated for the Los Angeles Times Book Award in 1992.

THOMAS DEFRANTZ is a dancer, director, and dance scholar. His writing has appeared in the *Encyclopedia of African American Culture and History* and the *Village Voice.* A Ford Foundation Fellow, De-Frantz's area of specialization is performed Afro-American art. He is currently dance editor for *Collage, the National Journal of African American Performing Arts.* He recently joined the faculty of music and theater arts at the Massachusetts Institute of Technology.

MANTHIA DIAWARA is a professor of film and comparative literature and director of Africana Studies at New York University. He is the author of numerous articles and essays and *African Cinema: Politics, and Culture* (Indiana University Press, 1992) and the editor of *Black American Cinema* (Routledge, 1993). He has also codirected two films, *Sembene Ousmane: The Making of African Cinema* (with Ngugi wa Thiongo) and *Rouche in Reverse,* an insightful review of the life, work, and mind of French anthropologist Jean Rouche.

STEVEN DRUKMAN is the theater critic for *Artforum* and the assistant editor for *American Theatre.* He has contributed to the *Village Voice, TDR, Theatre Journal* and many others. Book contributions include essays in *A Queer Romance*: Lesbians, Gay Men, and Papular Culture (Routledge, 1995), and Speaking on Stage: *Interviews with Contemporary American Playwrights* (University of Alabama Press, 1996). He is an adjunct professor at New York University.

GRANT FARED is an assistant professor of English and comparative literature at the University of Michigan, Ann Arbor. He is editor of *Rethinking C. L. R. James* (Blackwell, 1996) and has published in journals such as *Social Text, Research in African Literature,* and *Camera Obscura.*

ELENA GEORGIOU moved to New York from London eight years ago and recently completed an M.A. in poetry from the City College of New York. She has read her work extensively throughout the area and has been published in various literary journals both in the United States and abroad.

PAUL GILROY divides his time as a lecturer in the African American Studies Department at Yale University and at Goldsmith's College of the University of London. He has also worked as a musician and journalist. He is author of numerous groundbreaking works on Black diasporic performance and politics, including *"There Ain't No Black in the Union Jack": The Cultural Politics of Race and Nation* (1987) and *The Black Atlantic: Modernity and Double Consciousness* (1993).

MICHAEL A. GONZALES is a freelance writer whose column "Black Metropolis" appears weekly in the *New York Press.* He is also a contributing writer for *Vibe,* the *Source,* the *Village Voice,* and *Ego Tripping.*

NATHAN L. GRANT is an assistant professor of African American Studies of the State University of New York at Buffalo. He has written several articles on African-American literature, art, and film and is currently completing a book on Jean Toomer, Zora Neale Hurston, and modernity.

RICHARD C. GREEN is a Ph.D. candidate in performance studies at New York University. His work focuses primarily on representations of the "Black" body. His current research examines the myth and lore surrounding the Hottentot "Venus" and recuperations of this figure in contemporary performance. He is also a dancer-choreographer and has published several articles on dance and the work of Pearl Primus, Asadata Dafora, and Charles Moore. He is currently developing an essay about modernisms, race, and dance for a forthcoming collection of writings on Black dance 2nd performance.

MONIQUE GUILLORY recently completed her Ph.D. in Comparative Literature at New York University. She is currently a post-doctoral fellow at the University of California, Santa Barbara, where she is completing her work on the quadroon balls of nineteenth-century New Orleans. A portion of this research appears in *Race Consciousness: African-American Studies for the New Century* (New York University Press, 1996).

PHILLIP B. HARPER is an associate professor of English at New York University and the author of *Are We Not Men? Masculine Anxiety and the Problem of African-American Identity* (Oxford, 1996) and *Framing the Margins: The Social Logic of Postmodern Culture* (Oxford, 1994).

TRUDIER HARRIS is the Augustus Baldwin Longstreet Professor of American Literature in the English Department at Emory University. She has published articles and book reviews in such journals as *Callaloo, Black American Literature Forum, Studies in American Fiction,* and *The Southern Humanities Review.* Among her books are *Fiction and Folklore: The Novels of Toni Morrison* (1991) and most recently *The Power of the Porch: The Storyteller's Craft in Zora Neale Hurston, Gloria Naylor, and Randall Kenan* (1996).

JOHN L. JACKSON JR. is a National Science Foundation Fellow and Ph.D. candidate in anthropology at Columbia University. An excerpt from his thesis appears in *Race Consciousness: African-American Studies for the New Century* (New York University Press, 1996).

MAY JOSEPH is a Rockefeller Fellow and assistant professor in the Department of Performance Studies at New York University. She currently has two books in press with the University of Minnesota Press: *Transatlantic Dispersions* and *Young People around the Globe: Cross-Cultural Youth Studies,* both forthcoming in 1997.

MANNING MARABLE is director of the Institute for African American Studies at Columbia University. He is the author of eight books, including *Black American Politics* (1985), *W. E. B. Du Bois: Black Radical Democrat* (1986), *The Melody Never Stops* (1991), *Beyond Black and White: Transforming African-American Politics* (1995). He is also the founding editor of *Race and Reason.*

PORTIA K. MAULTSBY is professor of Afro-American studies and adjunct professor of music and folklore at Indiana University. Her research focuses on popular music and theoretical issues related to Black music aesthetics and performance. She has published chapters in *African-Americans and the Media: Contemporary Issues* (1996), *The Encyclopedia of African-American Culture and History,* vol. 4 (1996), and *We'll Understand It Better By and By: Pioneering African American Gospel Composers* (1992). She is completing a manuscript titled *From Backwoods to City Streets: Post–World War II Black Popular Music.*

TRACIE MORRIS is an essayist, poet, songwriter, and performer. She is the 1993 National Haiku Slam Champion and the 1993 NYC Grand Slam Poetry Champion. She has conducted creative writing courses for the Writer's Voice Program, the New York Public Library System, and numerous educational institutions throughout the New York area. Her poetry has appeared in various literary anthologies, including *Aloud: Voices from the Nuyorican Poets' Café* (1994).

MARILYN NANCE is an independent photojournalist/storyteller and recipient of a 1993 New York Foundation for the Arts Artists' Fellowship in Nonfiction Literature. Her work documents various facets of American life, from the Black Indians of New Orleans to Appalachian folk musicians and the funeral of an Akan priest in New York. Her work has been published in *Life*, the *New York Times*, the *Village Voice*, *Essence*, and numerous other magazines and journals.

ISHMAEL REED's bold work *Mumbo Jumbo* (1972) is but one of his many stellar accomplishments in literature. He is also the author of *Japanese by Spring* (1993) and *The Last Days of Louisiana Red* (1974).

TRICIA ROSE is an assistant professor of history and Africana studies at New York University. She has written and lectured extensively on black cultural theory and popular culture. Her first book, *Black Noise: Rap Music and Black Culture in Contemporary American* (1994), received an American Book Award from the Before Columbus Foundation in 1995. She is also the coeditor of *Microphone Fiends: Youth Music and Youth Culture* with Andrew Ross (1994).

CARL HANCOCK RUX is a Brooklyn-based performance poet and writer. He is published in the United States, Europe and West Africa in anthologies such as *Aloud: Voices from the Nuyorican Poets Café* (1994), *Fire and Spirit—African American Poetry (1996)*, and *Go the Way Your Blood Beats: An Anthology of Lesbian and Gay Literary Fiction by African-American Writers* (1996).

ANNA SCOTT, a conceptual artist working primarily in African diaspora dance idioms, is a Ford Fellow and doctoral candidate in performance studies at Northwestern University. She calls her mode of performance and research "Diaspora Doo-wop dance/memory" and prefers guerrilla performances. She recently adapted, choreographed, and staged Randal Kenan's *Let the Dead Bury Their Dead,* and an original work, *A Travelling Niggeratti,* is currently in production.

DAVID SERLIN is a writer, composer, and doctoral candidate in the American studies program at New York University, where he teaches courses on urban culture and identity.

RICHARD SIMON is a doctoral in American studies at New York University. His play, *Murder at Munsing Manor: A Nancy Boys Mystery,* was produced off-Broadway by the Ridiculous Theatrical Company at the Actors Playhouse in the fall and winter of 1995–96. His latest play, *Cruel Story of Crime,* was produced in the winter of 1997.

GREG TATE is a staff writer for the *Village Voice* and a founding member of the Black Rock Coalition. He is also a contributing writer for numerous other magazines and music journals, including *Spin, Downbeat,* and *Vibe.* He is author of *Flyboy in the Buttermilk: Essays on Contemporary America* and has recently been enjoying a thriving life as a musician with his band Mack Divas. He produced the group Women in Love's album *Sound of Falling Bodies at Rest.*

CLYDE TAYLOR, a well-known film critic and theorist, currently teaches in the Africana Studies Department at New York University. He was the screenwriter for the PBS documentary *Midnight Ramble: Oscar Micheaux and the Story of Race Movies* (1994).

GAYLE WALD is an assistant professor of English at George Washington University. Her book *Crossing the Line: Racial Passing in Twentieth-Century American Literature and Culture* is forthcoming from Duke University Press.

ARTRESS BETHANY WHITE is a member of the Dark Room Collective and received her M.A. in Creative Writing from New York University, where she currently teaches. Her work has appeared in the *Village Voice, Quarterly Black Review of Books, Ark/angel Review, Callaloo,* and the anthology *In the Tradition: An Anthology of Young Black Writers* (1992).

INDEX